Receiving
Juvenile Justice

Receiving Juvenile Justice

Adolescents and State Care and Control

Howard Parker
Maggie Casburn
David Turnbull

Basil Blackwell · Oxford

©Howard Parker, Maggie Casburn and David Turnbull 1981

First published 1981

Basil Blackwell Publisher Ltd
108 Cowley Road
Oxford OX4 1JF
England

The names of all the adolescents, parents and officials referred to in this book have been changed to prevent their identification.

British Library Cataloguing in Publication Data

Parker, Howard
    Receiving juvenile justice.
    1. Juvenile justice, Administration of — England
    2. Juvenile delinquency — England
    3. Social work with youth — England
    I. Title   II. Casburn, Maggie
    III. Turnbull, David
    346.6   HV146.A5

    ISBN 0−631−12727−5
    ISBN 0−631−12745−3 Pbk

Typesetting by Freeman Graphic, Tonbridge.
Printed and bound in Great Britain by Book Plan, Worcester

Contents

Acknowledgements

The project which led to this book was funded by the Social Science Research Council to whom we are particularly grateful. Our research would also not have been possible without the trust and help of some hundred Merseyside youngsters and their parents. Similarly, although they cannot be named, we would like to thank the police, court officials, social workers and probation officers who 'participated' in our research for their co-operation.

For their critical comments on early drafts of the manuscript we are indebted to David Downes, Mike Fitzgerald, John Paley, Laurie Taylor and Norman Tutt. Finally, we would like to thank Dorothy Lewis and Annette Power for typing the manuscript.

1

Making Sense of Juvenile Justice

DELINQUENCY CONTROL

Much nonsense is talked about English juvenile justice. Some is born of ignorance, some of prejudice — most is the result of confusion. At times, for instance, commentators manage to reduce analysis to the two notions of 'care' and 'control', suggesting that the present system is being choked by a tension between them. We shall consider these two concepts in detail throughout this book, implicitly rather than explicitly. That is, as we untangle and describe what actually goes on between local state officials administering juvenile justice and those families subject to their jurisdiction, we will be asking whether the 'exchange' is about care or about control or whatever.

Care seems a friendly notion, conjuring up images of shared understanding, of one human being providing, sensitively, those things required by another. Control, on the other hand, although by no means a sinister process, implies the desire by one party to exert influence upon another or direct him or her to stop or start doing something — to conform to a set of rules. These two sorts of processes overlap of course and, being relative concepts, may often be found in tandem, but, particularly at the poles of their relativity, they are quite different and produce for those on the receiving end different experiences.

This study deals with adolescents (12—17 year olds) who must pass through a juvenile court, which, certainly once they are 14 years old, usually regards them as culpable and largely responsible for their own actions. That is why the juvenile court sees fit to send adolescents to detention centre and Borstal for stealing, or to a community school for failing to heed warnings about the consequences of non-school attendance. Yet to date there has been no systematic examination of the perceptions of such juveniles — the acid test about 'care and control' has been avoided. Evaluating the perceptions of adolescents, of both sexes, subject to both criminal and care proceedings is one of the key aims of this study. The test results are actually quite complicated.

Significantly both magistrates, and the families that stand before them to receive judgement in criminal proceedings, are much less confused than most academic and political commentators. They both point to punishment, an obvious form of social control, as being the primary concern of juvenile court criminal proceedings. This stance is probably shared by most people in industrialized social-democratic societies. It is hardly worthy of being at issue and we have found no empirical evidence to suggest it should be so. Certainly there are some unfortunate words and phrases cluttering the system, such as 'care orders', 'intermediate treatment' and 'community homes', to mislead the uninitiated but once we hack away such packaging we are still left with, through criminal proceedings, a system of delinquency control which relies essentially on a range of punishments.

Working from within this perspective, there are two issues that *are* potentially problematic, however. First, which juveniles are processed through criminal proceedings and why? Second, what safeguards are there to make sure guilt is fairly established and punishment fairly distributed and that this administration does not clash with other lauded social values or principles? Test local juvenile justice systems – as we have done – in these quite conventional ways and they become manifestly defective.

As we will show in chapters 3 and 6, those who appear before the juvenile court on criminal matters are there in part because of the idiosyncrasies and contingencies of the selection process itself. In chapters 4 and 5 we demonstrate, by comparing City and Countyside juvenile courts, that the day-to-day production of juvenile justice is not comprehensively checked by the minimal safeguards of criminal justice (e.g. the right to competent legal representation or a consistent use of due process). Instead we find that juveniles from the same backgrounds (which we discuss more generally in chapter 2), charged with similar offences, are subjected to quite different court regimes, and receive widely divergent sentences, which have major and wide-ranging effects on their lives. A key task of this book is to explain how and why these injustices and inequities are produced and what juveniles make of them.

Yet the juvenile justice debate which has now raged for 20 years has not been about these injustices. At a national level, in particular, it has been an ideological contest between the two political parties and their supporters. The 1960s debate, now well documented (Parsloe, 1978;

Covington, 1979), which led to the original draft of the Children and Young Persons' Act ('The 1969 Act') was quite clearly influenced by significantly more left-wing aspirations, at their most articulate in Longford (Labour Party Study Group, 1964), who saw the continuing of the quest for *social justice* and a social-welfare-treatment approach to the care and control of children and adolescents as consistent since 'delinquents are to some extent a product of the society that they live in and the deficiencies of its provision for them'. The 1965 White Paper *The Child, the Family and the Young Offender* (Home Office, 1965) was consequently a radical re-appraisal of juvenile justice, calling for the abolition of the juvenile court, the de-criminalization of most young offenders and the extension of positive social work 'treatment' of the remaining young customers. The implementation of such a programme would have given great power and influence to the aspiring new social work profession (see Packman, 1975; Pearson, 1978). The political opposition from the police, the magistrates and clerks, championed by the Tories, was considerable and the compromise White Paper, *Children in Trouble* (Home Office, 1968) and the Bill which led to the original 1969 Act were considerably less innovatory. Nevertheless, had the 1969 Act been implemented in full, it would have redrawn the power relationships in the juvenile justice system very considerably. In fact, the change in government, just as the bill was to be implemented, signalled a massive change in intended direction. The new Conservative government resisted the Act. They suspended various sections of it and overtly rejected much of it, in particular the abolition of detention centre and Borstal places for juveniles. In doing so they threw it out of balance, leaving 'local' juvenile justice officials with a statute which, by recognizing two essentially conflicting ideological positions, but offering minimal guidance as to which should predominate, sowed the seeds for the next unhappy decade of delinquency control. Mark Carlisle, the Undersecretary of State, in the Tory administration announced the mutation:

> The age of prosecution will not be changed; children from ten upwards will remain liable to criminal proceedings. The courts will retain their present power to order Borstal training, to commit to junior detention centres and to order attendance at junior attendance centres. Probation orders will be replaced by supervision orders for those under 17, but courts will retain complete discretion to select probation officers as supervisors for children

of ten upwards in both care proceedings and criminal proceedings. (Carlisle, 1970, quoted in Packman, 1975)

The decade since the implementation of the revamped 1969 Act saw the build-up of a massive *dissonance,* a disjunction between the intentions and spirit of the original Act and the actual sentencing patterns. Apart from the increased use of cautioning, recently made citable on a criminal record and so undermining its 'diversionary' effectiveness, the sharpest image in the statistics is of the huge increase in the use of Borstals and detention centres, with community-based supervision, the linchpin of the original proposals, having declined somewhat over the same period. In fact only the use of care orders ('7 (7)s'), viewed in the original Act as a suitable treatment regime, have, when compared with the number of old approved school orders, developed in a way consistent with the social welfare approach — now itself under heavy attack from all sides. In short then, in criminal proceedings, more rather than fewer juveniles have entered the formal system; more rather than fewer have been dealt with through 'punishment' in custodial institutions and fewer rather than more juveniles have been subject to social welfare and treatment programmes in the community. We will demonstrate that this dissonance — indeed the turning on its head of the social welfare approach envisaged in the 1969 Act — has been made possible by the immense discretion which the implemented Act has given local juvenile justice systems, even further increased by modifications to the Act implemented by the New Right.

This discretion was built into the original Act, rightly or wrongly, as a prerequisite to a social-welfare-treatment approach to dealing with juveniles in need of care and control. However, the restructuring of the Act in 1970, despite re-introducing custodial regimes akin to a criminal justice 'tariff', failed to restrict the court's use of these disposals by offering sentencing limits, routine in adult criminal justice. As a consequence, the new overall juvenile justice system allowed magistrates a range of disposals, including custodial punishments, and no guidelines as to how to use them. Although much has been made of social workers' 'judgements' vis-a-vis supervision orders and care orders (see Morris and Giller, in Parker, 1979), in fact the sentencing trends show quite clearly that punishment and the use of custodial measures — the mark of magisterial preferences in delinquency control — have dominated. Yet, despite this overall trend, significant variations have occurred at a local level as juvenile courts 'settle' into their interpretations of the meaning of the 1969 Act and the relevance of traditional judicial safeguards. So, although dissonance is the key feature of the past decade, *diversity* runs a close second. There is in fact no juvenile justice as such in England and Wales but a montage of local interpretations. The contrast between City and Countyside courts, which we shall document shortly, provides a bitter pill for anyone who doubts this contention.

The third feature of the present system is much less well documented. It is a characteristic, a 'feeling', which hangs in the air, particularly the less clean air of our big cities, that justice for juveniles is, at times, rather rough. In short there is a third, controversial, feature — official *deviation*. The recent focus on police behaviour and misbehaviour on city streets, the occasional clashes between police and black youth, the call for the abolition of 'suspicious person loitering' as a charge and, indirectly, the public enquiries into police brutality are the 'public' tip of this iceberg. However, as we shall see, allegations run much deeper, once the opinions of streetwise youngsters and their parents are elicited. The receiving-end perspective we present takes the debate much further, leading us to consider in what sense juvenile justice can claim to have the moral authority to operate and thus to what extent it is merely repressive power focused on certain sections of the population.

Juvenile justice as delinquency control, 'law and order', has different meanings at different levels. The political discourse, which has been taken up by the New Right, in claiming the system is soft and in need of sharper teeth, presents quite a different picture from the one portrayed by actual sentencing patterns. Yet the sentencing patterns themselves provide only an overview and so fail to illustrate the major differences between local systems. The production of juvenile justice is also about other more complex issues: it is about the relationship between working-class adolescents and the local state; it is about the moral authority of the law; and, to return to Longford, about the relationship between criminal justice and social justice.

THE CARE SIDE OF JUVENILE JUSTICE

In analysing the production of welfare justice for adolescents via care proceedings (chapter 9), and comparing the agendas of that tribunal with juvenile justice produced through criminal proceedings, we will show that there is considerable 'spillage' or cross-over of agendas between the two court settings. They have much in common. In part this is explained by the fact that, since the Conservative government's insertion in 1963 of the 'control' requirement into the expectations of the care court and consequently the statutory child-care service, all manner of juvenile misdemeanour can be interpreted as suggesting there is a lack of parental control.

In order to reflect the reality of this cross-over we can, for the present, define the care side of juvenile justice as the business of care proceedings plus the making, in criminal proceedings, of supervision orders and '7 (7)' care orders. The impact of these interventions on the lives of youngsters, through time, can also be included. In chapters 6, 8, 10 and 12 we consider the meaning of the experience of this component of juvenile justice for working-class families, in their terms.

The grand political debate which has been waged over delinquency control has not been reproduced for the care side of juvenile justice, except in relation to child-abuse tragedies, beyond the scope of this study. Instead the increasingly vociferous criticism of the child care and control work of social workers and social services departments has been 'internal' and has come from academics and pressure groups (see Taylor *et al.,* 1980; Morris *et al.,* 1980). In particular anxiety has been expressed about the continued escalation of state intervention in the lives of working-class families, whether through 'at risk' registers, place-of-safety orders or the haphazard use of '7 (7)' care orders (see Thorpe *et al.,* 1979). These latter orders, because of their longevity, accounted for an estimated 19,000 juvenile offenders in care (England and Wales) in March 1978. The manner of accommodation of these youngsters has also been attacked, especially the rapid and significant investment in the number of secure places available in community schools. Other 'status' criteria for taking care proceedings, for example 'non-school attendance' and 'moral danger' have been equally castigated.

These are strong criticisms and we shall attempt to tease out their validity and whether they are commensurate with the views of those working-class families subject to the care side of juvenile justice and indeed with the perceptions of the social workers who orchestrate these interventions (chapters 7 and 11). We will then be in a position to begin to consider whether the legislative reforms proposed by pressure groups such as Justice for Children will really offer working-class families, the customers of statutory child care intervention (Holman, 1976; Thoburn, 1980), the support and guidance they say they need.

THE RECEIVING END

The validity and reliability of this whole study clearly depends on its methodology. In particular, because it attempts to provide a missing link in the understanding of juvenile justice — the views of those who must receive its jurisdiction — it is necessary to clarify at this stage how the hundred families we worked with were contacted, interviewed and re-interviewed. We must also anticipate the scepticism with which the receiving-end perspective will be greeted. One study of the views of Crown Court defendants, for instance, evoked much indignant rejection from the legal profession (Baldwin and McConville, 1977).

There are two strands of the receiving-end research tradition which we must look at: the receiving of social welfare and the receiving of criminal or juvenile justice — since the present study encompasses both. The most striking feature of the social welfare strand is its strong skew towards looking at the perceptions of the clients of small voluntary social work agencies (e.g. Mayer and Timms, 1970; Sainsbury, 1975) or alternatively the voluntary work of statutory agencies (e.g. Rees, 1978). Within this tradition the emphasis has been mainly upon the views of women (Marsden, 1973) and the elderly and handicapped (e.g. Goldberg, 1970). The notable exception to this overall trend have been the 'Sea-town' social services studies (e.g. McKay *et al.*, 1973; Glampson *et al.*, 1977). A recent study of 'home on trial' care orders potentially offered a focus upon both statutory and young clients of social welfare (Thoburn, 1980). However, although it is a competent and precise study of the views of parents, who are in a real sense also the subject of court proceedings, it actually fails to look at the perceptions of the youngsters themselves. The present study cannot, therefore, rest or rely on this overall strand of receiving-end literature and certainly cannot take on board well-formulated hypotheses about the perceptions of 'statutory' young clients of social welfare.

The receiving of criminal justice is slightly more developed. Studies of adult defendants, most notably by Bottoms and McClean (1976) and Baldwin and McConville (1977), form a useful base. For juvenile justice however, although some pre-1969 studies (e.g. Scott, 1959; Voelcker, 1960) and more recently North American projects (e.g. Langley, 1978) and a well-conceived study of the Scottish panels (Martin *et al.*, 1981) are available, there is very little about the post-1969 English system. The only published study of significance is that of Anderson (1978), which, although giving only brief attention to the perceptions of juveniles, does locate their views in a well-worked analysis of two juvenile courts. One or two pilot studies (e.g. Morris and Giller, 1977) and unpublished theses (e.g. Williamson, 1980) offer some insights and will be referred to in the chapters to follow. In particular the views of girls in 'trouble' and the views of juveniles subject to statutory community supervision (but see Jones, 1979) are largely unknown. It is only when juveniles became a captive cohort (see Polsky, 1971) that their views have been systematically elicited (e.g. Gill, 1974; Ericson, 1976; Walter, 1979) and we regard this aspect of the receiving of juvenile justice as already well researched.

Consequently apart from a handful of general appreciative studies of male adolescents (e.g. Parker, 1974; Willis, 1977) and despite the obsession of adult society with adolescents and the trouble they are deemed to cause, we know very little about the perceptions of those, predominantly working-class, youngsters who become 'official trouble' as the subjects of either criminal or care proceedings in juvenile courts in England and Wales. We have little idea what they make of the local state's intervention (i.e. of police, probation, court, social services, education and health agency involvement) and whether they accept the 'moral authority' of such intervention or regard it as repressive.

As interesting as the receiving-end studies have been, nearly all of them have suffered a major weakness. As one commentator (Shaw, 1976) on the tradition has noted they are, in particular, methodologically suspect.

> Samples consisting only of consumers, however representative they may be, inevitably give a partial, misleading picture by familiarizing the reader with only one set of values . . . sampling must be based on a population of relationships, not individuals.

Recent, socio-legal publications have also consistently failed to conduct case studies using a *holistic* approach. Perhaps the classic example is Pat Carlen's (1976) omission of the views and role of defendants in her otherwise seductive sociology of magistrates' justice. Having failed to explore this perspective, and thus its impact upon proceedings, she relegates the defendant to the status of 'dummy' player, constructing her thesis around this notion. Yet, as we shall show, this is to underestimate both the comprehension defendants have of their part and indeed their ability to develop tactical play. Yet alternatively a defendant study, without being situated in exactly the sort of world of interrelationships that Carlen offers, becomes just as problematic: the more so if researchers gain only either retrospective information, without themselves witnessing the process, or failing to somehow measure their respondent's perceptions against 'objective' criteria or alternative or independent perceptions.

THE RESEARCH STRATEGY

Constructing a research project to avoid such pitfalls and satisfy all these implicit requirements is extremely difficult. Even with a high level of cooperation from research subjects and a large input of research time, the building of a consumer study against a comprehensive background of alternative perspectives and 'checking' mechanisms is still practically impossible. We aimed to follow a sample of a hundred adolescents through most stages of the juvenile justice process, monitoring their passage independently and gathering potentially competing interpretations of what was happening to them. Ideally, for a criminal case a research project should be able to stay with the situation, for example – from street corner incidents, through the police station, the court hearings, to detention centre and then along to the probation officer's room where eventual 'licence' supervision occurs. Clearly this is the stuff of researchers' dreams. Such grandiose goals are beyond the scope of social scientists. However, we have tried to keep this ideal in mind and we have been able to detail and 'check' quite large sections of the passage of adolescents through both care and criminal proceedings.

First, we were able, thanks to the excellent cooperation of 'City' social services and 'Countyside' probation service to have access to all the 'paper work' relating to all the adolescents we approached. Consequently we had accounts of each youngster's criminal record, present alleged offence, and sight of any 'welfare' reports written. This data allowed us to build in 'tests' in our interview schedules with juveniles and their parents (e.g. Have you been in trouble before?).

Second, thanks again to the cooperation of the relevant court officials, the three members of the research team, working independently observed some 200 juvenile court sessions, each lasting about three hours. Fifty of these sessions were spent in criminal proceedings in Countyside, with 120 criminal sessions and 30 'care' sessions being observed in City. We were able to sit unobtrusively at the back of each courtroom, noting not only the various appearances of each and every-

TABLE 1.1 SAMPLE DISTRIBUTION AND INTERVIEWING PATTERN

Sample Categories	City				Countryside			
	Boys	Girls	Parents	Social workers	Boys	Girls	Parents	Probation officers
Criminal proceedings 1	12	7	⎫	⎫	8	—	⎫	⎫
2	5	5	⎬ 13	⎬ 16	5	—	⎬ 9	⎬ 15
3	4	—	⎭	⎭	7	—	⎭	⎭
Informal interview/ (refusal)	2 (8)	4 (10)			2 (4)	4 (6)		
Follow-up interview	6	2		5	9			10
Care proceedings	7	14	11	18				
Informal interview/ (refusal)	1 (1)	(5)		(1)				
Follow-up interview	3	8		10				
Groupwork project	9	8						

one of our sample, but situating them in the midst of the particular court regime and the several hundred cases we observed in process. This extensive observation allowed us to look at the production of juvenile justice at a local level (see chapters 4 and 5). Hence we have a major 'independent' perspective with which to analyse the perceptions of adolescents and their parents (and in fact court officials and social workers) of their passage through the juvenile court.

The sample of adolescents (see table 1.1) was constructed to represent the general range of candidates for the juvenile court, except that we inflated our analysis of female subjects slightly in order to focus on their position as females and compensate for the absence of previous analysis. For the care side of juvenile justice, we basically took all adolescents who were willing to cooperate, who came into City's care 'net', over a four-month period. For criminal proceedings we divided the range of disposals available to the court into three bands. Level 1 disposals, 'low-tariff' cases (e.g. binding over, conditional discharge and fine) are those which are unlikely to involve post-court contact between offenders and officials. Level 2 disposals, 'middle-tariff' sentences, are, in practice, attendance centre and supervision orders, involving continued community-based supervision of juveniles. Level 3, 'high-tariff' cases, involve the offenders being 'sent away' on a care order, for Borstal training or most often to detention centre. The reasons for our actual samples of boys at the top of table 1.1 not falling neatly into these groupings, despite our use of age, sex, offence 'seriousness' and antecedents in our sentencing prediction formula, are important, and will be considered in the coming chapters.

We contacted each of these 80 adolescents and their parents separately by means of very informal letters, seeking their help, in confidence and stressing the voluntary nature of this cooperation. Potential subjects were given their first opportunity to decline our attention by means of a pre-stamped postcard. We observed without their knowledge the court session in which each of our would-be subjects appeared and then, in turn, called at their home address, where they had a second opportunity to decline our request for help – if necessary by closing the door on us. The refusal rate, about 30 per cent, is shown in table 1.1. It can be seen that the refusal rate by girls is consistently higher than for boys, particularly in Countyside. In part we think this can be explained by the relative stigma attached to a court appearance for a girl. This stigma was clearly felt by many parents, who would not let us talk to their daughters. 'It's all over now . . . we just want to forget about it.' Our better success rate with City girls was produced by vary-ing our approach and contacting parents by letter asking them, as well as their daughters, for an interview, rather than merely asking permis-sion to see their daughters. Finally as we shall document, working-class girls are 'culturally' reserved when faced with outsiders and more nervous of such encounters (see also McRobbie, 1978).

This revised approach means that in City our sample of parents slants towards our female subjects. The conducting of depth interviews with over 30 parents (or sets of) is consistent with our primary aim of producing a study of inter-related 'populations'. The taking of samples from two courts allows a further set of comparisons. It allowed us to test how much families are affected by and 'take in' the nature of a particular court regime. It also allowed us to compare the work of Countyside probation officers, who dealt with criminal proceedings for 13–17 year olds, with City social workers and to see if their 'styles' affected client perceptions and satisfaction. We interviewed all the 50 social workers and probation officers involved in our sample cases, focusing on their work with the particular families, whether through preparing and presenting court reports or via community supervision. This allowed us a further check on other facets and another stage of the process, gained by juxtaposing these two perspectives.

In total then, the research team was involved in about 250 depth interviews as well as the court observations and informal and formal interviews with magistrates, police, lawyers, education officials etc. In all these interviews we tried to see the subjects on their terms, on their choice of territory and at their convenience. The interview schedules were constructed to produce cross-referencing and elicit independent perceptions of the same event or process. Our interviews with social workers and probation officers, because of our own backgrounds and experience, proved the easiest. However, although our interviews with adolescents and parents varied in quality, we found that, having agreed to meet one of us, most subjects were keen and perfectly able to talk at length. Like Kitwood (1979), we found adolescents were able to give detailed descriptions of their behaviour and views to a relative stranger. In many cases we were both able to sustain concentration for a good two hours.

One member of the research team contacted each triangle of poten-tial interviewees for a particular case, having also signed the letters and observed the court hearing relating to the case. This same researcher also stayed with the case for the follow-up interviews which aimed to explore how, if at all, adolescents' and social workers' perceptions of a situation (e.g. a DC licence) changed through time. We failed to complete as many follow-up interviews as we would have liked but still managed to recontact nearly 30 juveniles and their respective social workers and probation officers.

The final aspect of the project involved the running of two intensive groupwork programmes, one for boys and one for girls. These groups were again voluntary, involving court-experienced youngsters suggested by social workers and contacted by the research team. We spent one evening a week for 12 weeks on local leisure-based activities and two long weekends away with each of these groups: the second weekend being a joint venture. Much of what felt like an enormous amount of effort put into running these groups had little direct research spin-off. Although we conducted interviews with the girls' group (*not* included in our sample) and had endless conversations with nearly all the lads, the research pay-off was implicit rather than explicit, in that these close encounters gave us considerable insight into these youngsters' lives and helped us check again whether the interview data was similar to the 'natural' information given by group members, for instance in talking to each other. Perhaps, also, the summer groupwork programme allowed us as a research team to 'tune in' more generally to the subjects of our research. The hard data which was gained from this action research came in the form of video-taped cameos made by the youngsters themselves. We found that they thoroughly enjoyed role-playing their own previous experiences of contact with juvenile justice officials and we will use small transcriptions from some of these reconstructions in later chapters.

One of the difficulties we have faced in producing this book has been to present all our data in a limited number of words. Consequently we have not produced a separate, elaborate appendix detailing our research techniques. Instead we have referred to our methods in the text, providing notes for most chapters which usually relate to the aspect of the sample, detailed in table 1.1, we are working with. Those readers particularly interested in our research methodology and wishing to obtain copies of the various schedules used should now use this reference system.[1]

Finally, although we have had the good fortune to work on a project which suffered no major difficulties and although it was carefully prepared to avoid the blatant pitfalls of the receiving-end tradition, the methodology, even from our own biased point of view, has to be

criticized. First it will become clear shortly that our documentation of
the perceptions of our subject families involved recording severe allegations of official malpractice, particularly against the police. Yet we
present, and partly this is because of the police's reluctance to cooperate, very little independent checking of these allegations. We were
not present when a juvenile was arrested or questioned, for instance. We
feel that the discerning nature of these allegations, and the context in
which they were made plus the independent checks we have been able
to make of so many other parts of the process, will allow most readers
to assess for themselves whether these 'stories' are true. However, it is
only right that we point out the need for caution here. Second although,
for a qualitative study, our sample is fairly large, because of the dearth
of previous and alternative findings in this area, there is a danger of the
case study being expected to explain more than it should and abused
accordingly. We should state here and now therefore that the sub-
samples on which we base particular chapters are very small and not
statistically significant. They gain significance only when interlinked
and then only in terms of being a comparative case study.

2

Working-Class Families and the Local State

INTRODUCTION

We must start from the fact that the hundred families we selected because of their compulsory attendance at a juvenile court invariably turned out to be poor working class. The juvenile justice system does not deal with juveniles; it deals with juveniles from a particular section of society who in the main live in depressed urban areas: Merseyside juvenile courts alone deal with 7 per cent of juvenile crime in England and Wales.

We will gain little from analysing the specific perceptions of these families' views of juvenile justice without first situating these perceptions on a larger map. Unskilled working-class families living in urban areas judge specific incidents, such as a juvenile court appearance, not in isolation but in terms of an extensive background knowledge stemming from previous encounters with a range of local authority and 'law and order' officials, who represent the local state. Consequently in this chapter we will consider these families' views of home and neighbourhood, job prospects, social class, 'welfare' and law and order.

These poor[2] families live in a region which was once the wealthiest provincial area in the first industrial nation yet today share the experience of an environment now pitted with dereliction, an area which scores high on many indices of social deprivation. It is a region in which few adolescents can afford to adopt the commercially produced styles which a succession of rebellious youth movements — from the Teds to the Rudies — have made their own. Instead the region is characterized by a shared cultural milieu (see Mungham and Pearson, 1976) in which working-class adolescents and adults alike share both structural deprivation and leisure outlets. Theirs is usually not a world divided by inter-

generational strife, it is more often a world in which even the number
of years between parent and child is relatively small and where 'leaving
home' takes place only when children marry and begin their own
families (see Parker, 1974).

We start from this base: in general terms the relationship between
the adults and youth in our study is one of shared experience and outlook. This internal consensus is borne of a cultural tradition reinforced
and redefined by the deprivation which these families continue to
suffer as a whole. We will compare 'objective' measurements of social
deprivation on Merseyside with the perceptions of these families as we
progress. However, the findings presented in this chapter are better
understood if we introduce the notion of the *deprivation of knowledge*
at this stage. We found that our respondents' world view was basically
parochial: based on, and explained in terms of, concrete experience
rather than via abstractions or the use of theoretical ideas. This is not a
put-down, nor are we saying that the families had no theoretical tools
whatsoever, but that these tools were understandably crude and limited.
The circle is a vicious one: without some basic analytic equipment,
deprivation of knowledge simply grows and the immediate concrete
world becomes *the* world. At a practical research level this meant we
had to work very hard with our respondents in terms of questions
about social class. Such questions can best be answered by people who
have perceived or experienced the reality of several life styles — such as
the working-class 'scholarship' boy or girl who makes it to Oxbridge.
The adolescent born, bred and educated in one run-down overspill
estate simply has less comparative material in his head to use in constructing an answer.

However, the reticence and ambiguity of our subjects reduced considerably when they were able to consider issues which are naturally
topics of importance and daily dispute to them. On the question of the
value of schooling and job prospects their replies become more substantive. On the question of 'welfare' and law and order, its theory and
practice, they become both animated and assured, giving well-reasoned
answers punctuated by elaborate anecdotes. In this chapter we shall
move with this spectrum from the equivocal to the unequivocal, from
perceptions based as a result of a deprivation of analytic tools, because
of limited comparative knowledge, to perceptions based on extensive
and vital everyday experience.

OUTLINES OF THE REGION AND ITS WORKING-CLASS FAMILIES

The extent of both the absolute and relative social deprivation which pervades Merseyside is recorded in the census returns. Its pages catalogue immense poverty — detailing high indices of single-parent families, overcrowded and substandard buildings, ill-health and unemployment — and chart net migration from the city's heartlands, leaving behind the elderly and most socially disadvantaged members of the community (Evans, 1977).

Economically, the region has been described as an 'industrial graveyard' set to become 'the Jarrow of the 1980s'. A national economic recession, the long-term decline of the area's staple industries (such as shipbuilding) and the 'rationalization' programme of large, multi-plant businesses, particularly in the manufacturing sector, have combined to throw at least one in six of local workers on the dole scrapheap, a figure which escalates towards one in two in some districts. In the wake of this unemployment 'crisis', state initiatives in the form of regional policies and job-creation schemes — focused on the family unit and the male breadwinner in particular — can at best produce marginal and short-run palliatives.

Economic stagnation and decline is matched by the inertia of local statutory services, lacking real direction and left reeling by wave upon wave of expenditure cuts. As far back as 1965, the planning department, for example, conceded that over threequarters of the city's primary schools and nearly half its secondary schools fell short of the DES's own standards. These inadequate schools now offer a diminishing curriculum for local children, whilst the area's teachers, education welfare officers and social workers anxiously face redundancies, cut-backs in their resources and a moritorium on training opportunities. As public services shrink to a statutory minimum, some would contend that crime alone is a going concern and that the administrators of law and order are the only workers with a secure future. The region's recorded crime figures are amongst the highest in Britain, notably for such indictable offences as burglary, wounding, robbery and theft of motor vehicles. And, according to a member of the force patrolling 'one of Britain's toughest police areas', one-half of the serious crime (in the region) is committed by juveniles. The chief constable's annual reports draw special attention to 'young criminal drivers', 'gangs of youths' and

The cause of crime is very fundamental — greed, selfishness, violence — if we cannot prevent the dreadful increase in crime or at least contain it, the freedom and way of life we have been accustomed to enjoy for so long will vanish — either the thieves and vandals will take control, or restrictive legislation will be introduced to curtail their freedom and inevitably that of a decent society.

Although we felt it inappropriate and intrusive to quiz families about their standards of living, a wide range of indicators place them as poor, working-class families falling within the Registrar General's categories IV and V. The fact that, almost without exception, all these families were granted full legal aid affords the clearest marker of their low incomes. We also found that less than half the fathers were employed, and these in a variety of unskilled and semi-skilled occupations, whilst a considerably greater number of mothers, some two-thirds, were in part- or full-time employment, reflecting the traditional pattern in an area with a legacy of female factory employment. But we found that a significant minority of all families in our sample, and the majority of those families subject to care proceedings, were either fully or partially reliant on state benefits: in some families two or three members might be on the dole.

Whilst our sample families did vary considerably in their make-up, we found the majority of adolescents lived at home with two parents and about three other siblings, making up a total family membership somewhat above the national average.

There was a high incidence of 'second marriages' or marriage breakdown in the sample cases involving our girl subjects and those families exposed to care proceedings.

We also found parents and children living together in relative harmony (see Kitwood, 1979), but noted significant gender differences over issues of freedom and responsibility. Boys, perhaps freer from domestic and family duties, are certainly more visible on the region's streets and most we talked to seemed happy enough with their family homes, which were marred only by the occasional tiff, quickly brushed away. For girls, on the other hand, family conflicts and tensions proved a focal concern: for them, it seems, adolescence is not a time of youthful freedom but of persistent attempts to struggle and bluff their way out of family restrictions. Members of our girls' group were constantly devising strategies to spin out a little social space for themselves, resist parental inquisitions about their failure to stay at school, where they went in the evenings and what time they had to be back home by. A snippet of video role-play illustrates these preoccupations:

> DAUGHTER: Nag, nag, nag, that's all you do.
> MOTHER: I'll do more than bleedin' nag in a minute, girl.
>   . . . Anyway, get them dishes done – Get to bed.

The girls' concern with parental controls (but not with women's traditional and home-centred roles) could, in the face of their material limitations, prompt a shared fantasy of asserting their independence by setting up in a flat of their own:

> Having a place of your own . . . would be too quiet . . . but . . . suppose you could do what you want – and there'd be no drunks coming in and battering you.

Yet when it came to a juvenile court appearance 'mother' would almost invariably be the parent, taking overall responsibility. Three-quarters of our sample were accompanied in court by their mothers alone.

We also met a few girls who were so distressed by family frictions that they requested reception-into-care. And we will illustrate further the complementary and interlocking nature of family and statutory services controls, particularly for girls, in chapters 10 and 12. Sally, an adopted child, who followed through her request provides an extreme and poignant example:

> Since I'm five, I've never kissed my mam – I can't walk in the door without her nagging. . . . They said 'Behave or you'll go into care . . . behave or you'll go into care.' They even called out the social worker in the middle of the night. I said 'Call them, see if I fuckin' care. . . . I'll be better off in care.'

The girls' greater awareness of interpersonal issues and their paramount concern for the ways others, particularly adults, perceive them is a continuing theme colouring their experiences of the juvenile justice process. Despite these gender-specific problems and 'normal' manageable tensions, we did not find these families were marked by intergenerational rifts: rather, the overall picture is of poor, predominantly white, working-class families living in comparative harmony and housed on dreary municipal estates in a depressed area of the country.

PERCEPTIONS OF SOCIAL STRUCTURE

Images of social class and social space

Although 'objectively' these families were living on the baseline of the socio-economic scale, tipped there by political and economic changes spanning the last 30 years, they themselves tended to perceive their position somewhat differently: their outlook was more optimistic than official measures of their socio-economic position would allow.

Thus, when we broached the subject of social class with family members, we found that our questions and attempted explanations of them proved obscure to many families. For, whilst three-quarters of these parents did express some awareness of social-class divisions, the majority of their sons and daughters did not really know what we were getting at. They formulated their own partial ideas about 'the rich', 'the posh' and 'the snobs', since for the majority of these adolescents, born and bred within a few mean streets, comparative knowledge is as yet elusive. We found that those young people who were able to match their parents' concepts tended to be 16-year-old school-leavers:

> Some are posh . . . some are just low, all right . . . some are tramps. Posh people stick to themselves . . . they don't like mixing with us people . . . only their own kind.

Of those parents and the handful of adolescents who did detail social-class divisions, the majority saw three separate classes – upper, middle and working. Chris, for example, at 16, suggests the following:

> Working class – 'People who work for a living.'
> Middle class – 'Work but not as hard as the working class.'
> Upper class – 'Don't work – born into it.'

Families who favoured a schema featuring rather more divisions often included an underclass, a subgroup of 'dolites' and 'tramps', a sedimentary morass which they could look down on and take comfort from. This idea of a scapegoated sub-group providing a functional yardstick for poor, white working-class families has been uncovered in a number of urban studies (Coates and Silburn, 1970). The desire for family autonomy and respect, together with limited social horizons, helps explain the high class rankings which adolescents and their parents accorded to themselves, thus misidentifying their objective social-class position.

When we turn to the basis of class, both parents and their sons agree that it all boils down to money — which regulates consumption, housing and 'life style':

> Money talks — there's those in the money, in the know, with the connections. And there's everybody else.

> The upper classes have got everything — house, car — and one or two just toffee-nosed. They're not bothered with anyone else — they just don't want to know anyone under them.

But girls suggest structural divisions rest less on money *per se* than on conspicuous consumption: for girls, it seems, personal appearance is crucial, and an individual's clothes mark status divisions.

> Some in jeans, smoking and all that . . . some well-dressed and clean.

Or housekeeping:

> Scruffy houses to gorgeous palaces.

These comments provide give-away class indicators. The girls' measuring rod, a fascination with and assessment by looks, seems to mirror their own concerns with the way others see them and we will go on to illustrate this aspect further in chapter 6. Over and above these simple platitudes, we met very few girls or boys equipped with the comparative knowledge to weigh up the social order and assess their own structural place within it. One lad, for example, could only define a 'snob' by harking back to his home ground:

> Like her next door. She got a few bob redundancy money and is all stuck up. We don't talk to her now.

Exceptionally, we met adolescents like John, a school-leaver, who had considered alternative social models:

> Communism is an ideal — but is not practical. . . . You get your dictators.

But usually we found it was working-class parents, not their sons and daughters, who had the experience and acumen to expound such views:

The rich stole from the peasants and are now trying to pull the working class down. Class is about attitudes to life but money comes into it all the time.

Our subjects' views of social space reflected their limited social and geographical mobility. Most adolescents spend their 'free' time close to home: 'down the park', 'up the road', 'over to the shops', 'in town'.

For one or two lads, a term in a rural institution may provide a first glimpse of the world beyond the city boundaries. Others may plan an occasional day's outing with their mates, getting on a bus to a satellite town 'as far as "South town"'' or recall a Butlinland summer holiday:

Blackpool and Bournemouth are not like this concrete dump. Living in Countyside is like being banged up – it's just like being stuck away.

And those boys who joined our groupwork programme for residential weekends away from their neighbourhoods tended to view middle-class Lakeland tourists and overseas visitors with a good deal of suspicion, classifying all such 'strangers' as 'woolly backs' and 'divvies'. One girl asked 'Is this the countryside?', and another, 'Are the Lakes in Wales?' Thus, for the most part, these working-class youngsters were thrown back on their own local knowledge as a basis for making comparisons and, consistent with their overall views of social-class divisions, they could point away from their own homes towards the 'too quiet' outer suburbs where 'the posh' and 'the snobs' live, as well as to less salubrious parts of their own estates – invariably 'over there', 'the other end of the estate', distancing themselves from the residue of the 'dolite' underclass.

Most adolescents could also focus on the media's 'bad news' picture of their region, describing it as a 'rough and ready' area, renowned for:

Football, hooligans and vandals . . . football, comics and the slums.

Anita sums up press and TV coverage:

Hard, dead common, scruffy . . . none of yous over here has got a job.

From school to where?

Most of the adolescents we worked with were still on the roll of a local secondary or comprehensive school. Their views of schooling were neither consistent with marxist interpretations, which see it as a fundamentally controlling agency (e.g. Corrigan, 1979; Deem, 1978), nor with the views of education and court officials who, as we shall see in the coming chapters, saw secondary schools as a vehicle of upward social mobility. Instead, our sample tended to see school in a rather more matter-of-fact way, based on their experience of it rather than their analysis of its function in a political sense, except perhaps as a meal ticket, promising not jam tomorrow, just bread today:

> Learn you to speak properly — read and write — if you don't do that you get nowhere, do you?

Schools, they told us, are primarily in business to 'Learn you, get a job, and that', and they saw some local comprehensives as failing their pupils in even this basic task:

> Not very practical schools — you can't get a job with French or History.

But when we went on to ask these adolescents how they viewed the typical school day, we did not meet with the wholly negative response charted in some contemporary studies (e.g. Kitwood, 1979). We found, however, a clear gender split in majority perspectives. Only a few boys expressed outright dislike of their schools — 'boring', 'rubbish' — whilst for many there is a tendency towards toleration and compromise. For the boys, school is mainly 'all right' and 'OK', with certain teachers and lessons, games and football, and above all the chance to 'have a laugh' relieving the academic tedium. The boys, therefore, described their school survival kit in terms not unlike the 'counter-school culture' identified by Paul Willis (1977) featuring 'an attempt to weave a tapestry of interest and diversion through the day's institutional context'.

For girls, it seems, the school day is less a tolerable interlude than a more clearly liked or hated necessity. Working-class girls are especially concerned with what others, particularly adults, think of them at school and tend to seek teachers' approval, a finding paralleled in the *National Child Development Study*. Girls who told us they hated school resented regulations prescribing personal appearance and also seemed more anxious to get away before their 16th birthdays than the boys:

> I came high up in class — I didn't take no CSEs. They said I'd
> have got them. I just wanted to leave.

Perhaps, for girls like one 13 year old, this time away from home is seen
as increasingly irrelevant to an ultimate ambition:

> The subjects aren't any use — what do you want to learn needle-
> work for? I just want to get married and have kids. I want to
> dress them nice . . . I'd like to have coloured kids because you can
> make them look nicer than whites.

Given the disproportionate numbers of girls we observed who were
summoned before City juvenile court on grounds of non-school attendance, it is significant that over half these boys and girls told us they
'sagged' school frequently, mostly with mates, yet had avoided 'the
school board' checks. It is likely that if all these persistent school
truants were proceeded against, the 'care system' would buckle and
break down through overloading. Rick, for example, nominally in his
ROSLA year, has never been summoned to court for non-school
attendance:

> Go for a couple of weeks every six months or so — the new
> teachers don't know me — they think I'm new and say 'Have you
> got a book?'

Meanwhile, together with a mate, he has turned the family living room
into a workshop and spends most days doing up and customizing an old
motor bike. There they sit, drinking mugs of tea and talking bikes,
amidst bits of carburettor and pin-up calendars, adding there's no point
in going to school since their dads have lined up jobs for them anyway!

Our sample adolescents were ambiguous over the question of non-
school attendance. On the one hand most argued that teenagers had the
right to decide for themselves about their school attendance. Yet they
also accepted the fact that schools can take action against truants. They
were in the main against the use of care proceedings and being 'sent
away' for truancy and consequently fell back upon accepting alternative schools, parental sanctions and 'the cane' for non-attenders.

As their sons and daughters reach the minimum school-leaving age
and start job-hunting, many of the sample parents, with their own 'rat-
race' experiences of redundancies and short-time working, took a
sceptical line:

There are a few jobs if the kids look hard . . . but some of them don't care any more. There's so many on the dole, they think it's OK.

We found their sons and daughters were less cynical, in the main, being able to picture themselves in a number of traditional unskilled and semi-skilled waged jobs. Younger girls, for example, might fancy themselves as glamorous air hostesses but those on the threshold of leaving school tended to have their feet more firmly on the ground and saw themselves in a variety of secondary-sector women's jobs: care assistants, auxiliary nurses, hairdressers and shop assistants. Boys might have their hearts set on the Services, particularly the Merchant Navy, for this depressed region continues to provide a substantial recruiting ground; others would prefer civvy jobs, mentioning a number of traditional manual occupations, such as shot-blaster or sheet-metal worker. Yet despite their hopes, a clear majority of these adolescents were acutely aware of the region's job malaise and went on to rate their own real work chances poorly, as 'next to nothing' and 'nothing doing':

None . . . I don't reckon I'll get a job . . . some kids with qualifications can't get a job.

Many also knew from first-hand experience that their court appearances and resultant criminal record could tell against them; for, in an era of general economic recession, employers, even for the Services, can afford to pick and choose. Tom, for example, told us his solicitor advised him, in the face of weak prosecution evidence, to accept a binding-over from City juvenile bench. With hindsight, he wishes he'd stuck to his 'not guilty' plea, since he had been rejected by the RAF on the grounds of his 'criminal record' — and this in spite of his initial acceptance and successful completion of the entrance exams.

Parents, particularly those with older 'children' still out of work, tended to be equally pessimistic about their son's or daughter's 'nil' work chances:

He's got nothing to look forward to, only leaving school and going on the dole.

There's *good* children with 'O' and 'A' levels left school with not even a job after 12 months. She's got two and a half years left [at school] so even if she stays on a long time. . . .

But, we also met parents in more optimistic mood with undaunted faith in their own youngsters. Voicing an individualistic perspective, they clung to a belief that their particular son or daughter could rise above any local economic gloom and tenaciously win through:

> She'll make it in spite of the difficulties . . . Della is a very clever and strong person.

Mothers often expressed a further dimension of this unbroken faith. Perhaps they had come to terms with their own straight-jacket lot, but they believed their daughters might fare better and 'get more out of life':

> She says she's not getting married — she wants a full life . . . wants more . . . not a nine to five job in a factory like I had.

The way to 'making it' and securing a job, parents and adolescents agreed, does not lie through the formal employment agencies but depends on the lucky break reinforced by informal and family connections, with male relatives — dads, uncles, older brothers — putting a good word in. This predominant feeling — that what counts is less what you've done than who you know, with future work 'a chance configuration of family contacts and traditionally known job opportunities in the area' has been noted in several urban studies (Corrigan, 1979).

PERCEPTIONS OF THE LOCAL STATE

Principles not practised

Indirectly the views of our respondents, vis-a-vis the welfare state and law and order, are consistent with those liberal reformers who espoused the social justice principle during the post-war social reconstruction: for our respondents, in principle, saw the machinery of the local state being there to provide positive help and support. Their more definitive statements on these matters stem from the reality of both 'welfare' and 'policing' in their lives. Their views on these issues become less equivocal as a consequence. The unanimous and whole-hearted acceptance of an ordered society, necessarily equipped with police and welfare functions, was repeated in each family home we visited and endorsed by all members present. We would argue that this overwhelming consensus about the necessity of state intervention cannot be satisfactorily explained by these families' lack of comparative knowledge of alternative social systems. Rather, this endorsement repeats the findings of several studies concerned with working-class culture (e.g. Hall and Jefferson, 1976). The families we worked with all recognized the local state's potential as their guarantee against unpalatable social malaise.

The need for social and health workers and their right to intervene in family life where children are abused or neglected was firmly accepted. The need for the courts and the police was also unequivocally endorsed. Without the law, parents and children alike told us, mayhem, anarchy and chaos would ensue:

> Everybody would be getting their head knocked in. The rich would have no money and the poor would fight each other.

> Everybody could run wild and do everything they wanted; they could kill my brother. Then we'd get revenge and it would be crazy.

Thus, in principle, these families are wholly convinced of the need for basic statutory safeguards and services: their resistance and opposition is mustered not against the local state *per se* but stems rather from their own experience of the misuse of discretion and power vested in local agencies. We will consider these views in detail throughout the book by referring to the specific experiences and views of sections of our sample. All of our sample, however, distinguished quite clearly between 'the welfare' and the police, even though not all of them had first-hand experience of social work intervention.

However, all these families *did* share experience of 'law and order', of living in heavily policed areas and of observing, if not directly experiencing, the realities of routine urban policing. We will conclude this chapter with some discussion of their views of this process.

The police – need them, hate them

The region is not easy to police. Despite some years of relative containment, the recorded crime rates for the Merseyside metropolitan area continue to climb. The chief constable recently took comfort in the fact that, according to him, 80 per cent of his force were involved in 'community policing'. Race riots or the like, he assured the Police Committee, cannot happen to Merseyside. This optimism, combined with the unanimous support of the subject families — whose children actually contribute to the crime rate — for a well-ordered, fully policed society, might be seen as reflecting a healthy relationship between police and citizens in the region. However, this is not the case. The range of questions we asked concerning policing indicated an extremely high level of hostility and cynicism in both parents and adolescents.

For working-class families living within the region's police authority, the concept of community policing made little sense. Up to three-quarters of our sample adolescents for example, had never heard of juvenile liaison officers and could not as much as hazard a guess as to their function: just one or two lads with a previous police caution could grasp vaguely at the preventative task:

> To come and tell my mum to look after me properly and not get into trouble.

Rather, we found that police policies had succeeded in generating or sustaining an intense, consistent dislike, a distrust and hatred for the force, a unanimous venom shared by adolescents and their parents alike. And we also found that these families, living in quite different neighbourhoods patrolled by different police divisions, were more animated, more coherent and more self-assured in discussing this issue than any other topic we explored with them. The only point of contention seemed to be between households who said they 'hate them' and those where the police are merely disliked. Eric didn't mince words:

> Hate them, despise them, spit on them — to tell you the truth if someone around here saw a policeman on fire, they wouldn't even piss on him.

This agreed antagonism was often fuelled by the experience of recent bitter encounters with the police. Christine's view, for example, owes much to personal experience:

> I hate the police now everytime I see one. One of the detectives was my friend's Dad — I don't talk to her now.

Of course, the mutual dislike between police and working-class youth is well-documented (e.g. Gill, 1977) but the unequivocal way in which the vast majority of these adolescents, and particularly their parents, ex-

pressed their alienation to us was unexpected. There was a feeling that
the police were 'persecuting' their own estates, with many parents observing that the local force had changed from the peace-keeping policy
of 'the old days' to one of saturation policing, involving an ongoing
battle of wills between youths and the police on their own doorsteps.
For these families 'community policing' meant simply more policing:

It's like Gestapo round here: [the area's] blackened with police,
they patrol in mini-buses.

Loads of lads walking about — they — the police — jump out of
Black Marias and beat them up.

We found several boys who also told us that the police kept a high
profile around their homes and who felt any youth living in the vicinity
was likely to get picked up. One lad, for example, living in the docklands inner-city area, is adamant that he never goes out with his ring of
front-door keys now since, in a heavily policed neighbourhood, this
could amount to inviting a charge like 'going equipped'. For others:

They just pick you up for anything.

Think they're little gits 'cause they come round telling you to
move off corners and that when you've not done any harm.

Police pick on kids around here. You only have to be looking out
of the window when they come past — they ask you what you're
doing.

About a quarter of the boys we met, recalling their own brushes with
the local police, reckoned that 'the busies' have enough clout to deviate
from the rule book — to modify the legal code so as to suit their own
ends:

They must be getting something for getting you.

Most parents, too, had specific stories to tell about incidents they'd
seen of 'kids doing nothing getting picked on' and 'tiny children being
handcuffed'. Parents' widespread dislike and distrust of the police and
the subsequent taking of their child's side against outside authority
surprised us and indeed undermined one of our initial hypotheses: that
most parents would support policing practice in their areas.

It would be naive to suggest that these families' wide-ranging, bitter criticisms of the local police force may not be soured and inflamed by their recent court experiences. As we have no direct 'check' on these statements it must be left to the reader, having looked at the rest of our study and the 'safeguards' we build in elsewhere, to form a view. It may be, for instance, that lads are inclined to depict police practices as unjust in order to increase their own self-esteem: perhaps, as some adolescents outlined their views to us, they were trying, in effect, to neutralise their delinquent acts (see Ericson, 1976). Our group work programme with local boys also pointed to some significant modifications of this apparently shared antagonism towards the police. For we also found that the policeman seems to be a figure of secret envy: perhaps he is covertly admired because his job gives him the legitimate chance to assume the ideal 'macho' image which many working-class boys themselves aspire to. Certainly our group-work members shared a sustained infatuation with the trappings of modern police styles: they enjoyed wearing our video-making props including police-like hats and anoraks; they strove to sit at the front of the blue minibus and constantly urged the driver to go hell for leather. One lad, dressed up in police style, went so far as to stand in the middle of a country road trying to divert passing traffic. We would suggest, therefore, that for many boys the urban policeman represents an idealized 'real' man; he epitomizes those ascribed masculine attributes so highly rated in the working-class culture from which he comes – he has the chance to be hard, to be physically and mentally agile and to drive a powerful new car at speed. If young males are debarred, by reason of juvenile court convictions, presentation or whatever from joining such 'style' then they will try to outstrip its exponents.

Parents seemed to take little pleasure in developing their criticisms of the police. They recognized, like their sons and daughters, that some of their neighbours, particularly those without children and those with property of their own to protect, might maintain a high regard for the police. Yet their own endorsement of the need for a legal code and statutory control forced them into an ambiguous and circular dilemma in their thinking about the police: which is, in essence, 'We need them but we hate them.' Mr Clough provided an apt description of this dilemma:

I only like the police because we need them. I've needed them myself as a cab driver; they've helped me out. But I hate them,

I've been beaten up by them. . . . It's worse now; they get carried away: can't control themselves. We need them but I hate them . . . do you see what I mean?

Peter's perception of the police likewise contains the seeds of its own contradictions: perhaps his view best encapsulates how working-class adolescents view the heavy end of the local state and its various officials:

Don't like them . . . but we do need them, don't we?

SUMMARY

The hundred families who have made our research possible come from one of the most depressed and deprived regions in the United Kingdom and belong 'objectively' to the lower socio-economic strata of the local population. The are mainly families who in periods of economic growth provide the economy with unskilled and semi-skilled labour and who in a recession become the 'pool' of surplus labour. The children of these families are either soon to leave school or have just left school, mainly without either qualifications or any prospect of well-paid or rewarding jobs. Both parents and their children in the main appreciate this status in that it so obviously affects their living standards although their hopes for the future appear over-optimistic.

Like most other social groups in society, these families assessed their 'world view' in relation to their own experience. Although conscious of their poor job prospects and of living in neighbourhoods containing high levels of housing and social problems, their mood and their attitude to the wider society is not one of festering resentment. This is because their social and geographical position has not equipped them to develop sharp comparisons. Thus a deprivation of *knowledge* about their objective, relative poverty, can in itself be identified. Most people around them seem the same. Cheltenham and Oxford are not just a bus ride away. This is not to suggest that these parents and adolescents were unaware of material and status inequities. They were — as they were aware of the reality of 'rich' and 'posh' people. They did not use this group as a reference point, however, but instead more often located themselves above a more daily observable sub-group or under-class which allowed them to perceive themselves as 'better off' than official criteria would suggest. However, because of their position in society, the neighbourhoods in which they live and the attentions they receive from various local state officials, the parents and adolescents we worked with have complex and elaborate perceptions of the local state. In principle, they accept that welfare officials are there to help them. Again in principle, they accept the need for law and order, street policing and respect for authority. They are not overtly against the status quo. Yet in practice, and based on repeated concrete experience, their perceptions of local state officials are less positive and highly problematic. Whilst education officials, social workers and probation officers are judged diversely, the police are universally disliked, distrusted and even blamed for much 'trouble' by parents and children alike. The receiving of local 'law and order' has induced these families to withdraw their respect for the state. It is to this production and receiving of juvenile justice that we now turn.

3

Selecting 'Delinquents':
The Police as Gatekeepers

DECENTRALIZED DECISION-MAKING

As we have already suggested, discretion is 'embodied', through legislation, in local juvenile justice systems at all levels. The dynamics of street encounters between police and youths, the unofficial bargaining between police and young suspects, produce further diversity and sometimes official deviation over and above the discretion legitimated by the state; and we shall deal with these sorts of negotiations from the juveniles point of view in chapter 6. Here we are concentrating on the diversity produced by legitimated discretion. The actual bureaucratic structure in which 'sifting' decisions are made by the police about juveniles is well-documented by Priestly *et al.* (1977). Because they have looked at the police gatekeeping role so comprehensively, and because our primary task is to consider the adolescent's passage through the whole system, we will deal only briefly with the negotiating structure in which sifting takes place at the 'main entrance' to the court system: in the police command structure. The structure employed by Merseyside Police is, in formal terms at least, common to the whole police authority. Countryside and City juvenile courts, although serving separate petty sessional divisions, are thus in theory serviced by a sifting system which 'sends in' and keeps out similar types of alleged juvenile offending. Although this similarity of the sifting of juvenile cases for the two juvenile courts does hold generally, the actual nature of the Merseyside system, with decentralized decision-making about juveniles being made at a police sub-divisional level, does not necessitate this.

There are quite different decision-making structures operating elsewhere in England and Wales. Priestly *et al.*, for instance, found that in

Wiltshire the juvenile sift was made through a chain of command from constable, through inspector to divisional commander. There was no insertion of an assessment made by a police officer with special interest, or specialist training, in juvenile work. This structure contrasted with Bristol, where Priestly *et al.* found that the specialist 'juvenile liaison' function which had operated at a divisional level before the 1969 legislation, had been centralized into a specialist team of officers making up a juvenile bureau. Juvenile cases would be referred to this specialist 'main entrance' where decisions, based on similar criteria, would be made for the whole police authority.

In keeping with the failure of juvenile bureaux to develop in the north of England, Merseyside's decision-making structure remains decentralized. Merseyside having had one of the first juvenile liaison schemes in the country, did retain its juvenile liaison officers (JLOs) after the 1969 Act. Instead of decentralizing their specialist function, however, the then chief constable actually formalized their decentralization by basing them at sub-divisional level, the operational level furthest away from headquarters. On paper, and possibly for cosmetic reasons, the JLOs and their sub-divisional colleagues, assistant community liaison officers (ACLOs), are located within the youth and community section of Merseyside Police. This section is itself located, interestingly, within the public relations department! The youth and community section is 'HQ'-based and is headed by a superintendent who has under him a small team of inspectors, a sergeant and a couple of junior personnel. In theory, and on paper, this section has a staff of about 60, in that the JLOs and ACLOs, nearly all at constable and policewoman level, are a part of this section. These specialist officers operate at divisional and sub-divisional level. The ACLO's brief is a fairly broad one as his title suggests. He finds himself doing a lot of work with schools, church organizations, youth clubs, community groups and so on. He is above all acting as a link man between police and, in the main, community organizations. He will in practice share some of the JLOs work, largely as a consequence of the fact that he tends to share office accommodation with the JLO and is seen by his station colleagues, along with the JLO, as the 'soft cop'. The JLO is the key worker who does the spade work in preparing the background material for the 'sifting' of juvenile referrals. Each police sub-division will have one or two male JLOs and each division one female JLO who works across the relevant sub-divisions. The JLO initiates any consultation with the schools, social services and probation service. He makes recommendations about cases designated for 'consultation', that is 'due consideration' before a decision is made about whether, in the main, to prosecute, 'caution' or take 'no further action' (NFA). His recommendation passes upwards to the sub-divisional commander.

This sub-divisional superintendent has the additional title of community liaison officer (CLO). His role as CLO gives him total discretion vis-a-vis the fate of juveniles in process. Indeed the chief constable delegates responsibility for processing juveniles directly to his sub-divisional commanders. So again, in theory, the CLO's superior, his divisional commander, cannot overrule a decision concerning a juvenile. It is not surprising therefore that the JLOs and ACLOs in practice, see their boss as the sub-divisional commander. He runs their police station, he rejects or accepts their recommendations. He tells them, one way or another, what additional criteria he wants to be taken into account when sifting juveniles. The sub-divisional commander is a working policeman. He shares main-line policing goals; he is susceptible to the associated pressures and expectations. He runs a police station, not an assessment centre for adolescents. He has no specific lengthy training in youth work or social work nor is he expected to be conversant with theories of delinquency, delinquency control or child care. He is more concerned with catching criminals and sending them to court (see Jones, 1980).

In the circumstances, and given that the police are offered no clear legislative guidelines on cautioning, it should be no surprise that there is considerable diversity in NFA and cautioning rates and in what sort of cases go forward into the prosecution process (see tables 3.1 and 3.3). We spoke to some JLOs whose CLO nearly always followed their recommendations. We spoke to others clearly disillusioned by the frequency with which their recommendations were overturned.

The JLO's and ACLO's role, because of the decentralized structure in which they have no *de jure* power, is clearly not an easy one. Being 'on the ground' and 'at the front line' means they are totally aware of the policing difficulties and consequent ethos their colleagues share. Any attempts by them to foster a strongly community based 'softly, softly' approach are potentially undermined however, in a police force with a fairly basic attitude to policing. In particular the calling in to a sub-division of the equivalent of a special operation group to 'clear up' a particular crime problem can set back the work of an ACLO by months, since he must continue to work his patch and take the butt of locals' criticisms which routinely follow such operations. Similarly the

TABLE 3.1 CAUTIONING AND NO FURTHER ACTION RATES
FOR JUVENILES IN THE METROPOLITAN AREA

Petty sessional divisions/ police divisions	*Cautioned*	*No further action*	*Prosecuted*
Area 1 (City)	2313	198	4090
Area 2 (including Countyside)	403	47	1408
Area 3	786	67	
Area 4	825	82	
Area 5	624	57	
TOTAL	4951	451	9036

TABLE 3.2 RATES OF CAUTIONING AND PROSECUTION OF
MALE AND FEMALE (10–17 yrs) IN CITY JUVENILE COURT
AND CORRESPONDING POLICE DIVISIONS

| | *Males* | | *Females* | |
	Cautioned	*Prosecuted*	*Cautioned*	*Prosecuted*
1977	1825	2912	477	231
1978	1603	3464	645	264
1979	1590	3724	723	366

JLO must not only respond to the formal criteria concerning the sifting
of juveniles, he must respond also to the idiosyncrasies of his sub-
divisional commander, or else be seen to be out of step with the realities of policing!

THE 'PUSH-IN' TENDENCY

A Home Office research study (Ditchfield, 1976) has argued that the
official caution may not just be an alternative to a court appearance,
that is a diversionary tactic, but also an alternative to a 'no further
action' (NFA) or 'on the spot warning'. This, we content, is exactly

TABLE 3.3 MALES AND FEMALES (10–17 yrs) CAUTIONED AS
A PERCENTAGE FOUND GUILTY AND CAUTIONED BY POLICE
AUTHORITY, 1978

	Indictable		Non-indictable (excluding motoring offences)	
	Boys	Girls	Boys	Girls
England and Wales	45	69	39	39
Merseyside	40	75	48	60
London Metropolitan Police	43	64	40	38
Nottinghamshire	50	74	37	35

what occurs in the Merseyside system. Because the sifting is in the
hands of front-line policemen operating, quite appropriately, in organizational terms, traditional policing goals there is a 'natural' 'push-in'
tendency. It is easy to see from table 3.1 that only 3 per cent of all
juvenile cases that formally enter the system are dealt with by NFAs
and as this proportion actually includes those children under the age
of criminal responsibility the NFA category is almost non-existent in
terms of diversion. NFA figures are not available in the published
criminal statistics (perhaps a significant fact in itself in explaining why
the police prefer to 'push-in' and thus be seen to be clearing up crime)
and comparisons are hard to come by. However Priestly *et al.* (1977)
found that in Bristol with 25 per cent and Wiltshire with 10 per cent,
NFAs accounted for a much greater proportion of outcomes than in
Merseyside. Even more telling, Merseyside Police were at the time of
our research introducing an 'informal' cautioning scheme. This caution,
usually administered at sergeant level, also requires an admission of
'guilt' from juvenile and parent but instead of being citable from
criminal records, is recorded in the juvenile index, the local force's
intelligence system and 'black list', which is kept at a divisional level.
It seems quite clear therefore that the system is designed to formally
assess and record details about almost every juvenile who enters the
system (this incidentally includes recording 'run aways' and 'domestic
rows' and so on) on the juvenile index. The informal, and to some
extent the formal, cautioning rates are fed by 'trivia' which, it could be

argued, should make up the NFA category. We can observe a further feature of the push-in tendency in table 3.2. This illustrates, using the cautioning and prosecution rates for the city area (which deals with nearly half the region's juvenile cases), that although there was a *decrease* in the amount of crime recorded by the police both in 1978 and 1979 (though 1980 has seen a steep upward turn) the number of juveniles entering the court has steadily *increased*. We think, based on our courtroom observation, that this has occurred through the greater use of Route 1: 'straight to court'. Significantly, Merseyside Police claim that they don't know the facts on these matters as, they say, they don't monitor either the load number of 'consultations' they process during a year or the number of juveniles who go straight to court 'overnight' on Route 1 (see Fig. 3.1).

If we are correct then, the push-in tendency is very considerable and indeed much greater than the published figures would suggest. To illustrate this we must widen the focus and compare Merseyside's 'published' performance not with 'low-crime/high-caution' police authorities such as Devon and Cornwall, but with high-crime-rate areas similar to Merseyside. Table 3.3 shows that boys on Merseyside are cautioned at a comparatively higher level for non-indictable offences than in similar areas. This, we have argued, is because of the tendency to issue a caution for a very minor misdemeanour, rather than take no further action. The relatively low 'indictable' caution rate, we speculate, is a result of the strong tendency to use Route 1 for juveniles and send them straight to court without any 'sift' or consultation. We know that divisional and sub-divisional commanders are 'allowed' to use Route 1 freely. In a city division, for instance, all football match arrests go straight to court without any consultation. In a countyside division a similar blanket approach is used routinely to 'clear' certain main streets of 'loitering' youths. Regardless of the charge (e.g. obstructing the footpath) or the lack of any previous record, all juveniles arrested are prosecuted. Hence we observed large numbers of juveniles appearing in Merseyside courts for minor effences for which they received discharges who if they had been 'sifted' could have easily been given cautions.

THE SIFT IN ESSENCE

As we will show in later chapters, the formal rules, some defined by statute others by organizational procedures, of the various official agencies involved in juvenile justice are used by local officials in devious and unofficials ways. Sometimes this official deviation is designed to allow the working day to run smoothly; sometimes to actually serve more effectively the best interests of a child. On other occasions such deviation is rooted in ideological resistance to the official goals of the legislation. A central plank of our analysis, however, is that the 1969 Act legitimates so much local discretion anyway that most local state officials can pursue their own organizational and ideological goals without being tempted to resort to extensive rule-breaking. This, we are arguing, is exactly the case when we look at the police role as 'sift' in the local juvenile justice system we researched. The 'push-in' tendency we have detailed is in no way remarkable in the context of the crisis in the urban area which was being policed.

As we indicated earlier, we received only limited and carefully screened cooperation from the police. However, when we were allowed to talk to policemen about their role, the *struggle* between them and the adolescents on the street was clearly apparent in their definition of their function. Many of the comments were made 'off the record' and 'not to be quoted' of course and whilst we shall respect this confidentiality we can hypothesize that 'letting off' juveniles with minimal official action is unpopular with most urban policemen and anathema to others. We will present extensive observations from juveniles and parents to back up this contention in due course. Confirmation that this contest occurs in the beat policeman's thinking and that it leads him to 'forget preventative policing and concentrate on law enforcement' can be found in a recent analysis by a Merseyside police officer (Jones, 1980).

It is worth repeating that we are not arguing this position in criticism of the individual policeman but rather to illustrate that such an outlook is normal and routine in the policing of urban working-class youth. It impinges informally upon the operation of the formal sifting processes, thus creating a push-in tendency, which in legislative terms is not inevitable but merely a consistent use of legitimated discretion, based on certain ideas about how to deal with street-wise adolescents.

These formal rules and 'routes' are essentially very simple as figure 3.1 shows, although obviously the practice of the sift is complex. A full analysis would involve looking at the role of British Rail Transport Police, the 'Port' Police, Merseyside's links with other police authorities and the relationship between uniformed police and the CID. We cannot be concerned with such detail and will thus limit ourselves to a brief and oversimplified summary.

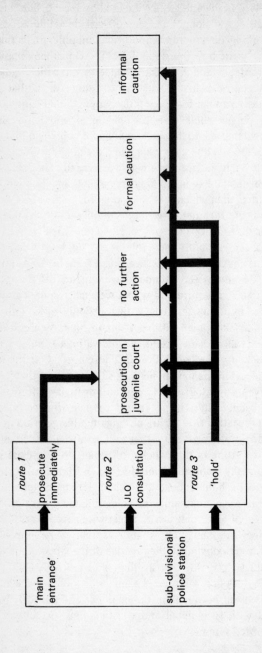

Figure 3.1 Main routes for 'offence' cases

We must assume that the majority of all juvenile cases dealt with by prosecution go directly to court along Route 1, after a brief front desk assessment in the police station. These cases simply do not enter the consultation machinery but instead go 'on the books and into court'. Key variables affecting routing include the suspect's background, his or her age and the nature of the offence. Route 1 cases will thus tend to be triggered by some 'previous' background, perhaps a previous offence or caution, if the juvenile is over 14 and/or charged with a 'serious' offence. Certain offences will automatically trigger a court appearance because of internal policy. 'street clearing' and football incidents have been mentioned as examples of this. These additional 'push-in' requirements may be transmitted from the chief constable, via his divisional commanders, down to the sub-division where the desk sergeant or CID inspector will operationalize them, or they may be based on a divisional commander's own discretion.

Route 2 cases will also begin with a brief front-desk assessment relying on criminal records, the local juvenile index, and age and offence criteria. If the front-desk decision is 'favourable', and the juvenile has admitted or seems likely to admit the offence, the case will be passed down to the JLO. Consultation should also take place for offence cases where the child is under 12, unless the 'nature of the offence' criterion overrides. On paper, consultation should also normally take place for all juveniles if it is known by the police that they, or their families, are on the case loads of social services or probation. In practice this criterion is only a rule of thumb, it is not always applied. The failure of social services to respond adequately to consultation forms in the early years of the system's operation is largely responsible for this. Consultation will also tend to occur when welfare or social need issues show themselves. A child who attends special school, for instance, will usually be routed for consultation.

The decision on whether or not to consult with other agencies lies almost entirely in the hands of the police. However, they have not received the cooperation and encouragement to maximize this option. We found their relationship with social services, in City, and social services and probation in Countyside was not very good, with some hostility and extensive 'indifference' occurring on both sides of the relationship. 'Good' communication occurred between individuals, rather than agencies.

Having completed his assessment of a particular case, a JLO makes a recommendation to his sub-divisional commander. The sub-divisional commander has, in essence, to choose from the four options shown in figure 3.1 although other possibilities, such as inviting social services to consider care proceedings, are available. The scope of these options are radically reduced if the assessed juvenile denies the offence. His denial rules out the two cautioning outcomes. The exact wording of the charge which, as we shall see in due course, produces so many other 'difficulties' in the juvenile justice system is most pertinent here, in that a juvenile or his parents will often not accept a particular charge as accurate, may question its validity and so tend to find their case pushed into the formal court system. Clearly there are also many juveniles who, rather than go into the prosecution process, *accept* a caution and thus an admission of guilt, even though not privately agreeing with the accuracy of the charge.

The third route indicated in figure 3.1 is not acknowledged by the police as being a formal route at all. Nevertheless we have shown it because in practice it is so clearly a reality. Why such a 'holding' system operates is difficult to tease out of tight-lipped officials. In part the fact that months sometimes pass between the case entering the system and the juveniles being informed of a decision is probably the result of the low priority given to such trivial cases; they simply hang around waiting for someone to process them. Perhaps, too, the sub-divisional commander responds to certain performance pressures from time to time and decides to be seen to be 'clearing up' effectively by prosecuting larger numbers of juveniles on his patch. We cannot be certain. From the point of view of this study it is the consequences of the 'hold' which are significant.

Each sub-division forwards its cases to be proceeded against to a central point: the prosecutions department. This department is not a final sift, except at a technical level whereby it will return cases or negotiate over details if they are not regarded as sound by the prosecution lawyer. It merely facilitates prosecution by collating and time-tabling. The prosecution personnel are well aware of the different thresholds operated by sub-divisional commanders, but do not regard it as their brief to comment on this. They merely process what they are sent.

SOME CONSEQUENCES OF THE 'PUSH-IN' TENDENCY

It seems quite clear that whilst sifting and prosecution decision-making remains in the hands of the police, who are given no clear guidelines about how such a process should operate, that the 'push-in' tendency is likely to dominate. This dominance is almost assured when local decision-making rests with front-line urban policemen. From the police-man's point of view there are major advantages in having this control. However, there are also serious ramifications, some unknown to the average policeman and some probably quite unintended. We shall men-tion three here, since they so clearly ripple through the rest of the prosecution process affecting perceptions of the quality of juvenile justice.

Firstly we must note the immense amount of 'trivia' which is pushed into the juvenile court. All the court officials we spoke to, as well as juveniles and their parents, agreed that this was the case. Indeed City magistrates themselves demonstrated this by dismissing or agreeing to the withdrawal of no less than 16 per cent of cases that came before them and using a conditional and absolute discharge in 23 per cent of cases that were proven. It is not unreasonable to equate a citable caution with a discharge in terms of significance on a criminal record. If we do this then it is not difficult to see that nearly 40 per cent of all cases pushed into the juvenile court could, and perhaps should, never have gone that far. Obviously this is a value judgement, but it is one widely shared by most non-police officials. In City one of the reasons so many cases were dismissed was again the result of the nature of the system. With sub-divisions using their discretion in isolation, unaware of the consequences of their policy, with the failure to use NFA and with the tendency to use Route 1 and push in 'overnight' cases being quite strong, many technically faulty cases landed on the prosecution lawyer's desk. We will see in the next chapter how much 'wheeling and dealing' he is then forced to engage in around the court.

Second, as we shall see, the wording of the charge is a fundamental issue. Again, the 'natural' tendency of the policeman to maximize the seriousness of an alleged offence by using a particular charge meets with immense hostility from juveniles and parents. The accused often respond to, in their eyes, the unnecessary severity of the charge by pleading not guilty. The outcome of this clash of perspectives at the police station is a full-blown trial, often involving a whole morning's work for numerous court officials. We witnessed many long-drawn-out criminal trials for trivial matters in both courts but particularly in City and these trials were the consequence of police inflexibility in the early stages.

A third dysfunction which has major implications for the moral authority of the juvenile justice system concerns the 'hold' phenomenon which we have shown as Route 3 in figure 3.1. These cases usually involve particularly trivial alleged offences. Consequently both parents and their children assume that 'hearing nothing' for weeks or months indicates that no further action is being taken. However, as we know, this is highly unlikely to be the case. Thus, when either a summons or a suggested caution is finally laid on them, their response is very negative. One reaction is to plead not guilty and so produce the trivial trial. Another reaction, as we shall see, is to complain bitterly *in open court* and so upset the quality of justice offered there. This second reaction is particularly likely when, at the time of arrest, a caution had been mentioned as a possible outcome by the arresting officer or desk sergeant, but the decision, some time later, was in fact a prosecution. Again, as we have shown, any specific information given in the police station about cautioning is potentially unsound since the decision-making is carried out higher up the line.

For our purposes the most significant consequence of these dysfunctions, *all a result of the 'push-in' tendency,* is the dissatisfaction and alienation it produces in juveniles and in their parents, which jaundices their views of justice as they are processed through the juvenile court.

We can now move on to those cases, nearly two-thirds, that pass through the police sift and get as far as the juvenile court. Although we have shown that considerable diversity can occur between different police sub-divisions in their sifting of juveniles, we have also suggested that this diversity is, in practice, checked by the 'push-in' tendency shared by most sub-divisional commanders. Their discretion tends to be used in a relatively uniform way. Thus, whilst the proportion of cautions as against prosecutions varies quite considerably between sub-divisions, these will tend to be diffused when we place a number of sub-divisions together into a division and so on, because of the *shared* 'push-in' tendency. Basically therefore the differences between Countyside division's cautioning rate of 26 per cent and City's police divisions' 28.5 per cent (of all cases referred) is not very significant, particularly when we note that Countyside's slight preference for NFA and the fact that their court's input was not increasing during the research period whereas City's was rising slightly. The enormous inequities in the production of juvenile justice begin with the police but, as we shall now show, are worked on and multiplied by juvenile court officials whose outlook, when we compare the two courts, does not even have the relative consistency which the police demonstrate.

4

City's Liberal Paternal Juvenile Justice

THE COURTROOMS

Situated in the midst of the municipal and business quarters of the city centre, City juvenile courts are housed in part of two large Edwardian buildings. City has four juvenile courts; No. 1 and 2 courts are in a recently modernized building. These courtrooms, designed to Home Office specification, have a totally modern look, being fitted out with industrial carpeting and bland office furniture. All desks and seats are on ground level. The clerk's and social service's desks have telephones which ring discreetly but regularly during proceedings. Both these courtrooms have desk/name plates designating solicitors, magistrates etc. The plates are now bolted to the desks after an unfortunate incident in which a mother used one of them to make her feelings known to a social worker at the back of the court. No. 1 and 2 courts have three doors, one for magistrates, one for the 'customers', who come from the waiting room, and one which leads from the cells. This third entrance allows police and warrant officers to do their handcuffing outside the court, so avoiding the in-court incidents which tend to flare up as juveniles are given custodial sentences and which did occur in Countyside Court.

The courts also have their own private entrance, which leads to a waiting area with public telephones, toilets, waiting room and a series of officials' rooms, including an interview room.

No. 1 court is used in the main as a remand court. It concentrates on a high through-put, taking pleas, dealing with guilty pleas and sentencing cases previously remanded for social enquiry reports. On a normal morning No. 1 court will process more than 20 cases. In the afternoon it will continue to deal with 'short' cases and some trials. No. 2 court also tends to be a 'quantity' court in the mornings, taking trials in the afternoon and being the forum for City's care proceedings at least a couple of afternoons each week. These two courts then tend to deal with the bulk of City's business.

The other pair of courts, No. 3 and 4, are housed in a separate building nearby. They have not been modernized or redesigned specifically as juvenile courts. No. 3 court in particular, with its raised platform for magistrates, large crest and mahogany wall panelling, has the smell and feel of a traditional criminal court. No. 4 court is slightly less austere but has the alternative problem of particularly poor sound-proofing. The outside noise level provides a major disturbance in this court, with officials regularly competing against articulated lorries and pneumatic drills. These courtrooms were hastily converted into juvenile courts some years ago to cope with the steadily increasing work-load and also to try to reduce the delay in dealing with juvenile cases caused by a backlog of work. They thus also lack support facilities such as interview rooms, refreshment facilities and an adequate waiting room.

No. 3 and 4 courts are used mainly for juvenile trials. They process trials day in day out and so deal with the lengthier cases. Nevertheless there is no sense in which No. 3 and 4 courts are 'quiet' or slow. The overriding impression one gets of this whole system is that it is bristling with activity. To process more than 4,000 cases, including the administration of the accompanying remands and trials, each year is a considerable organizational feat for one local juvenile court system. The bureaucratic apparatus is considerable. City's four juvenile courts are thus served by 13 clerks, several ushers, a social services court team of three, and a bench of more than 140 magistrates. There are correspondingly large numbers of defence and prosecution lawyers, warrant officers and the like.

City courts are very much in the business of people processing. Vast numbers of people have to be organized and timetabled five hours a day, five days a week. The size and complexity of the task creates a set of limitations and organizational constraints upon the styles of operation and the nature of in-court regimes which City can engender. For example, by definition, City magistrates are not going to be able to know their court's 'regulars' in any methodical way, as can occur in a small, quiet court. Similarly the chances of any one clerk 'knowing' his bench in a detailed way is slight. Indeed City magistrates themselves are timetabled in such a way that they tend to know only a small number of their own colleagues. Thus almost by definition City courts could not become cosy and 'in-crowd', through the extensive personal acquaintances of the court officials which characterize certain smaller court systems. On the other hand, the organizational pressures on City courts to become highly bureaucratized and impersonal, to the point of becoming a human conveyor belt, is obvious. It is therefore appropriate to evaluate the style and quality of City's version of juvenile justice with this structural backcloth in mind.

By sitting 'randomly' in separate courtrooms over our eight-month observation period, and keeping our three diaries independent throughout, we were able on completion of the fieldwork to offer a fairly rigorous check for both consistency and idiosyncrasy throughout the City system. Analysis showed a remarkably high level of consistency in the running of the whole system in terms of clerking in court, magisterial function, sentencing and overall treatment of defendants and their families. There appear to be three sets of operational rules in City which have evolved over time and become 'normative'. These rules revolve around the routine use of due process, an agreement that proceeding with civility should be the norm and the implicit acknowledgement that a consistent sentencing formula is normally used – the 'full tariff'.[3] These operational, but unwritten rules: *due process, civility and tariff sentencing* were highly functional. They allowed City officials to maintain a smooth-running yet complex people-processing system. In the discussion to follow we shall refer to these operational rules extensively. These rules, because they are normative and possibly even unrecognized by some court workers, are obviously not absolute. They are, in certain circumstances, stretched or even broken. In some cases the manipulation of these rules is purposeful in terms of organizational gains – as one clerk put it 'to get finished *before* the canteen opens'. In other cases they are broken by inept or inexperienced court officials. However, overall these rules were fundamental to the running of City courts and were celebrated and reinforced daily by court officials.

PROCEED WITH CIVILITY

We will show, when we discuss Countyside courts' approach to juvenile justice, that treating juveniles accused of criminal offences to displays of full-blown social and moral prejudice was not uncommon. In City, too, we often overheard or were offered personal opinions about defendants and their parents, which indicated that they were judged privately by court officials quite *outside* the formal proceedings. Before a morning session officials will often pass the time displaying some private views:

CLERK:	The customers are always late on Monday morning.
WARRANT OFFICER:	They don't get up . . . they miss the bus.
CLERK:	Bus, I thought they stole cars to get here.

Magistrates similarly displayed their attitudes between cases with asides to court officials and privately the ushers and police personnel also would often tell us what they thought *should* happen to certain types of offenders. One usher who'd had her house burgled felt strongly about such offences and was all for using penal colonies for that crime. Another became particularly vindictive about juveniles accused of bagsnatching. We no doubt all hold strong private views about crime and offenders. We should certainly not be surprised that court workers and particularly magistrates, with their predominantly affluent, upper-middle-class backgrounds, should hold ideological views including moral judgements about 'deviant' working-class youth. The significant feature of City courts was that, in general, this ideological antagonism and its accompanying prejudice and in some cases desire for strong retribution was largely *withheld* and did not routinely pervade the formal court proceedings except perhaps in the patronizing tone of some officials' attempts at courtesy or civility.

The key worker in setting the tone of the courtroom atmosphere is the clerk. City clerks, mainly young and recently trained, were, with one or two noticeable exceptions, keen on operating the proceedings with civility. They worked very closely to a due process model, tempering it where necessary with the need to treat the child or young person as less assured, articulate and knowledgeable than an adult. City magistrates either shared or complied with this style. Clerks and magistrates were not above thanking parents for their cooperation or at the end of a case saying:

Thank you, John, Mrs Robinson, you may go now. The usher will show you where to find the duty solicitor.

The participation of respectful parents in the proceedings, particularly for informal 'mitigation' before sentencing, was welcomed and well received by clerks and magistrates. For example, an articulate, well-dressed father in speaking up for his son who pleaded guilty to travelling on the railway without a valid ticket, was willingly given the court's time.

FATHER: He had a railway pass, so it was a familiar habit to get on automatically. He panicked at the barrier and said he had come from a nearer station because he thought it sounded better.

SENIOR MAGISTRATE: Thank you, Mr Fenney, we accept there was no deliberate fraud so we are going to fine you, Thomas, £5.

The norm in City court then is to proceed with basic politeness. This held, at any rate, for those families who behaved, in the circumstances 'properly' and deferentially. There were, however, three types of situations in which this was not the case: if defendants or parents showed disrespect for the court; if a few court officials were themselves difficult or ill-tempered personalities; or if a high workload for a particular session pressurized the clerk into taking 'unhelpful' short cuts.

DUE PROCESS AND REPRESENTED DEFENDANTS:
IN EVERYBODY'S BEST INTERESTS?

Nearly 70 per cent of City juveniles are legally represented, the remainder of defendants, mainly willingly, proceeding without representation. With a refusal rate of only 4 per cent for legal-aid applications, it is clear that City court believes representation to be desirable. Further, because City court clerks and magistrates do appear to be keen on 'justice being seen to be done', legal representation, as the most vital aspect of due process, is encouraged. Thus, not only does City court normally take great pains to explain the charge and elicit a correct plea by talking to both juvenile *and* parent, but clerk or senior magistrate will then go on to strongly encourage legal representation when it has not already been requested:

MAGISTRATE: I strongly advise you to seek the help of a solicitor. We'll stand the case down so that you can go and consult with the duty solicitor.

So regularly and unequivocally did court officials promote legal representation in court, and also privately state their belief that any defendant who wished it should have the right to representation, that it is safe to conclude that this was either a major goal and/or a device in achieving some other goal. We are arguing here that clerks and magistrates believed that two major aims are satisfied by a court basically run by 'professionals': first the court runs more smoothly and efficiently with represented defendants; and second due process is more easily secured and justice seen to be done, when defence solicitors are employed. One City barrister summed up a widely held view:

> This court gives legal aid as a matter of course on the grounds that it speeds things up and offers a better standard of justice. . . . I'm not just saying this because I'm in the business but everyone should be represented. They should all have the same chance. The prosecution is all geared up and knows the system inside out. I'm not saying that the barristers and solicitors are always up to scratch; I suppose you've realized that, but on the whole the defence should get the same expertize as the prosecution . . . the defendants don't know what they're doing.

To what extent is this contention true? Is the use of a 'generous' interpretation of due process and legal representation as the norm in everybody's interests and in particular do the court's best interests conflict with those of the defendant's?

As we have shown the 'raw material' that comes to court via the police prosecutors is not well refined, it is still problematic in itself and more particularly becomes so when defendants appear in the court to make a plea. In short, for the court to proceed smoothly in the official's eyes, there is a need to minimize the number of tedious, time-wasting, petty trials. Thus a good deal of pre-court, out-of-court and indeed in-court bargaining and negotiating takes place. The three key figures in this are the clerk, the prosecutor (who in City is nearly always a lawyer and *not* a policeman) and the defence solicitor. When a defendant is not represented the likelihood of pre- and out-of-court negotiating is reduced, although in-court bargaining, with the clerk as catalyst, is still possible.

Negotiated justice

The clerk to the court, although he might wish to busy himself in pre-court negotiations, tidying up and smoothing out potentially messy cases before they reach open court, has neither the time nor the authority to do so. He or she will get involved occasionally but not routinely. The defence solicitor on the other hand can and does make deals with his 'learned friend' and 'esteemed colleague', the prosecutor, quite routinely. Pre-court bargaining was regarded as both normal and acceptable in City court. We cannot say whether such negotiating is normal within the wider juvenile justice system as it clearly is in the criminal system proper (see Baldwin and McConville, 1977) as there is no analysis of the juvenile justice system known to us which deals with this stage of the prosecution process. We would speculate that in large, busy juvenile courts with high levels of legal representation such practices will tend to occur.

Although, as we indicated in the last chapter, many deals are made, at the time of arrest and charge, between police and potential defendants, we actually observed many deals being struck just before the actual hearings. Most of these negotiations were concerned with the nature and extent of the charges laid against a juvenile. They involved relatively simple modifications in the charge in order to seal a bargain: the pay-off for the prosecutor was that, by reducing the seriousness of the charge he could get a guilty plea and thus a guaranteed conviction rather than the possibility of losing the case or parts of it. From the defence point of view it meant 'getting it over quickly' and getting a lighter sentence for a less serious offence on the anticipation that the trial would be lost anyway. What is difficult to say, of course, is whether these deals were always in the defendant's best interests. In short, would the case have been lost? It is very difficult to assess this. All one can be sure of is that defendants usually went along with such modifications which would be routinely announced in court by the clerk:

> CLERK: Would you amend the charge for Remand 7 from theft to damage to the fire extinguisher, the value now being £8.

That the clerks nearly always accepted these last-minute changes is the clearest indication that they regarded such deals as being in the court's best interests. In fairness to them, we found no evidence that they undermined the defendant's best interests either. While the City magistrates were not always aware of why these changes occurred, they were almost totally ignorant of the extensiveness of attempted pre-court negotiations, particularly those which came to nothing:

DEFENCE: You haven't got enough for attempted theft.

PROSECUTION: I'll go and have a word with them (*police officers*). (*He goes away*).

DEFENCE (*to colleague*):   He's not got enough for attempted theft.

COLLEAGUE: That annoys me, that, trying it on.

PROSECUTION (*on return*): Are you prepared to plead guilty to going equipped?

DEFENCE: No, you won't make attempted theft stick you know, I'm trying to save *your* time.

PROSECUTION: Well, I'm instructed to lay on both charges.

As the attempted theft charge was dismissed, in organizational terms this breakdown of pre-trial negotiations wasted the court's time. That time-saving is a key issue in these negotiations is beyond doubt, since clerks themselves, who in City showed no signs of having any other motives, were often party to such discussions. The case of two girls charged with assaulting the police but with one girl, Noreen Jones, pleading not guilty was thus 'reconsidered' just before its official staging by a conference of clerk, prosecutor, defence solicitor and usher in an empty courtroom:

POLICE OFFICER: I'd be prepared to say that she was already
(*to both lawyers*)   heated . . . having been involved in a fight with another girl and that we don't know who started that.

Both lawyers go out to see the girls. Clerk goes out and returns. Then, in reply to a question from his assistant retorts

CLERK: No, the little devil's going to deny everything.

However, the prosecutor returns saying

PROSECUTOR: I'll accept a plea to breach of the peace for Jones if the other girl agrees to be bound over.

The clerk goes out and quickly returns

CLERK: Right. They'll both plead guilty to insulting behaviour liable to cause a breach of the peace.

USHER: I'll go and get the girls.
The clerk goes off to get the magistrates.
The show is on the road.

The most common deal struck in City juvenile court involved a defendant being bound over. Binding a person over to keep the peace for a specified period, and a specified surety, produces a compromise which is often attractive to both sides. It is an offer defence solicitors will make to the prosecution when a very trivial offence is being contested normally with a 'no previous' defendant thinking about pleading not guilty. The prosecutor might feel it worthwhile not offering evidence, and so avoid triggering a remand for a trial, but instead settling for an agreed binding-over. Similarly the prosecutor will, if he has a weak case, offer the defence a binding-over compromise. Prosecutors often use this tactic as 'a salvaging exercise'. For example, a prosecution solicitor will often find himself with several briefs based on 'overnight arrests' which are technically rather poor and liable to be dismissed. As one prosecutor told us:

> Monday mornings are hell. You get the briefs at 9.15 a.m. All weekend jobs . . . no one has looked if they're any good and you're expected to make something of them. When they're faulty then binding-over's not a bad compromise. We could ask for a remand and get the case organized but a lot of stuff's not worth it. Anyway it's best to get it away [bound over] there and then.

These negotiations allow the smooth flow of business in court. An unrepresented defendant, and hence an unprepared case, caused clerk and prosecutor to try to spot and stop any 'difficulties' from the outset. We found in Countyside court uniformed police prosecutors were not always as amenable to dropping or reducing charges in the interests of harmony and court efficiency. However, because City prosecutors were nearly all lawyers (i.e. not police inspectors) who were working for the police for a limited period they appeared to have a professional disinterest in their work which made them more flexible. This amenability meant that some pretty spontaneous cross-court compromises could be struck. Hence the case of a boy, with 'no previous', who was willing to plead guilty to taking a car but not to taking the tools from it, was dealt with swiftly. The clerk looks to the prosecutor with eyebrows raised. The prosecutor nods gently and then announces:

> In the circumstances we will withdraw the theft of the tools from the charge.

The sheets are amended and the case is rapidly remanded for reports and a long trial is averted.

If we had witnessed a clear picture of bargains which perhaps went against the best spirit of due process and justice being seen to be done we would suggest that City court officials were 'interpreting' due process for their own ends at the expense of the defendant. (We will in fact make this contention in the case of Countyside.) However, while some of these in-court deals seemed to 'ignore' the defendants' best interests others seemed designed to protect the young defendant. Some clerks would actually go to considerable lengths, and bend the rules, to reach a position favourable to defendants, especially when these corresponded with the court's best interest.

In one case in which two 11 year olds, jointedly charged with damage to a television aerial, appeared and one pleaded not guilty and the other guilty, the court was confronted with a difficult situation, which, had the children been represented, would probably not have occurred. The clerk intervened. He didn't want a trial for one boy with the other having to appear as witness. Eleven year olds are no joy in trials. He felt the case trivial and, even if finally proven, the sentence would be either a conditional discharge or a fine. The following dialogue then took place:

CLERK (*to prosecutor*): Can you help us here, Mr Hughes.

PROSECUTOR (*pauses*): Yes. We are not ready to proceed with the case. Eh, perhaps we could ask for a three-week adjournment whilst we make further enquiries.

CLERK (*looking at magistrates*): Perhaps we could remand the case for three weeks. Tony's plea [of not guilty] is sound but we need not record it. Perhaps we can take a plea on the 26th when Gary's reports will be available and they can both be dealt with then.

SENIOR MAGISTRATE (*puzzled*): You want me to scrap the plea.

CLERK: Yes, sir.

SENIOR MAGISTRATE: Well, as long as you know what you're doing, Mr Sykes.

The clerk did indeed know what he was doing. He had recognized immediately that the prosecutor was indicating that he would not be presenting any evidence against Tony in three weeks time and would then be asking for a binding-over. Three weeks was the exact period cases were remanded by City for reports. On the 26th a new bench would be presented with a report on a 'no previous' guilty plea report for Gary and a request for a binding-over for Tony. They would predictably 'agree' to Tony's binding over and deal with Gary very leniently and everyone would go away happy. Another messy trial avoided; two more cases cleared up by the police and two small, inarticulate boys being given about the right punishment on the City tariff.

Whether these practices are in essence 'rough justice' merely to aid smooth justice is a moot point. Should Tony have had the opportunity to go to trial and have his case proven or dismissed? More pertinently, should his case have ever come to court? We witnessed many situations like this in which a pragmatic interpretation of due process took place to smooth the running of the court and redefine an otherwise messy case. We did *not* note a trend whereby this interpretation was more often than not to the defendant's disadvantage. City court officials did not display this style, whereas in Countyside court, as we shall see in the next chapter, such tactics were observable.

Competent representation: in the solicitor's best interests

We can proceed no further in our analysis without taking a detailed look at the in-court role of the defence solicitors and barristers who work in City courts. However, before discussing their performance technically, we must first place the defence lawyer in his firm, and his firm in the market place. The lawyer is in quite a different position vis-a-vis his salary, or at least his firm's profits, than any of the other court workers. The lawyers are the only group of court workers whose salary is clearly related to their productivity. For the dozen or so solicitor firms who share the bulk of the legally aided criminal work in City, the formula is simple. The more work they can do, the more briefs they can deal with in any one day or week, the more money they make.

City juvenile courts provide a great deal of business, much more than most other local juvenile court systems both because of the large through-put of cases and the very high level of legal representation granted via legal aid and encouraged by a growing duty solicitor scheme. This excellent market and the facilitative working conditions make criminal advocacy in juvenile court highly lucrative. We interviewed several solicitors and spoke informally to many more about their work in City juvenile courts. They all agreed that the working environment there was nearly ideal. Further they also agreed that there was keen competition for legal aid business, intensified by the retraction of other sources of income such as conveyancing. The pattern of competition, via the duty solicitor scheme, documented by Mungham and Bankowski (1976), was evident in the case of City 'new boys' and old-established firms battling it out for business. A few of the solicitors we interviewed went so far as to say that legally aided criminal work was more lucrative than private, fee-paid work. These solicitors suggested that the cost ceiling, which most private clients would have to impose, also tended to reduce their performance in defending the case.

Placed in this context, City solicitors clearly have to be highly sensitive about their image amongst City adolescents and their families. They must enhance their own reputations as firms who 'get juveniles off' or at the very least obtain minimum sentences. Thus competent representation is essential to the retention of their market share, particularly in the inner-city neighbourhoods where efficient informal neighbourhood networks exist about such matters. Indeed several firms have actually set up branch offices around the city to practice 'in amongst them'.

In summary, therefore, legal representation is viewed by all the key court workers as being in their best interests. Lawyers realize that, in City, competent representation is in their best financial interests. This formula in the end means that competent representation can be said to be in everybody's best interests, including the defendants. This, then, is the position from which we shall start. We shall argue in due course that despite this general picture, there are a significant minority of represented cases where advocacy is unsatisfactory, ironically mainly because of the financially profitable nature of the work. More immediately we shall look briefly at the role of the defence lawyer in City juvenile court. We can divide his/her functions into four categories: the pre-hearing remand, trial advocacy, mitigation at the point of sentence and, the out-of-court negotiations discussed above. We shall concentrate on mitigation in the greatest detail, on the grounds that it is the most significant aspect of the representative's role.

The solicitor's role at the remand stage of a case is often very trivial. In most cases, he or she merely assists the court by having the right answers at the right time as routine unconditional or conditional bail is granted. Occasionally, however, the solicitor can become an advocate for his client against the police's request for a remand in custody or specific bail conditions such as a curfew at place of residence. We will do no more than mention this role here. It is a minor role which is significant in only a small minority of cases. Clearly though, if a solicitor successfully challenges a police request, his rating in the defendant's eyes must be very high.

Similarly it is difficult for us to comment very much on the solicitor's performance in trial advocacy. What criteria does one use and from whose point of view? And if a represented case is dismissed, is this always directly as a result of a defendant being represented? The mediation of an experienced solicitor or barrister does, of course, mean a very different approach to the conducting of the trial than if an adolescent defends himself, even with the help of a parent or the clerk. Criminal trials do not in fact reconstruct the previous reality, the distant event in question. When a defendant is represented, what the court hears are two alternative constructions both of which tend to manipulate and decontextualize the actual previous reality. Both sides are concerned with making certain critical points.

In the majority of juvenile trials we observed the issue was in the end about two conflicting views of an event or incident, with defendants holding to one account and a couple of policemen to another. There were often no independent witnesses and thus the defence solicitor's task was repeatedly trying to convince the bench that the police were wrong. This was occasionally done by confronting the police aggressively. In the main, however, solicitors operated on the basis that such an approach would not work and that the magistrates would always tend to believe the police. Hence solicitors would on the contrary usually compliment the police for their 'dedication', their 'honesty displayed today in court' and would talk of their 'most difficult task' but then suggest that on *this* occasion, 'in the heat of the moment', 'with poor street lighting' or 'large crowds of youths milling around', the police officer had been 'mistaken'.

Solicitors would also be very cautious about allowing their clients to take the stand and, if it was necessary, make excuses for their amateurism.

Juveniles have pre-occupations. Their recall is not as good as adults. Minor inconsistencies are not significant.

Your worships should accept that youngsters often see a police car and run away rather than try and give an explanation. This reasoning must be related to the juvenile mind.

In short then, the legal representative in City courts would try to produce a 'version' of a previous event in terms of his interpretation of the 'way the bench thinks'. He, unlike the juvenile, is less concerned with what actually happened or indeed he may try to avoid stating what actually happened!

Solicitors, being regarded by defendants as the 'experts', in terms of predicting an outcome of a trial and the likely sentence if found guilty, are obviously in a strong position to project their own professional identity. On the one hand they can tell their young defendant that there is very little chance of getting the case dismissed, and so in part cover their own performance. On the other hand, particularly in cases in which they are not convinced their client is telling the truth, or do not want to be seen to be believing him/her because of the nature of the implicit counter accusation (e.g. that the police are liars), they can 'signal' to the court in a code unknown to the defendant. They will thus open their speeches with phrases like 'I am instructed to say', or 'My client informs me that', to retain their neutrality and so retain the court's good will (see also Carlen, 1976).

In terms of their primary goal, of maintaining credibility with both court and client, they probably have little choice but to behave in this way. They are mostly pragmatists. They perceive their role as providing a reasonable standard of advocacy in a disinterested way. Most solicitors we spoke to accepted that they had quite limited communication, and even less rapport, with their young clients. They saw their task in trials as making the best of what information and 'lines' they had. They, quite realistically, assessed certain trial situations as 'losers'. For instance, in some theft cases in which the prosecution witnesses were policemen or store detectives, it was not unusual for them to claim that at the time of the arrest the defendants admitted the offence and then quote the defendant as saying something like: 'She said, sorry, we were going to sell them.' The loading against the defendants in such cases is substantial and solicitors are often simply 'going through the motions' of advocacy knowing the case will be lost.

Given the 'loading' of trials in certain situations it is very difficult to assess the representative's performance. The relatively high level of dismissed cases and our own court diary evaluations do support the view that defence solicitors and barristers were relatively well prepared for their trial advocacy, and usually turned in a competent performance on behalf of their client. However, we are not in a position to make any categoric statements about trial advocacy.

The mitigation formula

Williamson (1977) suggests that solicitors trot out one or more of a set category of mitigation stories. These deal with the 'good home backgrounds' of the offender, his involvement with 'bad company', the 'similarity of offences' he has been involved in, the 'adverse effect of dispositions', in particular custodial sentences on young offenders, the high financial cost of custodial sentences, the 'remorse' shown by the offender, the fact that he is at a 'critical stage in life' and about to settle down or that he 'cooperated with the police'. We recognized these stories quite clearly in our own observation. However, we do not accept, as Williamson implies, that they are rather simplistically trotted out. Williamson underplays the uniqueness of each local juvenile justice system, City's 'regular' solicitors developed their mitigation rules in relation to the operational rules of the court in question.

They certainly had tales to tell but they were more numerous than Williamson found and were reconstituted and inserted into mitigation in relation to a client's 'tariff score'. In short they operated strategically, based on a clear understanding, gained through experience, of City court's sentencing policy, which we shall further discuss in the next section. So clearly were City solicitors in tune with these sentencing principles that they can be seen as an integral part of a feedback loop which reinforced the very same sentencing principles. A competent, regular solicitor assesses a case, places it within a bracket of, say, three possible disposals on the 'tariff'. He then develops his mitigation within the context of this bracket but emphasizing the good points of the case via his tales of mitigation. Even if the mitigation plea does not secure the lowest penalty, it has the effect of preventing the bench sentencing 'over the odds', that is going for the highest point on the bracket. Thus, even when they respectfully decline the solicitor's minimalist suggestion, City magistrates tend to opt for the middle-bracket choice.

The solicitor, as in trial advocacy, can control his client's expectations about outcome by implying, for instance, that the highest point on his privately worked out tariff bracket is the likely outcome. Thus when a lower sentence is made, the client is well pleased with his solicitor's performance and will use him again if required. We should be clear this whole formula works *because* City officials implicitly agree and reinforce 'extended tariff' sentencing.

How does this mitigation formula operate in practice? If for the pur-

pose of analysis the range of sentencing disposals are divided into low
(e.g. conditional discharge), medium (e.g. supervision order) and high
brackets (e.g. detention centre) then a defence lawyer will tailor his
mitigation stories to make sense within each of these 'prediction'
brackets. A low- and medium-predicted disposal case for a boy or girl,
with evidence usually via a social enquiry report or else extracted from
parents during the hearing, of a good, caring and well-disciplined home
background will receive a quite different form of mitigation than a
similar case with a poor home background or indeed a high disposal
prediction with a good home background. For example a low-disposal,
good-home-background case will be reinforced in mitigation:

> The fact that he hasn't had a criminal record in a place like *City*
> is a credit to him and his mother.

> Paula comes from a good family. In these days to have 12 chil-
> dren all out of trouble speaks highly for. . . .

However, for an offender likely to be 'sent away' with a long list of
previous offences, it would be inappropriate to emphasize a caring
family too much, since that merely reinforces the black sheepishness of
the offender and his indifference to, and perhaps scorn of, caring
parents and a secure home background. Similarly no City bench would
be impressed by a claim that a 'recidivist' already far up the disposal
ladder was 'an innocent', 'an easily led child', 'vulnerable' and the like.
However embroidering this picture for a predicted low or middle disposal will usually 'work'. Thus even if 'home background' is not ideal:

> This is her first offence; she has never been in trouble before.
> She's never even received a juvenile caution before and in no way
> was she a principal in this offence.

The delinquent can thus be punished with something mild: the solicitor
will have in mind a conditional discharge, or at worst a small fine. Even
where there is evidence, via the nature of the offence, that the delinquent could be other than innocent his moral character can perhaps be
salvaged by the suggestion that he was led astray. Perhaps the offence
appears wicked, the bench is told, but it is not indicative of the offender. He was led astray by a bad person:

> He has since stopped going around with the adult Jennings and
> has thus not been in any further trouble since November. He is
> actively looking for work and. . . .

Paradoxically, if solicitors cannot make anything of a 'good family', they will often make much of a poor family picture by way of mitigation. This 'either which way' phenomenon can be found in social work 'stories' also (see Walter, 1979). This ploy will be used in particular if a supervision order is the best result from the defence's point of view (that is as opposed to a spell in a detention centre). On these occasions delinquency is seen as a consequence of deprivation. The juvenile is a victim of circumstances or family disorder. He needs the help, support and structure of a supervision order, not a further crushing blow which detention centre would offer:

> His father is in the prison service and has been posted to Northern Ireland, consequently the grandfather has to provide the discipline. . . . there can be few boys who have had such emotional traumas as he during his young life.

The supervision order need not be sold as a therapeutic device, however. At the wave of a magic brief it can:

> offer him the structure and guidance so clearly lacking at the moment. It will bring home to him that he cannot go on this way and that if he fails to follow the social worker's instructions he will be brought back to court, and might well lose his freedom.

Cases 'destined' for a custodial sentence cause the greatest problem for the solicitor, particularly if the offence in question is serious. The experienced City lawyer will not attempt an innocence plea, will not try a 'led astray' appeal and will only make something of home background if a specific issue appears helpful. Instead the defence will *accept* the gravity of the situation:

> John is aware that detention centre will be on your minds today. He has prepared himself for a custodial sentence.

> There can be no doubt that Stephen Hill's record makes depressing reading.

Having defused the situation in this way and established the worst point on the 'tariff' as common ground, the solicitor can then look for something positive which might be a sign that the recidivist is settling down. Perhaps the offender has 'seen the light', or 'realizes he cannot go on like this'. Perhaps he's got a job or a 'sensible girl friend' or has at least 'had the good sense to plead guilty and not waste the court's time'. The mitigator will attempt to build from bits and bobs a positive image which will show the offender in his best light, as a good risk for a 'final warning' or a heavy fine or deferred sentence.

Clearly, because City court operates a 'full tariff', the time comes when all the parties know that detention centre or Borstal is due. On these occasions mitigation is but a ritual which is briefly gone through, rather than an extended and unsuccessful plea which might be seen as wasting the court's time. Solicitors, with one eye on maintaining their credibility in the court, will tend to opt not to waste the court's time. They have other cases to win.

Williamson (1977) also noted the tendency for solicitors to take on the role of 'expert witness' in juvenile court. We found this also. In particular we noted a willingness on the part of some very 'regular' solicitors to use personal endorsements such as:

> Knowing him as I do I feel that the type of person he is he would respond to leniency.

> I know the family well and can say with some confidence that the family were deeply shocked by. . . .

> The owner of the hotel is a personal friend. He knows that the boy [in being sacked for theft] has lost a good opportunity.

The mitigation formula then is constructed within a set of boundaries which are generally agreed by clerks, magistrates, social workers and solicitors. The defence solicitor does tend to have some 'set speeches' up his sleeve. However, he chooses and restructures these to serve each individual case. In particular he implicitly places each case within a bracket of possible outcome. Regular defence lawyers are very accurate in this placement. The ensuing mitigation formula is usually successful. This also has the latent function of reinforcing future sentencing negotiations in that magistrates and solicitors find themselves agreeing on the sentence or at least the sentencing bracket.

Finally, we have analysed the solicitor's tales of mitigation somewhat in isolation. It should be remembered that in over half the cases they deal with fixing the sentencing bracket to mitigate within is aided by the social worker's report. Social workers themselves, as we will discuss in chapter 8, also predict the sentencing bracket. However, not being court 'regulars', social workers, although they tend to recommend 'downstream', are also likely to misinterpret the court's sentencing policy and if anything believed City court to be more punitive than it actually was. Hence, whilst normally being able to use the SER as a major prop, a fact which social workers greatly resent, defence lawyers can be occasionally heard arguing *against* a social worker's recommendation on the basis that it is too severe.

Sub-standard legal representation

Before moving on to consider the other side of the sentencing process — the role of the magistrates in City courts — we must deal briefly with the cases in which legal representation is not in everybody's best interest, especially the defendant's.

Based on our court observation and interviews with solicitors and other court officials we are suggesting that, in a significant minority of cases, the functional 'standard' performance, which is the norm, is not achieved and a sub-standard performance ensues. There are four sets of situations or factors which tend to lead to these poor performances. In a sense they are all related to the profit-making ethos outlined earlier. They are:

(1) Overload by 'legal aid' based firms.
(2) Overload by individual solicitors.
(3) Indifferent preparation and professional incompetence.
(4) Misplaced advocacy by 'non-regular' lawyers.

City lawyers would themselves admit that self-imposed over-commitment was in their financial interests and preferable to having only one brief at a time:

> It's not worth my while doing a morning in court if I haven't got two or three cases on the go.

When one of the key 'legal aid' firms has a busy week, its partners who advocate in the juvenile court feel the pressure. They find themselves with several briefs, perhaps spread over three courts in one session. Business is such on occasions that even helpful court time-tabling cannot alleviate the pressure. The consequence is that some solicitors who would normally put in a competent performance do not do so. They have not got their facts clear; they are late and flustered; they've not had a chance to clarify a few finer points with the defendant; or they hold a brief prepared by someone else in their firm which they misunderstand. Alternatively, barristers sub-contracted in to help cope with overload may offer a poor performance often having had the brief only for a few minutes and having never previously met the defendant.

There were a small group of 'lone rangers' in City courts who were trying to make their own mark in criminal advocacy. A couple of these solicitors would routinely take on very large workloads. Hence, when they suffered an organizational foul-up or were 'offcolour', their performance stood out as particularly weak. Where overload also means that an individual solicitor starts to keep the court waiting regularly, this solicitor finds himself becoming increasingly unpopular. Good will may eventually be withdrawn with perhaps a prosecuting solicitor taking the unusual step of commenting in open court about the behaviour of such a colleague.

The clients of these few solicitors are clearly likely to suffer; their cases will tend to be presented badly and they will also tend to suffer a 'harder time' because other court officials are out of sympathy with their representative.

The indifferent preparation of a case can be a result of overload pressure, resulting from avarice, but it may be merely the result of professional neglect. There were occasions when there were no obvious signs of overload on solicitors who simply came over as ill-prepared. They would either mumble out the social enquiry report's main findings and sit down, or stand up and proceed into a long, rambling, semi-irrelevant drone, clearly planning their case as they went along. At times their speech would be so wildly off the mark that a defendant would feel compelled to intervene and correct his lawyer:

No, I've finished that job. I'm back on the dole now.

We also witnessed occasions when solicitors forgot their client's name or, if there was more than one defendant, got the names mixed up. On one occasion a defence solicitor received his fee for this piece of mitigation after a guilty plea by his client:

What can I say? He's a young hooligan. His record's atrocious. How can I offer the court any advice other than to send him to the Crown Court with a view to Borstal training. I will not waste your worship's time.

Finally, there were occasions when poor advocacy can be seen as a result of the lawyer's lack of familiarity with the City juvenile court. Perhaps a 'family solicitor' who does little criminal work will appear for a particular client. Perhaps a barrister, sub-contracted as a consequence of overload by a particular firm, will misread the court's style and quote case law instead of keeping things simple.

Thus, despite the almost ideal setting, or, indeed perhaps because of it, there are a significant minority of occasions when legal representation appears to be only in the solicitor's short-term interests. He is able to draw his considerable fee and, when overload occurs, indeed maximize his financial rewards to the cost of the defendant. Perhaps therefore the solicitor who announced his 'difficulty' to the court a week before Christmas was being thoroughly professional by remarking that a trial date was unsuitable:

> I won't be at my best that day [27 December] and I'm afraid that if I don't do it counsel won't be available either as barristers tend to be in . . . eh . . . Ibiza at that time!

TARIFF SENTENCING, SOCIAL NEED AND SERIOUS CRIME

We found a very high level of consistency in all aspects of the magisterial role. Magistrates adhered very much to the three sets of formal rules which we believe underpin City courts — civility, due process with representation and 'full-tariff' sentencing. These operational rules are consistent with a liberal paternal ideological and theoretical approach to dealing with young offenders. Full-tariff sentencing in practice means moving through the full range of available disposals before resorting to the use of detention centre or Borstal, and, as table 5.1 (p. 79) shows, consequently not relying heavily on custodial sentences. We will begin by outlining the practicalities of this approach, before showing how two types of 'information' modify the use of this full tariff.

In contending that City magistrates adhere to a liberal paternal approach in dealing with juveniles we are not suggesting that all personally hold such an ideological position. We are merely arguing that in practice the sentencing policy they operate and the in-court discussions they initiate are consistent with such an ideology. It is more likely that the ideological input which sustains this policy comes from the strong influence of certain senior magistrates, the chairman of the juvenile panel and the training ethos offered by City's senior clerks through sentencing exercises with the panel. Just as we will argue in the next chapter that Countryside magistrates sentence punitively because they are not constrained by various checks such as civility, due process and the reinforcement of a rational sentencing policy, so we are arguing here that the more punitive attitudes of certain City magistrates are contained by the politics of training, chairmanship and the three sets of operational rules of the court.

These rules which we have already described are no less functional for City magistrates than the other court workers. How long the present operational rules have dominated is hard for us to say. Certainly for new magistrates and those becoming senior magistrates the message from the other court workers is clear — the system works very well, thank you, please leave it alone. Solicitors, as we have shown, pass on this message.

The tone and style of the regime set by the clerks at the beginning of a session impinges gently but firmly upon the magistrates. They do not wish to be seen to be the first people to be discourteous, the first to need 'checking' for their indifference to due process. Most will not wish to be seen as unreasonable, harsh and cynical sentencers. We do not want to overplay the notion of the bench having a structure imposed on it, but this should not be ignored. Magistrates are the only lay people in the court machinery: they are not there every day, it is not *their* court; they are not legally trained: they often sit not knowing their colleagues on the bench. They have no interest in making fools of themselves with Kamikazi dives into the unknown. They learn to value the formulae that they are given. Like the other court workers it is when they have the court's respect that they can stick their necks out from time to time.

The straight tariff

Ordering the range of penalties available in juvenile criminal proceedings in terms of severity is problematic. Is 24 hours' attendance centre a more severe penalty than a two-year supervision order for instance? Furthermore, some penalties such as a fine can be modified in size and re-issued at different stages of a delinquent career. (A first offender can be fined £5, a third-time offender fined £50.) Similarly a juvenile court's 'tariff' can be *in practice* short, as it is in Countryside, or fully extended as it normally is in City. In City for instance the deferred sentence might be used instead of a custodial sentence, acting as a 'final warning'. Similarly if an ex-detention centre juvenile re-appears in court instead of recommending him for Borstal, City magistrates might well use a minimal penalty such as a conditional discharge. Countyside juvenile court as we shall see would be unlikely to 'reverse' the tariff in this way.

The straight full tariff is thus an 'ideal type', a construct which is used by City sentencers and indirectly, by solicitors in preparing mitigation and social workers in preparing reports, as a guideline. They implicitly start with this model and then tune or modify it, depending on the circumstance. We shall deal with tuning first. *Tuning* is conducted in relation to a range of indicators — the age of the offender, the nature of the (minor) offence, the moral character of the offender, the condition of his or her family, the juvenile's attitude to school, his or her potential for 'settling' down into respectable citizenship. Tuning takes place within the same prediction bracket on the tariff which we have argued solicitors mitigate within. If for analytic purposes we divide the tariff into three we can illustrate the practicalities of straight tariff sentencing and related tuning.

Low-tariff sentences, like conditional discharge or a small fine, were routinely handed out for 'first-timers' found guilty of trivial offences (many of which we argued in the last chapter could have been kept out of the court system by a more progressive sifting policy by the police). These first-timers will tend to be seen as 'innocents' despite their 'slip up'. If mitigation, a social report or in-court questioning shows the juvenile to be 'sensible' this will tune his or her sentence down, within the low-tariff bracket:

> We are dealing with it leniently today because we think that you are sensible enough.

Juveniles considered too young to be regarded fully culpable, as with the 11-year-old boy who pleaded guilty to stealing felt-tip pens from a market stall, are also tuned downwards. He received a conditional discharge and was told:

> We're not going to punish you for this offence. You're only 11 and we don't want to see you here again.

The older juvenile (14—17) who is a first or second timer will tend to receive a similar low-tariff sentence but be treated as more culpable.

City magistrates were aware that fines were often paid by parents not their children. However, if the juveniles received pocket money or earned money, and they were culpable, a small fine was directed at them specifically:

> We fine you £5 and we want you to pay this out of your own pocket money at 50p per week. You're a sensible boy with a good future ahead of you now. Off you go. And Mr Clarke [father], he's to pay it *himself* please.

Middle-tariff penalties, including stiff fine, attendance centre or supervision order are routinely given for either a relatively serious offence such as assault or on the basis of previous offences being totted up and considered with a further minor offence.

The use of supervision orders can be 'routine' and used as part of the tariff or, as we will discuss shortly, be used specifically when 'social need and disorder' or 'inappropriate behaviour' in girls is uncovered.

High-tariff sentencing is usually the delivery of the inevitable in City courts. Since City magistrates do not, except in cases of serious crime, 'jump' rungs of the ladder the use of custodial measures, in particular detention centre, comes after previous middle-tariff sentences have failed. Indeed very often even after a final warning, a further piece of brinkmanship might be tried if new 'good signs' have appeared:

> The last time you were in court you received a stern warning. You were warned you would be sent away ... since you have now got a job we will not do this. But if you appear again you *will* be sent down. Instead today we are going to. ...

However, once the end of the line is reached, City magistrates *because* the tariff has been 'justly' used in the past feel confident in making their decision:

> I think you have been well prepared for the fact that you are going to detention centre. I hope you will take it as a just punishment and afterwards pull yourself together.

Or with paternalism to the fore:

> Mr Jute ... yes, we hope you'll have a few words with your son, see that he doesn't do this sort of thing again. We hope you'll take him back when he comes out of detention centre.

In each of these straight-tariff brackets the magistrates will finely tune in sentencing. Usually they will make their decision, at least in part, through information gleaned from a social enquiry report. Occasionally they will be persuaded to 'go ahead today', without a remand for reports by defence solicitors, and sometimes they will decide reports are not necessary. In the main though magistrates liked to have reports available. Certainly all the magistrates we spoke to said they found SERs 'useful'. We suspect they found it necessary to re-interpret some of these reports, however, by contrasting them with 'harsher' school reports:

> I always look at them side by side. Very interestingly they are usually rather different. The schools know the juvenile better; they aren't conned as much.

Nevertheless their keenness to take the child's background needs and difficulties into account was widespread, especially as all but the most trivial cases were monitored in relation to the parenting role and school performance. In particular caring parents who are seen to be trying their best, perhaps under difficult conditions, are 'rewarded' by their child being given a minimal sentence in the circumstances:

> Shoplifting is not a lark, it is stealing. We will take into account that you have not been in trouble before and have a good, secure background. We hope you will learn from today's experience.

An adolescent girl is reprimanded for shoplifting with paternal solmenity:

SENIOR MAGISTRATE: What have you to say about this, Pauline?

GIRL: Am sorry.

SENIOR MAGISTRATE: You're letting your family down, your mother has enough problems. We're going to give you a conditional discharge for two years. Now mend your ways.

Because caring parents are rewarded, wayward children have to be reminded that they are not getting away with things. Low-tariff offenders were regularly told that they were being punished, even if it didn't feel painful, which a conditional discharge rarely does:

> It doesn't mean you have got away with it. It will go down on your record. ... We are giving you a final chance because we believe that you have caring parents.

When parents have shown a 'sensible attitude' to their child's offence a minimal sentence will usually be applied. Social workers and solicitors, knowing this, will readily supply the magistrate with this information:

> We're very interested in the report ... we take into account certain action which may have already been taken by your family.

If City magistrates use parental attitudes and family dynamics as the 'key variable' in deciding whether or not a youngster is likely to stay out of trouble and settle down they regard the child's attitude to school as a very close second. A 'very good school record', 'your teachers speak highly of you' and 'you're in the Colts rugby team, keep this up' are passports to a minimal sentence in the circumstances of the case.

The straight full tariff then is the underlying sentencing structure in City courts. It is either confirmed or finely tuned by the consideration of a set of personal and social criteria. Each case is quickly assessed for the good, the bad and the ugly in relation to family dynamics and parental attitudes, school performance and a variety of signs of settling down, the significance of which varies according to whether the offender is broadly a low- middle- or high-tariff case.

Social need and the tariff

When the indicators we have already discussed swing violently off the norm, City court operates more dramatically. Thus whilst good, or at least 'neutral', school performance is hoped for and rewarded by in-court praise or a minimal sentence, non-school attendance or a negative school report rings a loud alarm bell. City magistrates regard such school problems as both a measure of social need and a sign of lack of control, or social disorder. When a 'major problem' surfaces, the tariff may well be significantly modified. *Modifcation* is more than fine tuning; it involves the sentencers in a redefinition of their guidelines which may lead to their 'jumping' a whole phase of the usual tariff. This process is particularly likely to occur for girls.

Although only 9 per cent of those proceeded against through criminal proceedings in City juvenile court were girls, it was quite clear that magistrates looked at their cases somewhat differently from boys charged with equivalent offences. In part this was a consequence of the fact that the tariff available for girls is different and more limited. The disposal range for girls has no attendance centre or detention centre on it. In a sense, therefore, whilst low-tariff cases can still be dealt with through conditional discharge and small fines, middle-tariff cases tend to attract a heavy fine or supervision order and high-tariff cases a heavy fine, care order or Borstal.

The City bench tended to show, in keeping with a liberal paternal approach, certain attitudes vis-a-vis female offenders. In particular, girls charged with offences of violence were regarded with a mixture of horror and amazement by many benches. Much more routinely, non-school attendance or disruptive school behaviour, although not on the court's official agenda, was highlighted as totally unbecoming. In keeping with the tendency to always have school and social reports for girls this alleged indicator of social disorder was more visible for girls than boys. For girls in particular this hidden 'offence' was quite inappropriately, in terms of due process, brought into the sentence.

In one case a girl, Sandy, charged with the theft of a doll from a shop pleaded not guilty. The case was proven against Sandy although her co-defendant pleaded guilty to the offence and giving evidence at Sandy's trial said that she was in no way a party to the theft. The senior magistrate, at sentencing, made it quite clear that Sandy's behaviour at school was being judged:

> She was out that day and she should have been at school. This is what I'm concerned about ... if you're not getting education, you are going to suffer the rest of your life.

To make a supervision order in such a case is to modify the tariff *upwards,* and not necessarily on the evidence of an SER. A Chinese girl, who had previously been in court for shoplifting on one occasion, was also 'bumped up' for supervision. Not least because:

> The school says you're uncooperative ... such an appalling school record.

Or again for shoplifting, two girls who, on the straight tariff would have got a fine, instead received supervision orders:

> We've read your school report with more than interest . . . a lack
> of cooperation from both of you . . . quite clearly. . . .

This bumping-up of the tariff is based on the paternal notion that adolescents need structure, discipline and an adult to care and control
them. The supervision order is seen as potentially offering a degree of
substitute care and control. If its paternal function is undermined by
poor social services delivery, magistrates get fairly upset. Thus, when a
case returns in which supervision has failed, they sometimes criticize
the surrogate parents, the social workers, for failing to see the child
regularly enough, or even more basically, for failing to see gender as
relevant:

> Why on earth was she not given a male social worker? A girl
> without a father would have benefited greatly from being super-
> vised by a man.

Thus mother-centred, single-parent families, when daughter appears
before the court, may well be the subject of a supervision order, when a
low-tariff sentence would have been given for a two-parent family or
for a boy:

> We can't let you go around stealing, Carolyn, because if you're
> doing this now goodness knows what you'll do when you grow
> up. . . . All this is a cry for help. Today you're being punished
> but you're being helped.

And for two other girls with family difficulties outlined in the social
enquiry report, who had committed a very minor theft of a ring, the
court actually acknowledges the trivial nature of the offence, yet goes
'up tariff':

> A foolish escapade, you're no longer small children. You both
> need help in this critical year before leaving school. The super-
> vision order is partly to help you, partly to punish you.

This tendency for 'welfare' criteria to increase the severity of sentence upon a juvenile is well documented in the States (see Lerman,
1975; Chesney-Lind, 1977) and more recently in Britain with the use
of a care order for 'punishing' an offender (see Taylor *et al.*, 1979;
Morris *et al.*, 1980). We must point out, however, that in City court at

least a '7 (7)' care order is usually only made after the strongest prompting from a social worker.

The social need—social disorder dimension, then, tends to lead to the bumping-up of the tariff and includes the notion that detention centre can be used as a therapeutic tool in the youngsters best interest (see also Thorpe *et al.,* 1980). Yet magistrates, particularly when dealing with girls, suffer some real dilemmas when recidivists, charged always with petty offences, have worked their way along into the high-tariff arena. The absence of an extensive tariff range makes the bumping-up from middle to high tariff much more problematic.

Serious crime and custodial sentencing

As we shall see, when we discuss Countyside court, the 'protection' of the community or 'other people's property' and retribution can become the court's major concern when producing juvenile justice. City courts had, prior to our research period, taken a hard line on taking and driving-away offences, particularly as the chairman of the bench put it 'where they were serious, dangerous driving and so on'. This period of exemplary sentencing was related mainly to a media and public outcry about several deaths caused in the region by youths in stolen cars. At the time of our fieldwork, this minor panic was receding, however, having been replaced by a particular concern for violence against the person, especially in relation to muggings and robbery. There was a significant increase of recorded violent crime in the region during the period we were engaged in our research.

Juveniles charged with these serious crimes were often punished by custodial sentences designed to protect the public and act as a severe warning shot for others. When an offender faces a 'serious offence' disposal, the traditional 'good points' to be found in the SERs and solicitors' mitigation will be of little consequence:

SENIOR MAGISTRATE: We take a very serious view indeed. ... Despite the social enquiry report and despite what your father says ... even though we were very impressed with what your father had to say ... we are thinking about a custodial sentence. ... Have you anything to say, Mr Orton? (*defence solicitor*).

> SOLICITOR: I appreciate the situation but would ask you to
> consider a deferred sentence. . . .

Or again:

> SENIOR MAGISTRATE: This one was a *bad* burglary . . . we
> cannot have elderly ladies burgled . . . the lady was
> very upset . . . we cannot overlook our public
> duty. Three months detention centre.

Similar statements concerning public duty were issued with most custodial sentencing concerning serious crime. For girls consistent *organized* shoplifting or a serious assault on a policeman would merit the same treatment. The 'serious crime' formula involves the City magistrates in rebalancing their scales. The protection of the community and a statement on its behalf concerning the need for law and order becomes paramount. No longer are the magistrates involved in the routine social control of urban youth. The steady climb up the tariff cannot be relied on or even tuned upwards. The use of a custodial sentence and the consequent modification of the tariff is required.

CITY COURT'S LIBERAL PATERNAL VERSION OF JUVENILE JUSTICE

The version of juvenile justice which City has settled for is not imposed from above. It is a largely local creation, a local response and probably therefore a unique response. This local context has been well documented. City juvenile court, because of its size and high workload, in order to function at all has had to develop a sophisticated, bureaucratic and cooperative organizational structure. Without a high degree of consensus and cooperation between the court teams, City courts would not be able to achieve their basic goal — the successful processing of some 4,000 criminal cases each year. Yet although under this relatively 'real' organizational pressure City magistrates and clerks have also, through their own experience, recruitment, training and in response to the amount and nature of juvenile crime paraded before them, developed the beginnings of a consistent policy for dealing with juveniles, their approach has clearly been influenced, ideologically, by many sources, especially the mitigation of solicitors and the explanations of social workers through their reports. These two sets of influences, one organizational and one ideological, though inter-related, should nevertheless be seen as distinct in that the priorities of one set of influences some-times undermine and undercut the other. We have noted that City courts do suffer from snarl-ups, over-long lists, disappearing solicitors, ill-prepared prosecutors, defendants being ushered in before their turn and the like. Yet in terms of the overall through-put of the system it basically runs fairly efficiently in organizational terms. We have argued that the regular courtroom teams operate in relation to three sets of normative guiding rules: proceed with basic civility to defendants and each other, proceed through due process and legal representation and sentence using the full range of disposals. These guiding principles are highly functional. They are understood and adhered to by the vast majority of court workers on most occasions. They allow professional disagreements to be amicably sorted out. They help prevent messy cases from upsetting and delaying the court. They allow court workers to predict sentencing and thus prepare accordingly and facilitate the court's smooth running without being out of step with each other. They allow justice to be seen to be done.

At the end of the last section we outlined the main features of City magistrate's sentencing approach. We have suggested that it represents the beginnings of rational approach to sentencing and is consistent with a liberal paternal set of beliefs about urban adolescents and social con-trol. In particular this approach is reflected in the disposal pattern as table 5.1 shows, and has the overall effect of avoiding the routine use of custodial measures, despite the relatively high crime rate. This approach is certainly in line with the findings of most empirical criminology, suggesting the presence of a 'delinquent career' for juveniles with a settling-down period in their late teens which will be delayed or damaged by custodial punishments. City magistrates do not seem to base their rationale on these findings, however. They seem to react more prag-matically: they simply note that 'serious crime' and recidivism is not the basic raw material of their court. Their definition of 'serious' of course is based on their experience of an inner-city court.

City magistrates' apparent tolerance is thus at least in part a prag-matic and, in the 'system's' terms, a quite rational response to the reality of urban crime. They use the full tariff, tuned by judging each case on its merits, or modified by a high social need or disorder indi-cator, or by a serious offence.

This sentencing policy allows the disposal agencies to *cope*. Put very crudely local detention centres could not cope if City magistrates started sending them juveniles whenever they stole a car, broke into a house or got into a fight. Nevertheless, this is itself a liberal position and as we shall see when we consider Countyside's sentencing, we should not take it for granted. Further, this degree of tolerance of routine juvenile crime is not in keeping with the punitive, retributive atmosphere in relation to juvenile crime pervading Britain at the beginning of the 1980s.

Yet despite their awareness and consideration of the personal and social disadvantages which inner-City's working-class youth must live under, City magistrates do not in the end engage themselves seriously in any sort of a critique of the urban environment which makes up the court's catchment area. They offer in particular no critique of the school, the opportunity pathways for unskilled city adolescents and local policing practices. Their outline theory of adolescent delinquency does not really grasp the monumental significance of these factors. Despite their liberalism, despite their well-intentioned paternalism, City magistrates are fundamentally very much a part of the local state control apparatus. Their ideological position is based on a consensus model of society.

School is seen as a good thing. It makes citizens; it is a pathway to respectability by opening up career possibilities.

This can be particularly depressing in a city with over twice the national average unemployment and 35 per cent youth unemployment in the inner areas. Similarly the relationship between truancy and crime is not a simple one and if the number of children who stayed off school decided to go shoplifting as well, the juvenile crime rate would be enormously enlarged. City courts operated as if truancy was some kind of pathology, a symptom of a wider social disorder. They had no grasp of the lack of meaning attached to school, quite rationally, by working-class adolescents (see chapter 2) or of the ways schools happily 'cool out' many kids. Nor were City magistrates willing or able to grasp the fact that particular juveniles appeared before them as the consequence of specific policing practices based on organizational goals. They rarely showed any willingness to doubt a policeman's evidence even when, in our opinion and that of many defence solicitors we spoke to, it was highly dubious. They never asked why a trivial offence was not dealt with by a caution but simply dealt with guilty pleas for stealing a pint of milk, riding a bike on the pavement, stealing a bar of chocolate or the ultimate, a mickey mouse badge, with conditional discharges. In short, they appeared to believe that what came before them came there properly and after due consideration by impartial professionals. The confrontation, the on-going contest between City youth and the police was not acknowledged in any way as being dialectical or problematic. In this sense we must doubt that justice is done on many occasions when it seems to be done. And, as we will show in chapter 6, from the adolescents' perspective justice is often not done.

Nevertheless, as we have shown, a liberal paternal outlook towards juveniles, even though lacking the necessary critical view of the local social structure does offer City adolescents, within the limits of the legislation, a juvenile court experience which certainly tends towards being consistent in atmosphere, keen on 'justice being seen to be done', and predictable in its sentencing. We must now consider the production of juvenile justice in a petty sessional division adjoining City's catchment area and in particular sample the very different atmosphere of Countyside juvenile court.

5

Countyside's Punitive Juvenile Justice

As we have already implied, despite the similarity of the urban populations and the socio-economic conditions they suffer, despite having
similar crime rates, despite the sifting and ages of juveniles for prosecution being generally similar, City and Countyside courts produce
dramatically different versions of juvenile justice. Differences occur
both in the mode of production, as we shall show in this chapter when
we analyse Countyside's in-court regime, and in the disposals produced
— the way juveniles are sentenced. Before describing the mode of production, which we contend also justifies our classification of Countyside as punitive, we must look briefly at the statistical evidence on
sentencing.

In many ways the methods of disposal given as percentages presented in table 5.1 speak for themselves. Our comments can be brief therefore but their significance for the quality of juvenile justice is extensive.
Table 5.1 is based on statistics gleaned from several sources. The
national disposal pattern comes from the Home Office (1979 and
1980) statistical returns. The Merseyside figures come from the relevant chief constable's report, the City figures from reports to the City
by the justices and the clerk; and the figures for Countyside from our
own analysis of the court lists. The calculation of figures from different
sources may involve some slight inaccuracies but the overall pattern can
certainly be regarded as correct. The metropolitan area in which we
undertook our research processes about 7 per cent of all young offenders in England and Wales. Although the region has the third highest
recorded juvenile crime rate, the actual pattern of offending largely
mirrors the national pattern. The region does have a higher level of unauthorized taking of motor vehicles than the national picture but, on
the other hand, it has less offences of criminal damage and despite local

78

TABLE 5.1 MEANS OF DISPOSAL OF ALL JUVENILES (10–17 yrs) PROCEEDED AGAINST AS
PERCENTAGES OF ALL CASES DEALT WITH FOR INDICTABLE AND NON-INDICTABLE OFFENCES

		Withdrawn or discharged	Absolute or conditional discharge	Other penalty	Fine	Supervision order	Attendance centre	Care order	Detention centre	Borstal recommendation
England and Wales	1978	7	19	1	43	11	8	4	4	2
	1979	7	17	1	43	13	9	4	4	2
Metropolitan area	1978	12	21	4	29	10	10	3	5	2
	1979	19	17	4	30	9	10	2	6	3
City juvenile court	1978	16	23	4	26	9	10	2	4	2
	1979	23	18	4	28	8	9	2	5	2
Countryside juvenile court	1978	12	14	6	25	10	11	2	12	6
	1979	11	17	2	22	14	11	2	11	8

Note: These figures are only accurate to within 2% for each category as they are calculated from different sources.

media suggestions to the contrary, it does not have an abnormally high level of violent crime.

Clearly the metropolitan area reflects the sentencing patterns produced nationally. The region as a whole does not appear idiosyncratic. Instead it is *within* the region that fundamental differences in sentencing occur. The pattern is by definition guided by the large City courts which deal with half of all the region's juvenile prosecutions. The other half are prosecuted in the four 'outer' juvenile court systems serving 'district council' areas: Countyside, as one of two juvenile courts making up one of the outer systems, itself deals with about 600 juveniles a year.

One in five of all Countyside juveniles proceeded against (and one in four of all those found guilty) receive custodial sentences compared with one in 11 for City and one in ten nationally. The implications of this wholesale use of custodial sentencing are enormous, particularly when one considers that the angry debate about the locking-up of more juveniles than ever before has been conducted on the basis of the national figures (see Crow, 1979; *New Approaches to Juvenile Crime*, 1979). Furthermore, Countyside decision-makers are much less likely to withdraw or dismiss cases than City and somewhat less likely to use a conditional or absolute discharge for minor offences, in comparison with City and the national picture.

This sentencing pattern may be viewed almost with disbelief. However, as we will show in this chapter, once one analyses the nature of the Countyside regime, it becomes quite feasible that this sentencing pattern may be a logical consequence of the ideological preferences of Countyside court officials, spilling over into their interpretation of court procedure and hence administration of juvenile justice.

LOSING JUSTICE: THE IMPACT OF INTERPRETING DUE PROCESS

The court setting

Countyside juvenile court occupies the rear section of a purpose-built judicial and administrative complex. Apart from the magistrates' courts proper, the complex also provides accommodation for the probation service and the police. The complex faces a modern planned shopping precinct and adjacent bus and rail terminals. This whole creation was part of the development of Countyside from a pre-war village in a rich and historic shire county into a large residential town — in appearance a montage of corporation overspill estates accommodating a largely working-class population previously housed, a generation before, in the inner area of City.

The juvenile court has its own entrance and, within the court, its own reception area and interview rooms: there is a small windowless waiting room of painted brick furnished with slatted wood trestles, one large cigarette tub and a very public telephone. There are no refreshment facilities. The courtroom itself is of modern appearance, basically furnished by tables and chairs without any name plates and indeed without any particular character or quality except a sense of order. The magistrates' desk was initially at floor level but, apparently at the instigation of one senior magistrate and sanctioned by a magistrates' meeting, this was later placed upon a raised platform where it remains today.

The clerk's central position, directly between defendants and magistrates, is not unimportant to the operation of the Countyside court, particularly when contrasted with City where the clerk sits to one side of the magistrates in a 'lower status' space. Similarly, defendants in Countyside are not seated close to their solicitors' desks or to social services or probation (themselves relegated to the back of the courtroom) but are spatially isolated. The 'smallness' of the courtroom, and the internal seating arrangements are not without consequence.

Countyside court is also 'small' in terms of the number of court officials who operate in it. There is a small pool of magistrates available, and in practice the court is routinely serviced by no more than a couple of dozen. There are only two or three clerks who operate in the juvenile court, only a trio of prosecutors, and no more than a dozen regular defence solicitors, most of whom work out of the 'shop front' premises set up purposefully in the nearby shopping precinct.

The setting for, and staging of, juvenile justice in Countyside is, then, very much a private affair. The small and select groups who gather in the courtroom meet very regularly to produce their version of juvenile justice. Unlike City courts, with its vast permutation of magistrates, clerks, solicitors and police personnel, Countyside's court workers are rarely subjected to new faces, new ways, unexpected interpretations of law or procedure. They know what's what and who's who. They are very much at home in *their* court.

'Interpreting' court procedure

We suggested in the last chapter that City court officials used due process correctly and fully, stretching or interpreting its principles rather
freely only occasionally and then not clearly to the detriment of the
defendant's rights. This did not appear to us to be the case in Countyside. In the first place due process was more regularly 'interpreted'
firstly in order to achieve goals which appeared to be concerned with
serving the best interests of the court personnel rather than justice, and
secondly, so that it could be used as a means of inflicting moral and
social stigma upon defendants and parents. The latent function of this
overall idiosyncratic interpretation is perhaps the most significant in
that, once established in a court culture, it can undermine the safeguards, embodied in due process, which prevent officials from adopting
personal interpretations of what is relevant and acceptable in the administration of justice. Such an interpretation of due process had
become a part of Countyside court procedure. How long and in what
way it had been accommodated is difficult to assess. We would hypothesize on the basis of our observation period that the manner involved
two analytically distinct processes: destructuring and restructuring.
Destructuring involves the tendency to take away certain safeguards
and courtesies — for example, not making much attempt to explain
jargon and check that a defendant understands what is going on. Restructuring involves inserting material into court procedure which
might be regarded as extraneous and which certainly was not routinely
included in City court's production. Examples of these processes will
be given throughout this chapter.

While Countyside often took several months to process legally represented 'not-guilty' plea defendants, the style of clerking during any one
session would appear at one and the same time to exacerbate delay, by
seeming reluctant to proceed in some cases, whilst appearing to move
with undue haste in others. This regularly repeated approach, set
against the claim of the court personnel that they were over-worked
and hard pressed, is difficult to explain since lengthy remands for trials
could be significantly reduced by the court's sitting a little longer each
session or by increasing the number of sessions for a temporary period,
and even appointing more magistrates. Yet Countyside, whilst in practice a 'quiet' court sitting only two days a week, appeared to regard
periods of several months as routine for a juvenile trial to be in process.
This attitude contrasts with City court, where by utilizing 'free' court-

rooms and recruiting more magistrates trial remands have been reduced from 12 to six weeks in recent years in the interests of justice. Countyside's atmosphere of 'pressure' was thus a self-created rationalization. It justified a myriad of in-court practices.

One example is 'herding', justified in terms of 'saving the court's time'. 'Herding' involves the usher leading defendants and parents briskly into the courtroom and, with the verbal help of the clerk, pushing and ordering them into their restricted space and then booming out: 'Parents behind their son, the defendant standing'. The clerk then reorders them to fit the order of names on the charge sheet and without looking up, and simultaneously shuffling papers, moves through rapidly, for the benefit of due process, the litany of name and address, the charge and the plea. 'Do you admit or deny the offence, in other words, are you guilty or not guilty' drones out, followed immediately by questions regarding legal aid, legal representation and remand. This complex and rapid routine appeared to cut dead the possibility of dialogue. It is a brave defendant who stops the flow. (This contrasts with City clerks, who almost always went out of their way not to 'incant' the taking of plea but used informal language to try to make sure that the defendant and parents *understood* the situation.) And when, after herding, father is not present, we observed that a further 'routine' question, a form of restructuring, was often slipped in as if it were legitimate and as if it were due process. A mother will be asked:

Is there any particular reason why the father is not here today?

The law requires only one parent or guardian to be present in juvenile court. We found that City courts respected this rule in keeping with due process.

These differences between the two courts are, we contend, connected with Countyside's particular approach to due process. Failing to offer defendants basic courtesies and civility, and perhaps reducing their chance of understanding proceedings, is an example of destructuring, so offering a minimalist interpretation of due process. Inserting extraordinary questions restructures procedure. Countyside officials wanted to know before the finding of guilt, whether or not they were dealing with a single-parent family, or whether father was in prison or even in bed. For, when both parents were present, the clerk often only referred to one of them and not necessarily the father. Father's presence was apparently not as necessary as his absence was unacceptable.

Only the working father was not chastised in, and for, his absence.

Countyside magistrates were superficially very inconsistent in their response to legal aid applications and in their efforts to advise defendants of the efficacy of being represented. It was not unusual for defendants or parents to state their desire to 'get the case over and done with', and thus dispense with adjournments for legal representation, or applications for legal aid, and simply ask 'to be done today'. Normally Countyside court would accept this from defendants although it was not always in the obvious best interests of justice being seen to be done. City officials, as we have seen, acknowledged this difficulty by always checking that the refusal by defendants to take legal representation was made in a rational and fully informed way. Countyside officials tended to behave somewhat differently, checking such matters only when they reached extremes. The classic example of this occurred when a defendant actually claiming innocence insisted on pleading guilty. Such behaviour was not allowed. The defendant was told he *must* plead not guilty and was granted legal aid, the case being adjourned for trial.

Countyside also appeared to encourage legal representation if a case looked 'messy' in some way. Perhaps the defendant was presented as 'stroppy' or badly confused; in either instance, to avoid any possible embarrassment, the advice would be: 'We suggest you see a solicitor right away, we will adjourn the case until. . . .' The defence solicitor would be expected to represent defendants in a manner acceptable to the court.

Nationally, the refusal rate for legal aid applications in juvenile court is about 8 per cent. In City courts, where officials were willing to encourage legal representation in the interests of justice and even against their own organizational interest, the refusal rate is only 4 per cent. Countyside juvenile court refused no less than 24 per cent of all applications during the year in question. This differential refusal rate largely speaks for itself and is a further example of the differences between City's and Countyside's approaches.

Legal representation: in whose best interests?

The refusal of legal aid, or at any rate the absence of a defence solicitor, might be regarded as less crucial in an informal court regime when dialogue is encouraged and the spirit of due process endorsed (see Anderson, 1978). Countyside court officials, on the contrary, created a very formal and rarified atmosphere in which defendants felt particularly uncomfortable and lost, which may be one reason for some defendants trying to 'get it over with quickly'. On the other hand, those who are aware they are entering a harsh court, accused of a serious offence or insisting on a trial, attempt as the statistics suggest, to seek the help of a solicitor. Countyside court granted 250 applications for legal aid during the year we are considering. These applications tended to fall into the 'serious' alleged offences, 'possibility of custodial sentence' and not guilty plea, categories. They were granted properly and were mainly indisputable as they fell so clearly into the criteria defined in the relevant legislation.

There has been a steady growth in legal representation in Countyside court in keeping with national trends. This growth in 'business' for solicitors is reflected, and perhaps partly created, by their investment in the Countyside scene. Their new shop front premises in the nearby precinct bear witness to this trend. These solicitors admit to playing a delicate game in Countyside. They had a 'foot in the door' during our period of observation but compared with the influence and presence of their colleagues in City juvenile court were still only tentatively established as normal and routine court 'workers'. On the one hand these solicitors had to 'keep in' with the court, in order that timetabling by way of remands, adjournments, etc. would always be in their best interests; on the other hand they had to 'educate' the court about their necessity and so reduce the refusal rate for legal aid and increase the court's spontaneous promotion of legal representation with new defendants. Hence, whilst normally being very passive and accepting of Countyside's atmosphere and regime (sometimes, in our opinion, to the detriment of the defence), solicitors would also occasionally attempt strategic advances and under the banner of due process, of course, make a 'strenuous application':

> In my opinion it is wrong for any juvenile to appear in court without recourse to a solicitor. ... If you do not regard it [the charge] as serious and refuse legal aid, then it is not right to tell him [the defendant] in summing up that it is a serious offence he has committed.

In suggesting that the granting of legal aid — and thus legal representation — is heavily influenced by issues other than 'the spirit' of due process and the quality of justice, we have highlighted the court's timetabling, the 'cooling-out' of potentially embarrassing defendants and the recreating of the facade of justice being seen to be done as the main items on the hidden agenda. However in the cases when defendants are legally represented and solicitors are not playing a 'court pleasing' game legal representation did appear to be in the best interests of the defendants. In these situations our criticisms of legal representation correspond to those we made vis-a-vis City court in the last chapter.

Proceeding unchecked

We have suggested that Countyside juvenile court, because of its smallness and lack of a critical audience, tends to produce juvenile justice in the absence of criticism and without a questioning voice. The danger of allowing officials to proceed unchecked is well illustrated by Countyside magistrates' tendency to paint over the weaknesses in their interpretation of due process by the practice of merely announcing that justice was done, and so should be seen to be done. The classic case of this has already been alluded to: the refusal of legal aid, representation, without explanation. Similarly magistrates regularly failed to give any explanation of their sentencing decisions, even when defendants were differentially treated. Nor were they any more inclined to string more than a dozen explanatory words together when sending a juvenile to detention centre on his first offence. They would simply announce:

> We find the case proven. You will go to detention centre for three months.

Defendants and parents were rarely offered any explanation as to the content of interruptions for private negotiations between clerk and magistrates, even when these clearly altered proceedings significantly.

One court team which might be expected to criticize and so check the Countyside version of juvenile justice are the social workers. The more so in Countyside because of the involvement of the 'court experienced' probation service. (Social services dealt with 10–12 year olds and probation 13–17 year olds in Countyside criminal proceedings.) Yet this social work service, with its constant presence in the court and its right and responsibility to submit social enquiry reports was not a major check upon the court's atmosphere and sentencing policy.

Probation officers accompanied only 'current case' clients in court, a minority of the overall input. They also operated a duty system to service the court, which meant that one officer did only one week's duty in the juvenile court, hence not really having time to tune into the in-crowd court atmosphere or develop the necessary social skills to influence procedure at strategic moments. Furthermore, unlike in City courts, where social workers had the policy of *not* producing social enquiry reports for trials until the finding of guilt, Countyside probation officers in the absence of such a directive tended to produce reports before trials. (The practice was fortunately stopped by the probation service about six months after our observation period, after receiving our research findings.) This meant that if guilt was found magistrates had only rather brief social enquiry reports before them, with no discussion of the juvenile's attitude to the offence nor any firm recommendation for disposal (since these issues can be addressed only after the finding of guilt), which has been shown to be a report's downfall in terms of influence (J. Thorpe, 1979). Full social enquiry reports can be regarded as vital to any juvenile court, offering sentencers information concerning the juvenile's culpability and having regard for his best interests. However, in Countyside, with its 'short tariff' and thus extensive use of custodial sentences, the passivity of the probation service was all the more harmful, both to the goals it espouses as an agency and to the chances of curbing delinquent careers. For example, in relation to taking and driving away offences (TDAs), we examined the antecedents of all offenders Countyside sent to detention centre in the year in question — 38 in all. Only four had previously received supervision orders, despite 80 per cent of them having only minor records and 37 per cent no records at all. Clearly probation officers should have been offering strong recommendations for supervision in many of these cases, or at least a non-custodial sentence. Their failure to offer a coherent alternative ideology to Countyside court was an opportunity lost to provide a check on its punitive sentencing, a failure to offer criticism. We will consider why probation officers 'fell in line' in chapter 8.

We have argued that Countyside's interpretation of due process, involving both destructuring and restructuring, is capable we believe of disadvantaging defendants in a variety of ways. We have given numerous examples of this and showed how it has developed, unchecked by the 'cautious' style of local solicitors and the passivity of the social work service. The resultant court culture can appear to be one in which *real* justice to some extent becomes lost.

ABUSING JUSTICE: THE IMPACT OF SOCIAL CLASS

It would be a naive argument that the social class differential between magistrates and defendants was in itself the key issue in the 'objectification' of defendants and the creation of punitive justice. To say that magistrates are middle aged and middle class seems almost a truism since it is clearly observable and documented (Burney, 1979). Most criminal defendants are from working-class backgrounds. In Countyside the gulf, the social distance between the bench and defendants, was considerable and clearly brought home by the frequency with which magistrates had to quit the bench abruptly for specific hearings because they knew defendants and their parents personally from acting as employer, head teacher, councillor and so on. The magistrates were, in the main, professional or propertied people and the defendants were, by and large, from one of the most deprived urban areas in the United Kingdom. It is obviously dangerous to generalize but so often did defendants and parents have the appearance of being materially poor that we feel obliged to refer to this. Even more so than in City, we were left with the impression of poverty.

We can hypothesize, on the basis of our work in City courts, that the social distance between judge and judged, which was present there also, need not produce either the 'objectification' of defendants or harsh juvenile justice. We would argue that City's operational rules, part of the court culture, honoured the safeguards of due process and restricted sentencing discretion, thus preventing social class prejudices and antagonisms spilling over into court proceedings. Such safeguards appeared less real in Countyside. Further, Countyside clerks and magistrates tend to make 'space' in the court proceedings for restructuring by inserting extraneous ideological and 'common sense' agendas about how justice should be administered.

An ideal way of disguising this insertion of a hidden agenda vis-a-vis administering justice is to claim, as many magistrates did in conversation with us, that 'each case is judged on its merits'. The dynamics of this operation are complex but we will be arguing in this and the next section that Countyside magistrates basically relied upon their own notions of adolescence, working-class family life, crime and its causes and the purposes of punishment. As a consequence of this, social class differentials, which as our analysis of City courts showed need not be influential, become so.

In this section we shall try to get over the obvious methodological difficulties of demonstrating the impact of social class on the administration of justice by using qualitative data taken from three sources. First, we had formal conversations with nearly all the magistrates who presided over observed sessions. That they happily met and talked with us, using the judgemental criteria we present below, is significant. Second, we draw on 'overheard' conversations between court officials, which took place during and after sessions, and between cases. Third, we draw on our own transcriptions of 'official' in-court discourse. We will deal with the impact of social distance by referring to issues of income, leisure and language.

First, we will consider Countyside officials' approach to matters relating to the income of poor people, the defendants and their parents. Fines in Countyside tend to be comparatively high and consistent with this was the magistrates' propensity to use compensation orders. In one case, which involved three boys convicted of stealing and joy-riding a Daimler saloon, the juveniles were all sent to detention centre and banned from driving etc., but were also ordered to pay £200 compensation each. The compensation order was made in respect of repairs to the vehicle, although the court was aware that the bill had already been paid by the insurance company. One might wonder if the status of the car influenced this decision, not least because the presiding magistrates went out of their way to state, quite unsolicited, that the compensation had absolutely nothing at all to do with the car being a Daimler. Nor is it irrelevant to our analysis that when a juvenile sent to detention centre and ordered to pay £1,000 compensation (at £5 per week for four years) appealed to Crown Court against the sentence he had the compensation order quashed. It could be argued that sentencers, because of their cloistered social position, are unaware of the impact of demanding that an unemployed juvenile should pay over a third of his income for four years. There were occasions when this benign interpretation was given backing, in that magistrates would preface their sentence with suggestions of leniency:

We're *just* going to fine you £30 and £30 compensation.

Yet on occasions when parents offered to pay the whole sum of a fine there and then, rather than on weekly account, they clearly took court officials aback. On one occasion the clerk repeated the fine's amount slowly and said:

You're sure you can pay this sum in whole now, today?

Thus even the parent who responds to the formal sentence correctly, and without inviting social comment, receives it. Having so often and routinely quizzed defendants and parents about how much money they received each week, their hire purchase commitments, how much rent they paid and so on, court officials regarded relative affluence in a juvenile or his family almost as a form of defiance.

Countyside's officials displayed conservative attitudes towards leisure and the use of social space. Because they failed to consider leisure in the context of the lives of working-class adolescents, these attitudes proved judgemental and restrictive. Thus, in interrogating a boy as to what he does when not in school, a senior magistrate was told:

We play footie, go places, go to the cinema if I've got money.

The reply from the bench was crisp:

Ah! You muck around all day and con your mother.

Adolescents are often reprimanded by magistrates for being on the street at all. Window-shopping is implicitly forbidden. Anyone window-shopping must be up to no good. One magistrate went as far as to suggest a kind of unofficial curfew for adolescents hanging around the village part of Countyside, with its proximity to the land of owner-occupied semi-detacheds:

It is a very serious thing to go wandering around the streets in Countyside village.

The use of complex language by court 'professionals' to 'cool out' defendants is well documented (Fears, 1977). We do not intend to dwell on this device here, except to say it was, as one would expect, a routine feature of Countyside court.

So far we have dealt with specific examples of stigmatization, which appear to be a product of the social-class distance between judge and judged. The clearest evidence that the social distance structurally present between judgers and judged affects court procedure concerns Countyside officials' development of a full-blown thesis about the nature of poor families and their 'criminal' way of life. Our fieldwork diaries became so laden with 'problem family' explanations that we were forced to identify this as a working model amongst court officials in Countyside. This model is basically pathological, corresponding in part with those explanations of social problems found in the 'culture of poverty' thesis. The central strand concerns the belief that Countyside is infested by an underclass of criminal families. We were sometimes briefed during proceedings when a reputed member of the criminal families brigade appeared. On one occasion we were passed a note:

> One of our regulars. They are one of our oldest customers . . . his name is sprayed all over walls in the area.

These families, so the thesis goes, generally tend to be socially disordered. We noted that clerks, perhaps unconsciously, confirmed this stereotyping in 'explaining' the sentencing decision to families, for instance by commenting in open court to a mother:

> I think one of your other sons is going to the attendance centre for a similar offence.

And to a boy disposed of with a fine:

> Perhaps, George, when your father comes out . . . er . . . comes out of prison, he'll help you pay.

Magistrates themselves expounded the criminal families thesis to us. One, for example, also a councillor, regarded them as nuisances and pollutants. He claimed to be pressurized by angry neighbours at his weekly surgeries, and favours a housing policy of moving them out, moving them on. In order to 'test' this thesis that there is a network of criminal families in Countyside, we analysed the names appearing on the juvenile court lists over the year during which we were observing. We found no evidence that such families existed as 'regular customers' of the juvenile court. When names did recur in the court, this was mainly the result of a series of remands. This might give an impression of recidivism but, certainly over the year's workload we analysed, there was no significant substantiation of the court officials' thesis. This particular ideological construction may stem from magistrates' other dealings with the local population as head teacher, councillor or employer. Whatever its source, it acts as a defence mechanism which can be utilized if the 'common-sense' principles court officials use in administering justice are ever challenged.

We have in this section relied heavily on extracts from official and unofficial discourse in and around the court to demonstrate our conten-

tion that the social-class position and subsequent cultural and ideological preferences of court officials spill over into the production of
juvenile justice in Countyside court. In the next section we shall deal
briefly with Countyside court's stand against the unlawful taking of
motor vehicles, normally expensive cars. The punitive nature of disposals vis-a-vis car offences is in itself important, but just as significant
is the way in which this policy illustrates the inconsistency, and thus
lack of rational sentencing policy, which is both created by, and reinforces, the administration of justice via class antagonism.

CONFUSING JUSTICE: THE IMPACT OF EXEMPLARY SENTENCING

Throughout the 1970s the taking and driving away of motor vehicles
(TDA) was defined by both official and media statements as a major
and worrying crime. With up to 20,000 vehicles a year being taken from
the metropolitan area annually, and with the majority of these offences
being committed by young men and juveniles, the spotlight was understandably upon those juveniles found guilty of car-taking. In particular
the spate of deaths, either to pedestrians or to car-takers themselves,
which occurred in the two years before our research period, had resulted in a stern approach from magistrates throughout the region.

Despite dealing with only 10 per cent of the cases of TDA processed
through all juvenile courts in the metropolitan area, Countyside managed
to sentence nearly half the grand total of juveniles sent to detention
centre for TDA and related offences. Nor was this extremely large
proportion the result of Countyside magistrates' resisting the use of
Borstal training. They recommended about one-third of the juveniles
sentenced to Crown Court with a recommendation for Borstal training
for TDA offences in the metropolitan area. In short, Countyside's
sentencing of TDA offenders was the centre piece of its generally punitive approach. It cannot be explained merely by the size and seriousness
of the general 'problem', as other local courts did not behave similarly.
City court, for instance, dealt with 40 per cent of all TDA cases during
a similar period and, although in terms of its own tariff took TDA cases
very seriously, still sentenced only the same number of offenders to
detention centre as Countyside, which deals with only 10 per cent of
the region's cases.

For the purposes of this section we shall limit our discussion of this
'early' routine use of custodial sentencing for one particular offence to

considering how it highlights Countyside magistrates' idiosyncratic sentencing. We must start by being aware that, having declared war on the joy-riders, Countyside officials announced to nearly all 'TDA' defendants:

> You should know that if you are found guilty on that day this court will be considering a custodial sentence.

> You must both come back on the 5th of   , and you should know that if, on that day, you are found guilty this court is taking an extremely serious view of this type of offence.

So often and clearly quoted was this exemplary approach in Countyside court that the declaration by some magistrates, that they had an agreed policy about sending car offenders down, appeared to be true. Certainly some court officials believed there was such a policy routinely operating.

A persuasive argument can be made for such an approach, of course, if one believes that custodial sentences, particularly detention centre, have a deterrent effect. In reality, as all penologists know, this is not the case. (Our analysis of the 38 juveniles sent to detention centre for TDA by Countyside during a 12-month period showed a 66 per cent reconviction rate within 14 months.) Whether or not Countyside magistrates were wholly concerned with mere deterrence is, of course, another issue. We would speculate that in keeping with their particular interpretation of the 1969 Act they were content to achieve the goal of retribution and perhaps of 'protecting the public' for six weeks. What can be said of such a policy, however, is that if it is exercised consistently it might gain deterrent strength through dissuading others who thus never come before the courts.

However, despite the categoric statements of some members of the bench, Countyside court was *not* consistent in its treatment of TDA offences. Certainly it was highly punitive but, far from sending 'everybody' down, it sentenced more than 10 per cent of offenders with attendance centre orders and fined a further 10 per cent. Another 5 per cent were placed on supervision orders. Thus, even on such a key issue, Countyside court was not able to present a consistent sentencing policy. It said one thing and to some extent did another. The reasons for this are complex. Certainly on some occasions there were simply no places available in detention centres and, whilst this fact was never publicly announced, it was at times the fundamental reason for a break in 'policy'. On other occasions, however, particularly for first time offenders with 'respectable' parents, good school reports and good job prospects, the 'criminal families' stereotype simply broke down and magistrates returned to publicly 'judging each case on its merits'. This was, of course, the crucial confusion in their whole approach to handing out 'universal' exemplary justice. The two sentencing approaches are in conflict: exemplary sentencing, with its need for a period of universality, is in direct conflict with individualized sentencing which, whilst not necessarily ad hoc can be reduced to merely 'judging each case on its merits'.

Thus Countyside court is consistent only in its general approach and punitive sentencing. This, we have argued, is partly the result of the lack of a sentencing policy which espouses any of the principles of the 1969 Act or, as in City, the consistent use of certain operational guidelines such as the full-tariff ladder. The inability of Countyside magistrates to reach consistency, even on an issue which some of their numbers claim is controlled by a policy of exemplary sentencing, is, we are suggesting, a crucial illustration of how resistant individual Countyside magistrates were to doing anything other than responding to their own inclinations and common-sense notions about the nature of juvenile justice. For some, this includes refraining from blatant retributive sentencing, especially if 'respectable' families are involved, and it is consistent with our argument that not all magistrates in Countyside would find the exemplary custodial sentencing 'policy' acceptable in all cases since it confounded their 'criminal families' ideology.

DISCUSSION

There is a sprawling over-spill estate, which we'll call Easton, which lies across the 'frontier' between City and Countyside. The district council and petty sessional divisional boundary lines run down the middle of many streets in Easton. Juveniles accused of committing offences inside the City boundary must, if proceeded against, attend City juvenile court and receive the version of juvenile justice produced there. Those accused of offending inside the Countyside boundary must attend Countyside court. We hope that readers of the last two chapters will not have too much difficulty in answering this question. If you were going to take a car which side of the street would you pinch it from?

We argued in chapter 1 that the 1969 Act, because of its partial implementation and consequent ambiguity, gave legitimacy to the extension of discretion in juvenile justice and that this discretion has tended to produce diversity in the production of local juvenile justice. This diversity was discussed by Anderson (1978) and has been confirmed by the present study. We have also suggested that, *overall*, discretion has tended to be administered in a traditional, punitive manner. Since this discretion is vested, fundamentally, in the hands of the police and the magistrates this should be expected. Mainline policing goals, in particular, are not normally consistent with diversion and the 'best interests' of juvenile offenders. The general sentencing trend has, as we know, been towards the use of more custodial sentencing. Community supervision has not flourished and in recent years has actually reduced its contribution. In short there has been a major dysjunction between the intentions of the original 1969 Act and its actual effect through partial implementation over the last decade. We also contended in chapter 1 that the creation of this dissonance is, in part, illustrative of official deviation. Here we have in mind deviation which flourishes in a system devoid of clear ground rules and objectives. We have in this chapter illustrated this practice in detail. We would hypothesize that both 'the best interests of the child' and the right to the principles of natural and criminal justice can be undermined simultaneously or separately. It appears to be possible for this to occur to a large extent without officials stepping outside procedural rules and by simply orchestrating and coordinating their extensive discretion.

Yet our discussion of City juvenile court suggests that such injustice need not occur. From within a consensus model, and using a reformist argument, we have implied that City is the sunny side of the street. City offers a clear model of how the spirit of the 1969 Act and the intentions of due process can be functionally combined to offer justice for juveniles. City does not even fall foul of the opponents of rampant welfare discretion in that it does not readily make 7 (7) care orders for young offenders (see Thorpe *et al.,* 1979). Compared with Countyside, it offered defendants and their parents more civility, more explanation, more legal representation and legal safeguards and more consistency. It sentenced more evenly and less harshly and in doing so took due note of the best interests of the juvenile, which it balanced with other more traditional considerations. We will show in the next chapter, when we compare the perceptions of juveniles processed through the two different regimes, that these differences are of great significance to those on the receiving end. The nature of the production of local juvenile justice has major implications for the moral authority of the local state.

6

Receiving Juvenile Justice

ENTERING THE SYSTEM: THE POLICE ROLE

We have already indicated the reality of the 'push-in' tendency, which sends large amounts of 'trivia' into the juvenile court. This process was recognized and resented by our subject families[4] who, as we shall see, highlighted another aspect of the pre-court stage of juvenile justice — the 'bump-up' tendency. It rests with the police, as law enforcement officers, to exercise their discretion in initiating action against suspected juveniles: the police can define and categorize their behaviour as specifically outside the law and can bring selected adolescents before the juvenile court itself. Cicourel (1968), in his participant observation study of police organization in American states, suggests that the very core of law enforcement is entrusted to the police's common-sense and intuitive notions, with the assumption of guilt based on considerable experience of typing offenders. He maintains that procedural rules and concepts like justice and 'fairness', are not applicable to routine street policing, where subjects are viewed as already guilty and therefore not entitled to any legal advantages.

When we talked with parents and children about the charges put to them, we found that the majority of families, because of their shared experiences of being on the receiving end of charge negotiations, recognized the definition of an offence as a social construct determined by the police. Moreover, more than half of these families, while not painting themselves whiter than white, were unhappy about the exact charges put against them. We met many adolescents who still felt aggrieved at police classifications of their behaviour and who continued to assert their innocence of specific allegations some months after their cases had been dealt with by the courts. These working-class youngsters held to the prevalent view that police allegations tended to distort, decontextualize and unduly criminalize their own actions as they saw

them. This view was particularly and consistently put to us by Countyside boys, for whom two-thirds of the charges resulted from police enquiries, whereas more City boys were arrested on the spot, being caught
in the criminal 'act'. But the majority of all these adolescents, both girls
and boys, felt vulnerable and powerless against the police. Whereas
middle-class families might have used their resources to obtain immediate legal advice, settle out of court or pack their children away for
special educational guidance, these relatively poor families were left to
face the discretion of local officials.

As they recalled their first brushes with the police, many adolescents
gave us an animated, detailed and personal dossier, indicating the scope
of police powers and particularly their power to create and 'bump-up'
charges.

> They can say what they like.

For many boys police discretion begins on the streets:

> Was in the right — was waiting for a taxi and he [police] was
> walking down. He asked me a lot of questions: 'Where do you
> live?' 'Have you been in trouble before?' I had to say 'Yes'
> because he could check up. Then he said 'What would you do if I
> took you to the police station and charged you with SPL?' I said,
> 'I can't do anything' — You can't do anything against the police.

> Once me and him [mate] saw a motor bike on the floor so we
> picked it up and put it on the stand. This car pulled up and a
> copper got out and said, 'You got a match?' Then he grabbed
> hold of me . . . he planted this iron bar and licence plate. When
> we got to the police station, he said he'd found them and 'I know
> you're always in trouble over motor bikes.' They picked some-
> thing off it to prove their say.

For others, the police seemed to apply their own definitions of the
offence at the police station, negotiating and constructing a criminal
charge. Simon, for example, remembers:

> One was for assaulting a police officer when all I done was swore
> at her . . . when they took me to the police station, they didn't
> know what to charge me with so they selected it from a list there
> . . . policewoman said, 'If I realized you came from such a good
> home, I wouldn't have arrested you.'

Another lad felt the police escalated his breaking-and-entering offence into a burglary charge:

> I asked them about it but they said it was burglary . . . it didn't used to be.

Most girls, too, were perturbed by the extent to which the police themselves can apparently bend procedural rules. Above all, the girls' sense of police discretion and inconsistency seemed to centre on feelings of being picked on and picked out from potential co-defendants, often other girls, who they reckoned were of equal or greater culpability. Mandy, for example, charged with shoplifting, told us: 'The other girl wasn't charged, just got a form to fill in (i.e. a caution). A couple of coloured girls also felt they alone were processed on through the court because "There aren't many dark policemen" and the police discriminated against them — "The police made them say it was me".'

When we went on to ask our sample adolescents how they were treated at the police station, we found most boys felt all was fairly above board; only a handful, mostly from the Countyside police division, recalled undue verbal pressures:

> They dictated it [statement] . . . I wouldn't write it . . . I wouldn't have made a statement.

A police officer had said:

> I can be violent when I want, so you'd better start telling the truth.

A few boys did mention physical intimidation or bullying at the hands of the police but did so with resignation rather than outrage. These boys, who live in heavily policed areas, gave the impression that they expect the police to take a firm line with them and so are slower to take offence than would members of liberal, middle-class pressure groups. For the girls, on the other hand, rough police treatment seemed more frightening, an altogether less expected and accepted experience:

> Fella had hold of my arm dead tight — dumped me in a room on my own and wouldn't let me go to the toilet.

> When I was in a cell on my own this big fella came up to me and said, 'Plead Guilty and I'll give you a caution.'

Most parents were also present at the police station but a small percentage, about 1 in 6, did not attend. Apparently (and we have no way of checking this), in some of these cases the police decided to proceed without a parent present, ignoring procedural rules, although in fairness a minority of parents, like Mr P, who was angry with his son for this latest escapade, refused to attend. In any event, those parents who did go to the police station seemed considerably less satisfied about procedures there than their children. Indeed, some 60 per cent of parents we met and talked with were unhappy on this score. Their dissatisfaction centred on the long period their child had been locked up, often in solitary confinement, on the failure of the police to notify them in reasonable time and on the routine use of verbal threats, occasionally backed up by physical intimidation:

> Della is only 12 and they treated her like a hardened criminal.

> They picked her up at 3 p.m. I didn't get told and only got there at 6.30 p.m. It was too late to be much help to her then.

> He broke down when they threatened him with his job when he didn't own up . . . said they would tell his boss . . . he'd only been working for two days.

We are far from suggesting that these families alleged that all police personnel, protected by their uniform, routinely brutalize young children and strip them of their legal rights. For their own accounts pointed not to a dogmatic and conspiratorial view of police operations, but rather to one infused with clear distinctions, both between cases and between different police officers dealing with one and the same case. Tony's experiences, for example, illustrating police attempts to accommodate suspects, must be juxtaposed with other accounts of police incivility and verbal maltreatment. Caught up in a Saturday afternoon town-centre skirmish between groups of National Front and Socialist Workers Party supporters, Tony was eventually charged with 'disorderly behaviour'. Apparently, he was first put in a cell with National Front members but didn't see eye to eye with them so the police took him out and confined him to a cell with the left-wing group. Finally realizing that he didn't fit in there either, Tony was allotted a cell to himself! Again, a mother who had been most impressed by the detective who advised her to get a solicitor for her daughter and not allow her to make a statement said that she had been terrified just a few hours earlier by the way the police had come to her house and:

grabbed Susan by the arm like a little criminal . . . I assumed I
could be with her but the other constable said I couldn't — she
was there three hours — never had a cup of tea or anything —
must have been very frightening for her.

For boys in our sample, it seems police charges were generally put
on the day of the alleged offence, although several weeks or months
could slip by before a case finally came to court. But for about half
these girls a time lag of three months or more could stretch out before
the police got round to putting formal charges. Perhaps this lapse, with
parents and their daughters often claiming the police originally advised
them that a caution rather than a prosecution would be arranged, reflects the low priority the local police give to girl offenders, and the low
organizational status attached to securing a conviction against a teenage
girl. In any event the stories told independently by Della and her
mother reflect a fairly common experience:

DELLA: They said they would let me off but they came back
and charged me.

DELLA'S MOTHER: The police sergeant laughed. He said it
would be forgotten. Then four months later we got a
summons and she was charged with breaking into a car
and stealing a pen worth 50p.

All in all then, these families' face-to-face experiences of policing
fuelled a good deal of anger and resentment, and their initial encounters with the forces of law and order helped colour their overall impressions of the juvenile justice process, as we will illustrate in the following
sections.

SUMMONED TO COURT: AN OVERVIEW

Waiting and worrying

Our courtroom diaries suggest that very few adolescents are ushered
into City or Countyside juvenile courts without parental support.
Mothers were present in court with some 80 per cent of our sample
adolescents. Occasionally father might share or shoulder his responsibility too but, as we noted in chapter 2, for these working-class families
child-care most often rests with 'Mum'. When we asked parents how
they felt about accompanying their children before the juvenile court,

the majority told us they thought this their right and proper duty although a few, perhaps reflecting the relatively brief financial dependency of working-class adolescents on their families, suggested that, by 16, children should be regarded as adults in their own right and fully culpable:

> At 16, they're old enough to know what they're doing.

Most families also told us they 'would have liked to get it over and done with in one day'. But in fact nearly all these adolescents were remanded — perhaps for further police enquiries, for legal representation, for trial or for reports — and were, nearly always, required to attend court on several further occasions before their cases were finally dealt with. For many parents, these rescheduled visits created real difficulties and inconvenience: those with other and younger children had repeatedly to ensure alternative child-minding arrangements, whilst several working parents lost pay or used up holiday entitlement. Mrs A for example, a single parent, told us she had to take three separate days off work, losing a total of £69 in wages and bonus payments. She saw this as the court's hidden fine. One Countyside boy, who also put in three court appearances in all, reckoned this series cost his family £200 in terms of lost parental earnings and travel to court, on top of a £30 fine.

About half our adolescents said they could put impending court appearances out of their minds — 'just forget about it between' — but for others consecutive remands proved unnerving and unsettling, the more so in Countyside, where the juvenile court's punitive tendencies were becoming legendary in some circles:

> Everybody round here reckons that if you're remanded more than twice, they're looking for a place to put you.

All these families up before both City and Countyside magistrates had to wait about outside the courtroom before the usher called out their names, in a sequence to suit solicitors, and motioned them forwards. The amount of time adolescents spent kicking their heels outside the courtroom varied considerably, both between cases and between each separate appearance, and could range from 15 minutes to anything up to four hours. Most of our sample families had been kept waiting for two hours or more on at least one occasion. We found adolescents tended to accept this delay, expecting no right to more comfortable and punctual arrangements, but for some young defendants this seemingly arbitrary period helped compound feelings of injustice:

> We were one of the first in and, by the time we went in, they'd nearly all gone.

> Just put in a room upstairs and left there.

Families' experiences outside City juvenile courtrooms reflected the quantity of work in progress. One boy noted:

> Packed — couldn't move; packed all down the stairs . . . was bad.

And the way cases could be timetabled for solicitors' convenience:

> Had to wait about an hour 'cos we had a solicitor.

Despite their common waiting experiences, about half these adolescents felt these delays did not unduly ruffle them, but others admitted they found the waiting period a worrying interlude, a time for stewing over possible outcomes and fearing the worst:

> Like to go in and get it over with — if waiting thinking this or that might happen.

These lasting impressions of a nerve-racking and confusing experience were particularly acute for adolescents without previous court appearances for, despite the recidivist stereotypes so popular with Countyside court officials, most adolescents have not been up before the local bench regularly:

> I think sometimes they don't know where they are . . . you get a lot of people lost in there you know.

> When I went in I sat down 'cos everyone was sitting down she [solicitor] told me to stand up.

Nor was this fearful ignorance allayed by routine preparatory advice from solicitors, social workers or probation officers. The result was that most families were thrown back on their own information resources. Most parents generally seemed to have picked up some ideas of what to expect from their own previous experiences or from those of neighbours and friends but few knew the procedural ropes as well as Mrs J who told us:

> I've known about courts all my life − from the experiences of my ex-husband. He was in prison when all three of my girls were born.

Many adolescents were forced to rely on the popular press and TV series such as *Crown Court,* supplemented by snippets from mates and older brothers. Often these impressions proved misleading and foreboding: they pictured an austere, larger than life scenario − 'dark', 'scary', 'a wicked judge who'd shout at you and all that' (see also Martin *et al.,* 1981).

Making a plea

When they at last got inside the juvenile courtroom and a plea was taken from them, our sample adolescents divided equally in admitting or denying the charges put. Owing to the qualitative nature of our research, with sampling designed to reflect the broad range of juvenile court cases, we are in no position to suggest that this tendency typifies plea-making in the juvenile court. What we can say is that these figures would belie the complexity of adolescents' feelings as to the extent of their culpability, and the degree of congruence between formal charges and their own views of their law-breaking behaviour. Only a minority of the boys and girls we spoke with seemed to regard their pleas in a straightforward way:

> I was guilty and if I tell lies I'll get into more trouble.

Rather, for most, the charge remained a contentious issue: they spoke to us not as sophisticated bargainers but as people who plainly asserted their innocence or who continued to hold reservations as to their actual guilt in the face of particular charges laid against them.

Amongst our sample we found that juveniles appearing before Countyside bench pleaded guilty more frequently than their City counterparts. Thus Carl, who denied the unauthorized taking of a motor vehicle which he claimed he had found abandoned on waste ground, settled to plead guilty to an alternative charge of 'stealing by finding'. Similarly, we met two other Countyside lads, originally charged with 'burglary' who agreed to make a guilty plea to 'trespass with intent':

> He [solicitor] said it was not worth pleading not guilty if we were going to take the stuff — said he would try and get the charge dropped from burglary if we pleaded guilty so we said 'All right'.

In City court too, we met boys who pleaded guilty more for strategic reasons than anything else. Chris, for example, pleaded guilty to TDA but told us his mates had forced his hand. He said he had not taken the vehicle of his own volition. He decided to go ahead and plead guilty, anyway, knowing a lengthy trial and further remands would mean loss of earnings for his parents and he just wanted 'to get it over and done with there and then like'.

A third of our City sample told us they were advised to plead guilty by their solicitors (see Tomlinson, 1971), a trend which clouds the stance of pressure groups such as Justice for Children, who urge legal representation on the grounds that it always serves 'the best interests of the child'. We found girls in particular recalled examples of such persuasion, for perhaps girls are reckoned more pliable, or their offences more trivial and not worth a trial. Shirley's experiences, on a charge of shoplifting a baby's coat worth at most £10, help illustrate these pressures. When she was first charged she says she argued her innocence, claiming that, had she intended to steal she would have gone for something worth having. She maintains she then made a statement to the police admitting guilt, on the understanding she would then receive a caution, but some six months later she was summoned to attend the juvenile court. She told us that she duly entered a plea of not guilty but, after hearing the prosecution case, her solicitor requested an adjournment. Then he put it to her that if she continued they would 'tear her apart'; better, rather, to save face with a conditional discharge or a fine. So, she says, she relented and she left City juvenile court with a conditional discharge for two years and justice said to be done. Certainly it says much for their tenacity and self-assurance that three other City boys chose to ignore similar legal advice and persisted with not guilty pleas:

> She [solicitor] wanted it cut and dried. She thought it was too trivial but it was not trivial to me. I didn't want to plead guilty.

Prosecution in process

Once a plea has been made one way or the other, the court is ready to proceed with the case. For juveniles pleading guilty, the bench will hear a brief account of the circumstances surrounding the offence and then come to a decision, usually — but not necessarily — with the help of welfare reports: the 'hearing' may be over and done with in just a few minutes. Where the young defendant pleads not guilty, the court will adjourn until a trial date. Sometimes, as in Countyside juvenile court, this can be fixed for several weeks ahead. Then, on the day, the bench hears evidence from both sides and, depending on the numbers of witnesses and contested points, this stage may take up a further hour or more.

When we asked these adolescents whether they could hear and understand the courtroom discourse we found City adolescents could generally hear quite clearly but two-thirds of our Countyside sample said they could not hear properly:

> The magistrates mumbled amongst themselves — would like to have heard what the magistrates were saying.

Whilst the majority of the boys and girls could identify the various key court officials, as we illustrate in the following section, and also claimed they could follow the gist of what was being said to them or about them, they tended to lack full comprehension. In the main, they found long words and legal terms alien:

> The woman [prosecution solicitor] spoke in a roundabout way, she said 'I put it to you.'

> No ... not really ... no ... you understand part of it like, but. ...

A quarter of these adolescents went on to suggest they saw this formal courtroom language as part of a conspiracy designed to exclude, ensnare and befuddle them:

> I think they try to fool you. Ask you questions with those big, long words to try and catch you ... when you slip, they've got you.

> Think they should be open ... was like I was left out of the conversation.

This finding will come as no surprise to readers familiar with the American juvenile justice literature which highlights the routine exclusion and objectification of young defendants: 'The defendant is the subject of a debate between people whose relationship to himself is always vague and whose relation to each other is mysterious' (Emerson, 1968). More recently, a study of process in a London magistrates' court concludes that defendants are like 'dummy players', pushed unrehearsed into a theatre where the established cast systematically deny them a speaking part (Carlen, 1976). Our court observations also point to the relative silence of adolescents and their families before the juvenile bench and well under half our sample youngsters, while happy enough to speak with us in their own homes for well over two hours, took no verbal part in the courtroom proceedings. Those who did venture a few words mostly confined themselves to saying 'Sorry' or replied shortly to specific questions. Martin, 14, did try to tell his own story but took care to keep it uncontroversial:

> Said what I was doing — just waiting for the taxi and where I'd been . . . not worth saying the policeman wasn't telling the truth because the law would have proved he was.

We met marginally more Countyside boys who felt they were denied the chance to have their say:

> I never got a say of my own . . . told to keep quiet . . . gagged . . . there wasn't time . . . that wasn't fair.
>
> We never said ourselves like . . . what we wanted to say.

Although similar feelings were expressed to us by a few boys who appeared before City benches:

> When stood up to say something, they said, 'Sit down, we're talking to your father.'

Moreover, passivity may be expected from girl defendants, viewed as appropriate behaviour and even encouraged by some court workers, as we will illustrate in the following section. Girls may find it doubly difficult to break through this ascribed passivity and speak out in the juvenile court, the more so since a shame at being on view and weighed up in the eyes of unknown others featured in these girls' reflections on their juvenile court hearing:

Thought, God, I've got to stand in the box — but had to stand in
the middle . . . were only two of them looking at me.

Carla, too, was frightened she might 'have to stand on view in a little
box', a feature, she says, the girls at school had gathered round and
quizzed her about the following day.

There was also a feeling amongst adolescents that it would have been
futile anyway for them to try to participate. Better rather to leave
things to a solicitor, since by speaking out they could have let themselves down:

Probably could have made it worse.

I'd probably have got six months though.

A further variation on the theme concerned the use of passivity, or
silence, as a tactical and ultimate line of defence, a final guard against
loss of one's self-respect and dignity. This may well have been over-
looked by courtroom studies which have also neglected the defendant's
point of view (see Parker, 1979).

Weighing-up court officials

When we asked these families to describe in their own words what they
made of their respective hearings on the day, and specifically to what
extent they felt the various court personnel were understanding or sympathetic towards them, we found a marked contrast in their perceptions
of the two different in-court regimes.

Thus Countyside families in the main talked about feeling degraded
and belittled before the bench: For them, the lasting impression was of
an alien forum in which the court officials were 'all trying to bring you
down'. Although Countyside parents and their sons occasionally
remembered a helpful probation officer, many families felt they were
denied due courtesy and respect before the court:

All seemed against you as if you'd done it. The way they looked
at you and talked to you.

And, whilst we might have expected these families to describe such
officials as police and prosecutors as 'difficult', a significant minority
viewed the magistrates, particularly the senior member, as aggressive

and hostile towards them. Some Countyside parents didn't mince words and described senior magistrates variously as 'bombastic', 'cows', 'gloryhunters':

> She didn't even look at us — she looked down at us. We heard her giggling in the backroom and she grinned when giving the sentence.

City parents, on the other hand, tended to picture their experiences in less emotive terms: they seemed to perceive the courtroom process in a more routine and impersonal manner. To them, in the main, courtroom officials were empowered to do a job of work and treated them equitably: many of their sons, while conscious of their own relative powerlessness, remembered the courtesy of specific officials towards them. Thus the majority of City boys told us the courtroom personnel 'listened' and tried to tune in to their lives and circumstances:

> They felt sympathetic because I was the only child and my mum was crying.

But these boys' feelings were not echoed by the City girls we talked with. Rather, for girls, the overall impression, it seems, was one of feeling 'scared' and 'frightened' and, as we will illustrate in the next section, few seemed to take in what was being said in court because their minds ran on fatalistically to their chances of being 'put away':

> When they said I had to come back, started thinking about it — the social worker was saying mightn't have a chance this time . . . kept thinking about it.

A previous study of process in two different juvenile courts speculates that only young defendants with long records, like the girl above, are aware of the different court personnel and their distinctive tasks (Anderson, 1978). When we asked the sample adolescents whether they could place the various key personnel on to a pre-sketched courtroom plan, we, on the contrary, found most subject to criminal proceedings were familiar with the principal parties. A recent analysis of the Children's Hearings in Scotland has also noted this general comprehension amongst adolescents (Martin *et al.*, 1981). Magistrates were often picked out as 'judges' or 'those powerful people who judge' and defence solicitors as 'my solicitor', whilst other assorted officials (and research worker) were invariably passed over since 'a lot of them sit there doing nothing'! City boys scored higher than their Countyside contemporaries at this task, probably because the desks in numbers 1 and 2 City juvenile courts are equipped with name plates. City girls, although slightly more reticient, nevertheless could also remember and identify the key courtroom officials.

Police, prosecutors and witnesses

We have already noted that the definition of an offence is a social construct determined by the police, and have indicated that many of these adolescents took issue with police definitions of their behaviour. Similarly, over half these adolescents continued to feel that specific charges put to them in the courtroom were inappropriate and at worst:

> I shouldn't have been there in the first place.

There was a recognition that in the courtroom the police had the upper hand, with the power to further criminalize and decontextualize their own actions as they saw them:

> Was unfair ... police put damage cost [to off-duty police officer's own car] up dead quickly, said £50 at police station ... in court police made it up to £145.

> The policewoman said I swore at her five times but only swore once ... she said there were loads of pedestrians; was just an old lady.

> The policeman who brought the records up ... he has been there before and he can say what you're like and what you've been up for and he doesn't even know you.

For girls accused of shop-lifting, other prosecution witnesses may seem tarred with the same brush:

> When the security woman swore on the Bible, think she was telling lies ... said she was following me from shop to shop but I never saw her.

We have also pointed out the reluctance of these adolescents to come forward and speak their own minds in court. Those who disputed police evidence reckoned:

> The court nearly always believes the police.

And in the face of the prosecutions' big guns it was politic to say nothing:

> They all seemed to be working together — the detective and the floorwalker.

The knowledge that 'it is not worth contradicting the police' is, Carlen contends, prevalent in magistrates courts also and certainly other court officials we talked with, including defence solicitors, sometimes endorsed this viewpoint.

'My solicitor'

It is consistent with the high level of legal aid granted to young defendants before City juvenile courts that nearly all these adolescents were legally represented in court. Indeed one City lad told us his solicitor was 'forced by the court'. Apparently, in Jim's case, his dad had wanted to speak for him, feeling he knew his own son better than any lawyer and was best placed to outline mitigating circumstances. After three adjournments, the bench refused to decide on this case without a solicitor and their scrupulous concern for justice to be seen to be done struck Jim's father as 'mental pressure'. Thus City juvenile court invariably gave these young defendants the opportunity to seek publicly funded legal advice although, in the event, one or two families decided against a solicitor, reasoning they 'didn't want one' or 'didn't need one'. By way of contrast, Countyside juvenile court, as we have shown, was less concerned with safeguarding juveniles' legal rights in this way. This is reflected in the fact that one-third of our sample appeared without legal representation.

Although local solicitors told us continuity of representation is especially important for juveniles, some two-thirds of all these adolescents were passed on from one member of a firm to another so that, whilst all could remember their firm's name, only about half could recall the name of the solicitor who had turned up for them on the day.

We found legal representatives generally approached families for a brief preliminary discussion, with their timing varying from a few minutes before a case was called to a good half hour or so in advance. Exceptionally, one or two City adolescents said their solicitor failed to make prior contact with them on the day and these cases help illustrate the busy nature of City juvenile court and the booming business of juvenile criminal advocacy:

She was late the last time . . . no one knew where she was.

He didn't turn up in court . . . he was on holiday in Greece.

Where solicitors did give and take last minute instructions, this brief discussion might be confined to parents. It seems solicitors seldom used this time to give advice about courtroom procedures, and some restricted themselves to trying to minimize their client's participation in the coming proceedings:

He said 'I'll do all the talking.'

Girls, in particular, tended to remember their solicitor advised mute passivity:

Solicitor said just sit there and listen and then if they ask questions to answer.

Whereas one or two boys say they were encouraged to assert themselves, 'to speak up loud'.

It also seems solicitors more readily volunteered predictions to their young clients where they anticipated a non-custodial decision, telling their clients they'd:

Probably get off with it.

Commentators who have analysed the solicitors' task in the juvenile court, point out that a legal training is often inappropriate to this forum, where many cases are not contested. Moreover, in the juvenile court, where ideally the bench is concerned to match a child's needs, considering personal and social factors, with his or her deeds, the solicitor may be poorly equipped to offer competent advice and support (Anderson, 1978). But we found the majority of legally represented families were satisfied with their solicitors' services, so much so that they would use the same firm again if needs be. We also found City parents seemed slightly more enthusiastic about their child's solicitor than their Countyside contemporaries who, whilst usually pleased with the quality of work in court, were less convinced of the solicitor's impact:

For what he said, I thought he did quite well . . . but I'm not saying he was listened to.

This slight discrepancy between the perceptions of City and Countyside parents did not feature, however, in the views of the boys and girls we talked with. Adolescents generally remembered their solicitors as effective, helpful and supportive people and it may be that they recalled their solicitors all the more favourably because they were seemingly given so little guidance by any other courtroom personnel. They remembered, in the main, that it was their solicitor alone, with the 'gift of the gab', who had spoken up for them:

> Said we'd kept out of trouble for two years and probation had done some good . . . said about wanting to go in the Merchant Navy and taking exams.

> He was good . . . said I was intelligent and do all my jobs around the house.

Solicitors put across their stories:

> Was pleased with him . . . was saying how could she have stolen them and walked into the shop when she could have walked away.

And sometimes got them off:

> Good, he got a fine.

But a few adolescents told us they had misgivings about their solicitors, describing, in accordance with our own courtroom observations, a small number of incompetent and ill-prepared representatives. In particular, some legal professionals seemed out of touch with their clients' own worlds: adolescents criticized this small minority of solicitors for presenting the court with a partial, bumbling and inaccurate account, and faulted them for disregarding and distorting events as they themselves saw them:

> All right at the beginning . . . said we were good lads at school but didn't put in about the cut eye I was supposed to have done.

> We told him things he could have said to catch them out . . . it was February . . . snow . . . poor light . . . couldn't see well. They [police] said it was a sunny day, in court.

Social workers and probation officers

We have already noted that for these families social workers and probation officers were not forthcoming with comprehensive advice and information about the juvenile justice process: they did not offer
systematic guidance about the legal aid scheme or courtroom procedures and in particular it seems they did little to allay the fears and
anxieties of first-time defendants. Nor were social workers and probation officers routinely present in court on the day itself. And where
families did remember 'their' officer was present in the courtroom, this
was often a coincidence of the department's court duty rota rather than
the result of a coherent policy requiring them to attend. It is also consistent with our courtroom observations in criminal proceedings, that
even in those few 'current' cases where a family's social worker or probation officer was in court, they seldom recalled 'their' worker speaking
up for them. Thus these families told us of a silent and passive presence
who 'never even got up'. Perhaps this low profile led adolescents to
reserve their invectives for courtroom officials they could see and hear
– the police and the 'judges' – and to attribute the social worker's or
probation officer's potential influence on the proceedings to the social
enquiry report.

The function of the social enquiry report (SER), a background summary of the child within the family, is described in the 1969 Act as a
vehicle for individualized justice. Some commentators, however, like
the French structuralists, see the report as a punishing exercise:

> A mechanism of interminable investigation and perpetual punish-
> ment – an investigation of the minor and his milieu carried out
> by a host of experts in social pathology (Donzeldt, 1980).

This view was endorsed by some parents who viewed the social worker's
or probation officer's visit to their home as a 'nosey' and unwelcome
intrusion:

> They want to know how you're getting on with your husband,
> how much he earns and all that.

Some parents had felt threatened when the officer requested to see
their child alone:

> You shouldn't ask children how their parents treat them behind
> the parents' back.

Or felt the report implied they were not up to scratch as caring parents.

Although an SER is not routinely prepared for all juveniles facing criminal charges (see Priestley *et al.*, 1977), English juvenile courts do request them in the majority of cases. Similarly, we found that City and Countyside benches were presented with social enquiry reports, detailing individual circumstances, for some two-thirds of these families.

When a report was prepared we found most parents, while lacking complete knowledge, were aware of the report's drift and its recommendations, but sometimes their children, the subjects of these written summaries, were totally unaware that any report had been written about them. This lack of knowledge was particularly evident in Countyside, for in a half of all cases for which a probation officer had in fact submitted a report to the bench, the young subjects told us they knew nothing of any report. Again, even if adolescents were aware of some kind of report, the knowledge was second-hand, coming from their parents. Few seemed to grasp the full impact of these written summaries of their lives. We found their understanding was at best vague and partial.

> Background and all that . . . see if I come from a good background, a good house 'nd all that.
>
> For the court to see . . . said how many times my mum's been married, all the kids' names and schools.

And fewer still were allowed sight of the report before the hearing. Pauline, for example, said she first saw her social enquiry report on the way home as her dad re-read the much folded copy he had hung on to from the courtroom. For although some pressure groups assert that according to 'natural justice', a social enquiry report should automatically be available to the child, his or her legal representative and parents (Taylor *et al.*, 1980), social workers and probation officers are not required to show these reports to their young clients. All in all then, for these families social workers and probation officers did not play a significant part in the juvenile court's decision-making.

Magistrates and 'judges'

The importance of lay justices as a group of unpaid public servants, drawn from local communities and equipped with limited powers to deal with the anti-social activities of their neighbours forms a basic tenet of magistrates' justice (Burney, 1979). The concept of lay justice was further strengthened and endorsed during the post-war reconstruction era:

> It is an advantage that a justice should have a knowledge of the way of life of other classes than the class to which he belongs and it is essential that there should be many among justices who know enough of the lives of the poorest people to understand their outlook and their difficulties (Royal Commission on Justices of the Peace, 1948).

Yet we found these ideal qualities had not entered the head of the majority of the poor working-class families who contributed to our research. Adolescents did not picture their judges as ordinary lay people but as paid court officials. Defendants saw the magistrates as remote figures:

> Just nobs who live in big houses . . . they don't know what goes on in this area, just what they hear.

They were earning easy money for little graft:

> Only work to 12 o'clock, don't they? Only do half a day.
> Managers of big firms . . . they have a day off from the office and get paid so much for doing it.

Nearly all these adolescents also pinpointed the magistrates as the most important courtroom officials: in their eyes the 'judges' were the crucial decision-makers:

> Magistrates have the power to do what they like with you . . . could play eenie-meenie-mo with you.

For adolescents appearing before the Countyside bench, the magistrates' power could become overbearing and wielded with a view to degrading and humiliating them. It tallies with our own analysis of these two different in-court regimes, that we found Countyside families were more ready to judge their judgers, and quicker to condemn the bench, for their crushing and imperious attitudes towards them, than their city counterparts.

RECEIVING JUDGEMENT

The 'sentence' of the court

Before the partial implementation of the 1969 Act, with its concern to tailor the juvenile court's decision to the individual circumstances of each child within the family, it was argued that young defendants viewed the juvenile court's function strictly in terms of punishment (e.g. Scott, 1959). One long-serving juvenile court magistrate writes that children looked on the bench's decision as a sentence and expected a scale of legitimate penalties to be applied, according to the seriousness of their offence and the extent of their criminal record. Concepts such as treatment, she continues, including the provision of social and educational facilities are neither envisaged nor understood (Cavanagh, 1959). The debate which followed throughout the 1960s failed, like more contemporary discussions about reorganizing and revamping our health and personal social services, to consider the perspectives of those subject to the juvenile justice process. A small pilot study concludes that, despite the welfare polemic which inspired the 1969 Act, young defendants themselves continued to favour a traditional sense of justice with a scale of penalties tuned proportionally to the nature of a proven offence and the number of antecedents (Morris *et al.,* 1980). We indicated in chapter 2 that, whilst our sample parents looked to the bench to provide some help and guidance for their children, the majority of boys subject to criminal proceedings still regarded the juvenile court's prime task in terms of punishment and control:

> Is all punishment — just stick you down and that's it. They're not even talking to you — talk to your family and your lawyer — just around you . . . so that can't help you . . . magistrates should know what *you* feel like.

The girls, it seems, would partly go along with this prevalent view although they tended to recognize, perhaps on account of their different and culturally ascribed socialization patterns, that the bench should also try to help young defendants by means of shock tactics — 'scares them'. Yet, for most of our sample, concepts such as 'care' and 'treatment' seemed bewildering and alien: mention of the word 'treatment', for example, frequently met with a puzzled frown or a stab at the local psychiatric hospital whilst the term 'care' was invariably transcribed into getting 'stuck away' in a home (see also Martin *et al.,* 1981). Indeed, for families subject to criminal proceedings the care order looms as a harsh punishment:

> Is punishment for parents as well because you're away from home, they don't see you, could hurt mothers, they could commit suicide.

Further confirmation that, for these working-class families, the care order amounts to a severe and indeterminate punishment is afforded by the way our sample consistently noted this sentence. For, when we asked these families to rank the range of disposals available to the juvenile bench by means of randomly numbered tariff cards, we found they invariably placed the care order high up in a hierarchy of graded punishments. Thus three-quarters of our sample agreed the juvenile court works with a scaled tariff, peaking with 'put away' penalties – detention centre, care order and Borstal – and, whilst the girls seemed less confident of themselves than the boys in sorting out our (tariff) cards – with their reticence perhaps coloured by the fact that attendance centre and detention centre remain outside their own experiences – they ranked the care order as the juvenile court's worst punishment:

> They take you off your parents, don't they, until 18 or 16.

One 13 year old girl, for example, could see no end to a care order, unlike the more finite terms of detention centre and Borstal. Again, despite these families' broad agreement, Countyside boys, sometimes with their own experience of the more rigorous probation model (see chapter 7) tended to regard the supervision order as marginally more punitive than their contemporaries in City, where the local social services department assumes responsibility for all supervision orders made by the juvenile bench. Girls too, with half of our sample drawing on their own experiences, seemed to regard the supervision order as relatively punitive.

This broad agreement on the juvenile court's actual schedule of punishments has led the Justice for Children lobby to assert that those subject to criminal proceedings will perceive 'justice as fairness' if the bench adheres to a policy of graded disposals, taking into account the seriousness of an individual's offence together with the extent of previous convictions: in short, this pressure group contends, with a swipe at professional 'do-gooders', 'justice as fairness' demands consideration of juveniles' 'deeds', not 'needs'. This neat conclusion, however, must necessarily negate the full complexity of the views of those subject to the juvenile justice process and the often bitter and problematic nature of their own experiences. Rather, we would argue that whilst working-class juveniles do voice a broad agreement in ranking the juvenile court's range of disposals, their accumulated and experiential knowledge challenges the appropriateness and efficacy of these available means. In particular, they felt that the charges as put to them tended to be 'bumped up' thus invalidating the fairness of the broadly 'agreed' sentencing tariff. Half the overall sample also noted that a juvenile court record becomes a public badge. Hence 'You're branded once you've been in trouble'. Being 'branded' will lead to being picked out in particular, in the future, for another push up the tariff ladder. We noted in chapter 2 that both parents and their children were convinced that 'delinquent' street behaviour was defined and categorized unfairly by the police, so undermining the potential fairness of even a set tariff ladder.

In addition to these major reservations there was a minority feeling amongst adolescents that the tariff is unfair anyway because:

> You should be done for what you're there for — you're not there for doing other things you've already been punished for.

Many parents also felt that the use of detention centre and Borstal merely compounded the problem of juvenile delinquency: as they saw it, by indiscriminately sending their sons away, the court had created 'bitter', 'tougher' and 'rougher' angry young men who wear their sentence 'like a cloak'.

Thus for these families a stockpile of personal experiences, together with an appreciation that the discretion vested in the police could never be removed, served to erode notions of juvenile justice as fairness. Under the present legislation, with official discretion rampant, at all stages of the process consistency and predictability is low. Indeed, our own predictions of the bench's likely decisions for our sample adolescents, based on such objective criteria as age, current charge and antecedents, proved badly astray: in City juvenile court our calculations were about 50 per cent correct, erring on the side of over-sentencing, but in Countyside juvenile court our margin of error escalated to 70 per cent since we grossly underestimated the punitive nature of 'juvenile justice' dispensed there. We found that for these working-class families

— who, we must emphasise, believed whole-heartedly in a well-ordered society and did not place themselves above the law — thwarted expectations, together with the magistrates' apparent failure to convey to them consistent explanations on sentencing, merely compounded their over-all feelings of injustice and unfairness, fuelling a consensus of hopelessness and powerlessness before the law. We also found this sense of rough justice was more evident amongst the Countyside sample, where the bench's final decision came as a harsh surprise for two-thirds of these families:

> It was a stiff sentence because he's hardly been in trouble.
>
> We wouldn't have minded it (DC) if he had a record.

One Countyside father added that detention centre seemed fair enough for his son who had a previous conviction but:

> The other two hadn't been in trouble before; they shouldn't have gone down. What's his name's Mum [Tommy] — Yes, Tommy, she couldn't believe it — it nearly made her sick.

Surprise was also a lasting and prevailing reaction among City adolescents. Although the majority of their parents told us they had been expecting the magistrates' decision, for over three-quarters of these youngsters the decision seemed unexpectedly lenient:

> Was lenient what they gave me for that offence [TDA] — was scared to start with when they said three months but could have been two years Borstal.
>
> Was expecting DC because I've been before for cars and they'd said next time it happens you'll go down [2 years SO].

It seems City juvenile court's preference for full-tariff sentencing and the reservation of custodial offences for particularly serious crimes helped preserve its moral authority amongst these families. Whereas Countyside juvenile court's exceptionally punitive stance stoked up anger and resentment, many of those subject to City's jurisdiction agreed: 'I've been quite lucky.' Nor was this feeling of surprise tempered by recollections of painstaking explanations from the bench and attempts to clarify and justify their decision in either court. For obvious reasons Countyside adolescents were more aware of this. They

told us that magistrates seldom took the trouble to explain their final
decisions, an impression which tallies with our own courtroom observations. Rather, Mick's perception of the sentencing process seems close
to the Countyside norm:

> They went out into a room to talk about it: then the clerks came
> back. Then three policemen came in. The red light came on and
> the magistrates came back and said we've decided to send you to
> detention centre.

One or two City youngsters did seem to pick up the gist of brief homi-
lies and lectures:

> Don't remember — they said I must be a good girl and try hard.

But for the most part our sample were thrown back on their own intuitive rationales:

> Couldn't understand at the time but my mum said it was because
> I hit him when he was down.
>
> I have got a job in ICI and I think they probably decided to give
> me a chance.

Most families also reckoned personal appearance could influence the
bench and said they took care to turn out well-groomed and in their
smartest clothes — 'no tatty jeans'. But our courtroom diaries, especially
detailing Countyside juvenile court, record the down-at-heel aspect of
many families, with their overall shabby appearance highlighting their
material disadvantages relative to the salaried court workers.

We have stressed that 'juvenile justice' neither begins nor ends with
the decision of the bench: rather the local state's net fans out to take in
routine surveillance and the social construction of a charge and its aftermath in terms of continued supervision and surveillance, whether in a
secure institution or the community itself. The breadth of these
families' own experiences is best illustrated by their assessment of
juvenile justice as fairness according to Matza's five-fold classification, a
schema which tries to measure 'fairness' according to such key concepts
as cognizance, consistency, competence, commensurability and comparison (Matza, 1964). Overall we found that five out of every six
families included in our study would take issue with more than one of

these criteria — that is they sized up their own experiences against these ideal standards and found them wanting. For Countyside families this figure was more like nine out of ten, making up a total which strains absolutely the moral authority of the juvenile justice system, and this from ordinary working-class families who, at one and the same time, lend their support to the construction of a legitimately ordered society. Thus, in the end, even amongst City youngsters who did not generally feel aggrieved at the bench's final decision, the breadth of their own stockpiled street encounters and their experience of the construction of criminal charges undermined the overall moral authority of the juvenile justice system. Their perceptions chart a system riddled with official discretion and deviation. In the circumstances their conclusions are quite rational.

MAKING SENSE OF SENTENCES

The liberal reformers who campaigned for the full implementation of the 1969 Act were fired by the desire to further the cause of social justice for working-class children by building into the disposals a variety of treatment programmes. They pictured 'a gateway through which children would pass into a rich supermarket of salvation services' (Parsloe, 1978). Although the Act has never been fully implemented part of this ethos can in theory be identified as operational via the work of social work — probation supervision billed — 'to advise, assist and befriend'.

Our sample included 16 adolescents whom the court made subject to statutory supervisory orders, eight on supervision and eight on licence after a DC term. It is consistent with the approach in these two different local courts that the majority of lads placed on supervision received their orders from City's juvenile bench, whereas Countyside juvenile court was largely responsible for those sent away to detention centres. It is also pertinent to note that only one of these supervision orders included a condition of intermediate treatment provision.

In this section we will concentrate on the views of these families, subject to social work intervention, in order to measure the extent to which the present system, officially incorporating 'compulsory help', is perceived as being concerned with help and treatment. We talked to this sub-sample about the impact of social work intervention shortly after the court decision, then again some months later. We found their

views complex and at times contradictory, ranging over a spectrum of
attitudes, and, because of the qualitative nature of our research, it is
difficult to do them justice in a generalized summary. Here, therefore,
we will merely touch on majority viewpoints and will go on to draw out
and examine the complexity of their feelings by detailing the views of
individual families and their respective social workers and probation
officers in chapter 8.

For these adolescents the extent and nature of social work supervision hinged, as ever, upon the discretion of the local social work
agencies: Countyside probation and City social services each followed a
different policy. Within these agencies further discretion, implemented
by individual supervising officers, also had impact on each youngster.
We should, of course, make it plain that in so far as the statutory basis
for supervision is concerned, we are not essentially able to compare like
with like here, for, in line with the different tendencies of these two
local juvenile courts, our Countyside sample includes a bias towards
views of detention centre licence supervision and our City sample,
representing the views of both girls and boys, focuses more on perceptions of the supervision order in practice. What we can say is that for
Countyside boys supervision invariably meant a regular routine of
weekly office reporting, sometimes gradually tailored off at the discretion of each probation officer. For those committed to the local social
services department, on the other hand, supervision could in practice be
a more haphazard and spasmodic affair: City adolescents might see
their social worker alone at the local office, at home with their families
or hardly at all:

I've seen him twice because he calls when I'm at school.

Social workers could vacillate between weekly contact, fortnightly or
three-weekly intervals or perhaps a more lax and laissez faire approach:

Don't know — have only seen him once — he's on holiday, said
he'd call round when he gets back.

Nor, it seems, did social workers explain their intentions properly to
their young clients — rather, like the magistrates, they tended to keep
them in the dark. Left to construct their own rationales, some adolescents, like Eric, concluded:

They automatically finish you once you leave school — they
don't bother.

Since a half of these adolescents subject to a supervision order made out to the local authority transferred social workers at least once in eight months, the overall impression is one of confusion with the social worker often featuring as an elusive and anonymous figure.

> Mr L something, er—no—er—that's the psychiatrist.

Those youngsters who did manage to see their respective social workers, and saw their probation officers at the office, describe the nature of this contact similarly, with interviews generally taking the form of routine and repetitive questions as the officer reviewed what they'd been doing and how they'd been getting on at school and with the family, occasionally offering advice about state-financed work-experience schemes. Unlike social workers, we found probation officers seldom called at their young clients' homes to involve parents and siblings in their work, whilst both agencies rarely provided alternatives to the casework interview. Martin, a member of a social work group project, affords an exception:

> Go to office — like a group — you go out one week — play football, go swimming, bowling — and stay in the other talking, like games, for example, what would you do if you was going to buy and sell a house?

These adolescents saw the supervisor's primary task in terms of checking them up and checking them out: they accepted the social workers' and probation officers' authority to ask direct questions with a view to keeping them out of further trouble with the law:

> They just ask the same questions — they find out what you're doing at night time — your interests, hobbies, they always ask you questions.

> Just check up on you a bit, take you out camping and that and try and keep you out of trouble — know other lads who've had probation . . . social workers are a bit soft aren't they?

This last lad's comments help illustrate the different regard these families seemed to have for probation officers and social workers. For we found adolescents and their parents were generally more appreciative of probation than social services' intervention into their lives. Perhaps this discrepancy is partly explained by the social workers' more generic role and power to remove neglected and abused children from their parents, and by the sustained and sensational media coverage of social work's disasters, as much as by diverse supervision practices. Yet we found parents were ready to praise the probation service. Probation officers offered their children a period of structured supervision – they did not come door-knocking and bringing 'the problem' back home. And, whilst the office-based probation interview is not without its drawbacks, as we will illustrate in chapter 8, most adolescents reckoned their probation officer was 'all right' and 'OK', a person (armed with the power of a report recommendation) who is basically on their side:

> He's all right – like him – he lets you discuss your family problems and your home. He's trying to get money to take us on a holiday but will be all canoeing and that.

And the probation officer will, within supervision time, offer a listening and potentially helpful ear:

> Someone to talk to – tell him all your troubles – you can speak freely down there – he doesn't mind what you say.

Social workers, on the other hand, seemed less straight-forward. Although parents generally felt 'their' social worker had their child's best interests at heart, the less structured way of working, and, particularly, the extent to which some social workers opted for a non-interventionist line, gave City families a more equivocal picture of the supervising officer. For their young sons and daughters, social workers were 'all right' too, so long as they took trouble to listen and talk to them. Good social workers conveyed an active interest in their clients:

> Is interested in what you're saying.
>
> Is a young fella, about 25 like – he talks the way you talk to him.
>
> Liked her – when got in a bit of trouble at school she used to go and see the teachers and ask about it.

Bad social workers conveyed bored indifference:

> Is a waste of time going.
>
> She wasn't concerned – was a waste of money – just nothing.

Thus, for some City adolescents, the social worker remained a remote and peripheral figure; probation officers, could, as the supervision session developed, become more like adult friends:

> I talk about myself and he talks about himself. He got married this year and went to Yugoslavia.

But social workers, with one or two exceptions, took and demanded less 'bother'. For many clients, as the supervision order slipped away, the social worker offered a superficial and fleeting presence amounting to 'no more than contact' (Rees, 1978).

> He doesn't do or say much — just soft questions — can't understand him most of the time — is like a record player.

Almost without exception, both parents and adolescents, whatever their criticisms of social workers and probation officers, and however great their uncertainty about exactly what they were, knew for sure that they were 'nothing like the police'.

SUMMARY

We argued in chapter 2 that almost without exception the parents and children in our sample supported the idea of 'law and order'. They saw the need for street policing in their neighbourhoods and they largely accepted the principles of criminal justice, seeing punishment via the courts for law-breakers as legitimate. However, the practice of law enforcement and criminal justice was found wanting.

In this chapter we have detailed their dissatisfaction with the application of law and order through local juvenile justice. We have shown that for most of our sample, subject to both juvenile court regimes, their pre-court experiences of police attitudes and behaviour, particularly in relation to charge definition and the decision to prosecute or not, soured their respect for the process. In terms of City court this was particularly regrettable since both adolescents and parents tended to judge their in-court experience favourably, believing they had been treated civilly and sentenced in keeping with the tenets of 'just desserts'. This satisfaction and respect for the moral authority of the City court, although it survived in some cases, was undermined by what was, in the youngsters' eyes, pre-court official malpractice.

In Countyside court the pre-court resentment was merely sustained and aggravated. Both parents and their children generally bitterly resented their treatment at the hands of court officials and took issue with the severity of the sentence. In short they comprehended and 'felt' the very same in-court processes which we attributed, independently, to Countyside court in chapter 5. Furthermore they withdraw or continued to reject the police and court's right to function as administrators of law, order and justice. The local state in their eyes is repressive, exerting its will by the weight and force of its powers, rather than its accepted right. Moral authority is absent.

In the next chapter we will consider the perceptions of the social workers and probation officers involved in our sample cases. We will show that they are highly critical of the performance of defence solicitors but less critical of their own. Their young clients, as we have shown, see things differently. They saw their lawyers, fairly positively, perceiving them as the only officials actually 'for them' during proceedings. Whilst social workers and probation officers were seen as influential officials, they were explained in somewhat neutral terms. In the courtroom social workers and probation officers, although clearly not seen as opponents of the defence, were equally clearly not perceived by defendants as unequivocal advocates.

This clash of opinion over the efficacy of solicitors is in part explained by the lack of analytic and comparative knowledge defendants have with which to judge the performance of their legal representatives. We would contend that defence lawyers are judged over-favourably by their clients. However, as we have demonstrated, the failure of social workers and probation officers to take any consistent active part in helping the juvenile defendant and his/her parents prepare for court in part produces the defendant and parent dependency upon, and consequent appreciation of, the solicitor.

Finally, accepting that juvenile court disposals are perceived primarily as punishments by adolescents and parents alike, we looked at the impact of statutory social work supervision, which represents the 'helping' element in the present system, upon subject families. We noted some differences between probation and social services supervisory procedures and found that these did affect client perceptions. Overall, however, the impact of social work on the 'criminal' side of juvenile justice, whilst regarded relatively favourably, was perceived as marginal rather than central. The grand words of the drafters of the original 1969 Act, concerned with treating the young offender in his family, seem not to have been realized in the two systems we have looked at. We can now shift our focus to this social work function in criminal juvenile justice and consider, amongst other things, why this should be.

7

Social–Probation Work for the Juvenile Court

MARGINAL PERFORMERS

In this chapter we will examine the social work contribution to criminal proceedings in City and Countyside juvenile courts. We have already implied that this contribution is marginal in our two local productions of juvenile justice. We will here try to tease out why this should be so by looking at the politics and practice of social work in and around the juvenile court, referring frequently to the results of our interviews with the social work sample. In Countyside court the social work role in relation to 13–17 year olds is carried out by the probation service. In City court, social workers, employed by the social services department, provide a comparable social work service for all youngsters between ten and 17 made subject to criminal proceedings. Our research deals with 13–17 year olds.

As we have shown, the amount of discretion licensed by the 1969 Act has functioned to produce a diversity of practices, all of which 'legitimately' constitute the juvenile justice system. The social work role in the system reflects this diversity. Not only do these neighbouring court systems use different social work agencies to cater for a similar age group, but each agency has a different organizational structure, and resources, and their operational ideologies, although broadly similar, are based on different job definitions, with different histories and sometimes different aims. We have argued, that the work of each welfare service is dependent on, and often determined by, the nature of the local court culture. Nevertheless we will attempt to delinate each service's role and attitudes, and focus on points of integration and difference where appropriate.

Just as for parents and juveniles their local system tends to be *the* system, so too for social workers and probation officers, although they may have experience of other courts and will almost certainly have a theoretical understanding of the possible variables in justice systems, the local system becomes, over time, *the* system. They comprehend their role largely in terms of their daily concrete working experience. They become socialized by its particular culture.

The profile of our sample group of probation officers and social workers[5] shows that two-thirds of them are from the region, three-quarters of them have been in social work or probation for more than three years and two-thirds of them are qualified, most having obtained their qualification in the past two or three years. In the probation sample only a third had more than five years' service while a half of the social worker sample had been working in social work for over five years. Most of the social workers had been based at the same district office for more than two years while just under half of the probation officers had been based locally for that time.

The probation service has always been troubled by the dilemma of serving both the courts and the 'customers' (Bottoms and McWilliams, 1979). Local authority social workers now share these contradictions or dilemmas through their responsibilities as co-officers of the juvenile court. There are some differences in their relationship to the court however. Whilst some social workers may work almost exclusively with juvenile offenders, most will work with all children and young people in need of 'care and control', as well as with other client groups who have nothing to do with the courts. As a result of their wide brief many social workers will attend criminal courts only irregularly. Their relationship to the court is therefore not intimate. In our sample social workers saw themselves as the 'ugly sisters' to a court system which, in criminal proceedings, appeared to treat them as a poor substitute for the probation service. As one social worker put it:

> A probation officer's work is pin-pointed. Social workers still suffer from this 'any problem anywhere' – the whole generic thing. Probation officers have the freedom to develop on their well-acclaimed image in the court. There is still generally a massive misunderstanding of what a social worker is.

In Countyside court it was not the practice of individual probation officers to attend court unless it was a current case for which they had statutory responsibility or they were recommending supervision or detention centre (DC). For our sample juvenile cases only a third of the officers attended the court hearing and a half of those were there primarily because they were acting as the court duty probation officer. By contrast, half the City social workers were present in court, despite the fact that the social services department were represented in court by a permanent team of social workers. (Given our sample size little should be read into this, however.)

Within the courtroom the performance and presentation of both the social workers and probation officers was characterized by passivity. None of the few probation officers who were present in court spoke, or were asked to speak, to the bench, either to elaborate on the SER or make any comment about a case. Of those social workers who were present in City court, only one spoke to the bench when requested to provide further information on the juvenile's situation at school. The peripheral relationship of the social work role in criminal proceedings, which our adolescent samples themselves noted, is thus confirmed by our court-observation diaries.

Apart from actually providing the SER, both probation officers and social workers took a very low profile in the actual courtroom. Somewhat ironically, as we stated in the previous chapter, this passive performance appeared to benefit the probation officers, for, in the eyes of the juveniles, they were not identified as being responsible for Countyside's punitive behaviour and attitude towards them. The youngsters were relatively ignorant of the content and function of the report and hence underestimated its significance. As a consequence of their lack of knowledge about the report and the probation officers' passive presentation, many of the sample appeared to give the probation officers the benefit of the doubt and concluded that, in the absence of actively doing anything 'against' them, probation officers might well be 'for' them. Paradoxically, partly because more City adolescents were at least aware of the recommendation in the SER, and thus had some, if only partial, understanding of the report's importance, social workers did not appear to benefit from such irony and instead their young clients took a more critical view.

SOCIAL WORK PERCEPTIONS OF THE COURT

Views of function

Despite their criticisms of their physical placing in court, the probation officers generally felt comfortable and relatively at ease in the court setting. Although there were varied views on the relationship between probation officers and the other court officials, dependent largely on the degree of each officer's previous experience of alternative court systems and on their particular relationship to the personalities in Countyside, most of them subscribed to the necessity of 'game-playing':

> Clients know that you go to court a lot — they know that you are part of the court. They would feel let down if you didn't act the part in court.

> You have to get on with them [court officials]. You have to play the game.

They basically shared the view that a helpful working relationship was necessary or useful to achieve the probation officers' goals which were, 'good for the clients'. Some officers at the same time doubted whether this approach was really in good faith, feeling that they should be more oppositional to Countyside's sentencing approach. The overall picture is of a disparate group of probation officers spread across the three district teams serving Countyside court who, in the absence of any clear leadership or overall strategy, merely react pragmatically and individually to an 'unfortunate' working environment.

Turning to City social workers, although the more court-experienced of them subscribed to court gamesmanship, many lacked, or felt they lacked, sufficient experience or confidence to enter into such manoeuvres. In criminal proceedings, many of these social workers shared the adolescents' sense of being outsiders and expressed similar feelings of unease at being in an unfamiliar social setting:

> All separate — we just sit there and are rarely asked anything.

> They all have great ignorance of our role and our part in the proceedings. They see us as a necessary appendage to a court of law, as elements of do-gooding.

City social workers then also responded to and fitted into, rather than shaped, the City court's regime. They however had the good fortune of finding its structure and approach less in conflict with their own ideological and professional goals.

The history of child-care legislation in the twentieth century has been about striking an acceptable balance between considering the child's interests and needs and punishing him and protecting society.

Both the social workers' and probation officers' sample reflect a variety of views but most subscribed to the need for balance. As one put it:

> Help kids where possible and punish them when necessary. To do this in an environment which does not dramatize the offence and which protects the juvenile from the possible effects of publicity and contamination.

Countyside probation officers were conscious that the emphasis was too much on punishment and not enough on help and consideration: they knew that they worked in a punitive court and that:

> According to the '69 Act it's meant to help — but I don't think our magistrates have caught up on that yet. Many of our magistrates still simply like to punish.

By contrast with Countyside, some of the social workers in City court thought that the emphasis on helping was not always appreciated by the youngsters on the receiving end:

> Helping them — giving them every chance. I think they're a bit soft in City and the magistrates go too far — some of the kids are then amused.

However, both groups felt that their local juvenile courts were about punishing first, helping second, and in practice accepted their consequent marginality. They were more critical of the *manner* in which decisions were taken in court than of the actual decisions themselves. Almost half of the social workers thought that a more participatory court, one which was more informal, with greater child and parental involvement, would provide a better forum for decision-making:

> Somewhere where you could get round and talk about the child.

Although most probation officers would like to see some changes in the system — for example fewer middle-class 'professional' people as magistrates and more solicitors who 'specialize' in juvenile work — they did not want to see the system changed. Their general attitude is summed up by one probation officer:

> It is imperfect but I would like to see it used more perfectly, the imperfect system that we've got.

Only a few of either groups endorsed a change towards a panel system along the lines of the Scottish model: many had no concept of an alternative system at all. Very few supported a complete return to a straight justice system as advocated by the Justice for Children lobby. The majority of probation officers and social workers, despite their criticisms of the present juvenile court, did not want to see it dismantled. They accepted that justice for juveniles was not an easy task and that the present system of quarantining children from the possible rigours of the adult justice system was necessary if the children were to be treated with tolerance and compassion. The major reform they would like to see, apart from more participation by children and parents, was a greater role for their own profession. Like most professionals they tended, with some significant exceptions, to correlate their own self-interest with the interest of the client.

We will examine perceptions of the actual social work contact later in the chapter but it is perhaps appropriate to say at this point that although many of the sample were aware of the possibility that social work intervention might, in a few cases, make the problem worse and so exacerbate a child's deviant behaviour, most of the probation officers and social workers were fairly convinced that social work intervention did not usually result in drastic failure:

> I suppose it could, we're not perfect. I hope that it doesn't!

> It varies from case to case. I don't think it ever makes things worse. Usually the kid would have got into further trouble anyway, and in some cases I feel I've had a positive influence.

Social work intervention might not improve matters but it was hoped that it only rarely made things worse. For one person the question itself was quite shocking:

> Who could suggest such a thing? Who would formulate such a question?

Views on other court workers

Social workers' perceptions and assessment of the other court workers tended to be coloured by the extent to which their roles complemented or contradicted their own. When we elicited their views of the other court teams — police, solicitors and magistrates — it was clear that they held similar levels of hostility and prejudice for these groups as were held about them by these groups.

The significance of the adolescents' contact with the police, and the dissatisfaction which this produced, has been emphasized in the previous chapter. Neither the probation officers nor the social workers were fully aware of this dimension as it affected the adolescents' view of the criminal justice system. Although a few probation officers were aware that some of their young clients disagreed with the form that a particular charge took, most of them, and most of the social workers, thought that the charge was not in dispute, accepting it as a reasonably accurate description of the alleged offence.

Generally most probation officers and social workers thought that their relationship with the police was quite good although hingeing on the personalities involved and the local set-up. Many of them appreciated a cooperative JLO who was seen as an 'essential link', who could 'act as a buffer between the do-gooding social worker and the tough copper'.

Most of the sample were aware that each agency had its stereotypes of the other and that these reflected, to some extent, real ideological differences in their approach to juvenile delinquency, which created a barrier to effective communication. Mostly the contact between social workers, probation officers and the police was about exchanging information, although this was not a regular practice – except for a few probation officers who had struck up a good personal contact in the local police network.

We indicated in the previous chapter that our sample adolescents were generally well-satisfied with the service of their solicitors because they saw their lawyers as being the only court worker *for* them and their 'story'. Social workers and probation officers were not so easily satisfied with the performances of many juvenile court solicitors, who were almost universally seen as 'money-making, middle-class plagiarists', many of whom did the minimum amount of work necessary on a case and exploited the client's ignorance of the law, the court and the local tariff.

Replies to questions about solicitors were peppered with invectives, representing the solicitor generally as something of an unsavoury – if very eloquent and sophisticated – character, for whom juvenile representation is an easy way to make easy money. Yet in the final analysis, most of our sample thought that, given the present court set-up, legal representation was much needed so solicitors became a necessary evil. They should be retained but modified by way of encouraging them to specialize and thus become more committed to juvenile court work.

The social work critique of the magistracy flowed similarly from the sample's inability to conceive of a different juvenile justice system. Hence, whilst most benches were criticized for being middle-aged and middle-class, often lacking insight into the social world of those they judged, most of the sample could think of no viable alternative:

> I can't think of a good substitute. They don't take their jobs lightly . . . they try very hard.

> In the absence of a positive replacement, magistrates do not do a bad job.

In the circumstances then, and because the social work sample accepted the need for an independent arbiter, the magistracy was given a conditional thumbs-up.

Finally we noted a sense in which these criticisms of solicitors and magistrates were based on the joint sample's belief that they, either by virtue of their own working-class roots or their daily experience of working-class culture and life style, were more able to represent and understand the juvenile court's customers than other court professionals.

Working with the local tariff

There was agreement by the social workers and probation officers that a 'tariff system' operated in court, but there were a variety of views as to what actually constituted the tariff. Social work commentators, such as Curnock and Hardiker (1979), appear to imply that such a basic tariff can be perceived as existing nationally and 'objectively' and suggest that a practical or 'operational' tariff develops in each court according to the extent to which 'social need' is accepted by the individual courts, when it is presented through SERs. Our research in juvenile court demonstrates that the situation is more complex.

As we have shown, the basic tariff can exist in a 'shortened' or 'extended' form, regardless of a specific consideration of 'social need' or mitigating circumstances. In Countyside the shortened tariff operated, offering young offenders few chances before they received a custodial disposition. In City the fully extended tariff ladder was normally used. The notion of *the* tariff as the backbone of a theory of practice in social enquiry report writing would thus seem suspect. Moreover, we must cast doubt on Curnock and Hardiker's notion of the 'reverse tariff', in which the selective introduction of 'social need' via a report may reduce a tariff's punitiveness. We have argued that over time it is possible for the social need — 'special circumstances' — agenda to become 'internalized' into a local court tariff without the specific prompting of a written report with a strong recommendation.

Another significant factor which influences any social enquiry assessment is the social worker's desire to maintain his or her professional credibility in court. Curnock and Hardiker's work hints at the importance of this but does not make it explicit. They state:

> The legitimation of social work should be a potential safeguard against violations of due process in the courts.

Indeed it should. However, the social workers'/probation officers' need to maintain or build up professional credibility may dilute such safeguards as it did in Countyside. In Countyside the probation officers appeared to accept the shortened tariff and, particularly in TDA cases, usually accepted the 'inevitability' of a custodial disposition and did not attempt to counteract it by regularly emphasizing high 'social need' and/or recommending a non-custodial sentence. Instead, officers wrote their reports according to what they thought the magistrate might accept as 'reasonable' and their conclusions often enhanced the tendency for magistrates to follow their own punitive approach. Probation officers' tendency to write pre-trial reports, devoid of any recommendation, produced a similar effect. Yet, even when they made strong recommendations, their opinions were not given a great deal of consideration by the bench. We looked at 16 SERs: five made no recommendations and, of the 11 which did, the magistrates only accepted the probation officer's recommendation in six cases, and only four of those were accepted unconditionally, the other two having extra punishments added to the recommended disposition. In five of the other six cases the bench chose to increase the severity of the recommendations and in one case the actual disposal was less than that recommended. Such rejection must clearly undermine probation officers' confidence and without any overall strategy or collective support it is likely to lead to them internalizing the reality of the court's approach. We interviewed several officers aware of being caught in this dilemma. By contrast City social workers had their recommendations accepted fully (or coinciding with the outcome) in 12 out of 18 cases.

In City court, where the magistrates were seen to be less punitive and more flexible in treating each case on its merits and giving due consideration to social need, the social workers saw themselves as using 'social need' to modify the tariff more often. They claimed, in almost a third of the cases, to have used the introduction of high social need, combined with a strong recommendation, to affect the 'normal' tariff in a less punitive direction — in several cases avoiding what would almost certainly have been a custodial disposition. Our own observations would suggest that such reports usually endorsed by mitigation did at least 'tune' if not modify sentencing. City social workers were only confident that their recommendations would be followed in about 50 per cent of the cases, yet their actual success rate was significantly higher, at 67 per cent. The discrepancy between the predicted and actual success of recommendations could indicate that these social workers underestimated their influence in these specific cases: more likely it confirms our general impression that they attributed to City court (because they were not court regulars) a more severe or shortened tariff than it in fact operated and failed to fully understand its liberal paternal nature.

Most probation officers and social workers in our sample wrote their reports with the magistrates' attitudes in mind. They thought that magistrates did read reports and took their recommendations into consideration, along with other relevant factors. It is significant that both groups thought the magistrates paid special regard to parenting, school and the offence, along with the recommendation, as the most important areas of information in the report. Our examination of 16 probation and 18 social workers' reports indicated that these were the areas most widely covered. The main focus of the reports was the individual youngster in his personal and family situation, rather than, with a few exceptions, references to wider structural or societal issues. But most reports did comment on the type and standard of accommodation: 'clean, well-cared for, comfortably furnished', and placed the family in their environment, 'high levels of unemployment, delinquency and other related social problems'. In making the recommendation, apart from those which merely established culpability and indicated an acceptance of the inevitability of a punitive sentence, the rationale was based mostly on the youngster's need for individual treatment or help, 'to help her use her time more constructively and be more responsible for her actions', 'support and help D as he develops in his adolescence in an overprotective atmosphere'. The probation officers' reports tended to say very little about the neighbourhood and both groups' reports had sparse information on the youngsters' relationship to his or her peer group.

Whilst there was little difference in terms of content between social workers' and probation officers' reports, there was, as we have said, some difference in their tendency to make, and the strength of, recommendations. These differences occurred because each social work sample *reflected* rather than created the court regime, and responded to rather than defined the local tariff ladder and the impact of the social need—mitigation dimension. The probation officers' desire to maintain their professional credibility and their general lack of overall strategy, despite their antipathy to Countyside's regime, led them to acquiesce to a 'short' punitive sentencing ladder, based primarily on deterrence and retribution. The social workers, on the other hand, were profoundly fortunate in that their professional credibility was not often put to the test and could be maintained by little more than endorsing a court regime which accepted the social need dimension as legitimate and normally sentenced up a fully extended tariff ladder, even without strong social work prompting.

CONTACT WITH CHILDREN AND THEIR PARENTS

Social enquiry work

The normal pattern in preparing an SER we identified was for the social worker/probation officer to see the juvenile with his parents or family at his home and, again, preferably on his own, at the office. This pattern did vary, however, with the youngster sometimes not being seen at all, or seen just with his parents. The report is therefore prepared from, at most, about two hours of interview, and sometimes much less, depending on the complexity and seriousness of the case and the time available for preparation. Many of the social workers and probation officers appeared to think that this time was sufficient to provide a limited, but fairly accurate, picture of the juvenile's situation. However, others were less sure:

> I think we make sweeping generalizations from a brief visit. I just stick to the facts I can prove. I wouldn't be prepared to tell a probation officer much on a short visit.

Although half the social workers knew the youngster at first hand or knew of him through prior contact with the social services department, for most of the probation officers their contact with the youngster and his family regarding the SER was their first contact. Thus many of the social workers and most of the probation officers had to gather information, assess the situation and make a recommendation on a juvenile on the basis of one or two hours contact.

We have noted in the last chapter that overall the parents had usually seen, or were aware of, the contents and recommendation of the reports but that half of the youngsters were unaware of a report and those who were aware had at best a vague and partial idea of its content and purpose, although they knew about the recommendation.

This triangular communication pattern of using the parents as a sift to inform the adolescents as appropriate is acknowledged by the probation officers and social workers, although it is not a deliberate policy as such. The fact that some parents never saw, or were aware of, the contents of the report prior to the court hearing is explained, or excused, by lack of time and effort. By informing most of the parents of the contents and recommendations in the report and leaving it up to them to explain it to their children, the social workers and probation officers were perhaps offering the parents the right to control the youngster's access to the report, but they were effectively denying the subject of the report access to it or possibly giving him only a relayed and thus distorted picture.

That over half of the probation officers and social workers actually discussed the report with both parents and youngsters, or sometimes even showed it to them, indicates that many of them made an effort to do more than they were legally required to do. If an 'extra' home visit is not done to show the parents and child the completed report prior to the hearing, then the last opportunity for them to be shown the report is just before the hearing itself. Since few of the probation officers and only half of the social workers actually attended the hearing, many of them were dependent on the duty officer to carry out this function. Although some duty officers fulfilled this task, many did not. As a result, unless their solicitor or the magistrates enabled defendants and their parents to obtain a copy of the report, those who had not seen the report through their social worker or probation officer, were effectively denied access to it.

We noted a tendency among the probation officers, in particular, to be keener on discussing the report with parents and children in those cases which were likely to become the subject of probation involvement or if their agency already had statutory responsibility. First offence cases and less serious cases, on the other hand, were often seen as 'straight-forward' and therefore merited a low priority in terms of the officers' time and effort. Thus parents and children in these cases were less likely to be shown the reports or have them explained. In the absence of a set policy to show reports to parents and children generally, access to the reports was limited by the policy and practice of individual probation officers and social workers and the exigencies of time, effort and organization.

Preparing clients for court

Since social workers and probation officers were not routinely present at the hearing, the opportunity for them to advise juveniles what to do in court was limited to the occasions of their home visits or when the youngster was seen at the office. Our interviews indicate that the social workers claimed to have advised the youngsters or their parents about obtaining legal representation and about the nature of the SER recommendation (and thus what they could reasonably expect to receive as a disposition) in two-thirds of the cases. However, both social work groups were, by their own admission, inconsistent in offering such information and rarely concentrated on telling families what the court experience would be like and 'coaching' them accordingly. They failed to cover these areas of possible advice to clients in any systematic manner. Usually it depended on the discretion of individual officers or workers as to whether they discerned a 'need' on the family's behalf to have such information and advice.

Yet, as we have seen, the adolescents in our sample often went into court ill-prepared and unsure of what to expect. Further, they very rarely mentioned the social worker or probation officer as a pre-court source of information and help. From the receiving-end perspective, the social work samples' claims about this help, marginal as it is, still appears to be over estimated vis-a-vis their preparation of clients for court. This relative neglect of client 'preparation' is all the more surprising when we consider that both social work samples agreed that only court-experienced juveniles had much chance of really understanding what was going on or had sufficient confidence and competence to convey *their* point of view to the juvenile court.

Patterns of community supervision

This section is based on a small part of our sample — the 16 'supervised' adolescents we followed through the criminal justice process and interviewed again at the point when they had been in receipt of social work supervision some six to nine months after the disposition was made. The statutory nature of this involvement was eight supervision orders, three of which were the responsibility of probation officers, and eight detention centre licences, all administered by probation officers.

Of the ten adolescents dealt with by probation, the officers thought that six of them had not been re-offending mainly because they had 'good parental support', were settled in employment or had avoided returning to 'bad company':

> He has been astute enough to keep himself to himself.

Only in two cases was it thought the youngster was deterred because he still 'recalls the pain of DC'. Two of the lads were known to have committed offences and were pleading guilty. Another two were appearing in court, one for non-school attendance and the other for an alleged offence which was being denied. There appeared to be no clear link between the development of a positive relationship between client and probation officer and the juvenile ceasing offending. The probation officers were realistic enough to appreciate that other factors, such as those mentioned above, were often more critical variables than a 'good relationship' in determining a juvenile's tendency to re-offend. However, a positive relationship could function to 'de-brief' the juvenile coming out of DC – and ease his re-entry back into society, complemented by some assistance regarding employment when necessary.

Most probation officers were pessimistic about the positive effects of DC. They acknowledged too that many of their young clients saw DC licence as an extra punishment, a sentence which the court had never fully explained to them. We found probation officers operated the licence in a structured and consistent manner, directing the juvenile to report weekly, then fortnigntly and finally monthly until at around six months, if there was no further offence, they moved to discharge it. One of the supervision cases followed the same pattern, while the other two involved more intensive, weekly reporting because the officers identified problems which had to be ironed out:

> He still has problems, he needs someone to be there for him – for support.

Most supervision, whether under licence or a supervision order, was done on a one-to-one basis, usually in the office, but occasionally a lad was seen at home, either alone or with his family. In our sample, three youngsters were offered an alternative to individual office-based contact, in the form of some kind of group supervision — a football group and the like — but this was either declined or proved to be ineffective:

> I have tried him with a group situation but we were getting nothing done — they try and see who can be the biggest clown.

We could only follow up five cases in the social worker sample, all of which were supervision orders. For some of the social workers, supervision was seen as a 'correctional' exercise and the reporting aspect was seen as important but the limitations of supervision were evident to most of them:

> It's very rare that you feel they are any good. Really it is pretty superficial. The only time it works is when the kid develops an attachment to the social worker. As a means of keeping kids out of trouble, it's suspect.

Two out of the five youngsters had been in trouble since they were placed on supervision: one for non-school attendance, the other for a criminal offence. Three out of the five youngsters were thought to have kept out of trouble with the police, but one of them, because of the 'highly delinquent area' in which he lived, was considered likely to re-offend, although apparently he had not actually come to notice. Three of the social workers thought that supervision had been effective in as much as the youngsters concerned had improved their relationship with their parents and one had had a greater 'insight' into his problem. Two of the lads took part in IT schemes, one of which was a 90-day residential placement which, by substituting for individual social worker involvement, effectively excluded the social worker and relegated the role to that of a distant 'official caretaker', rather than the central worker.

One social worker though that supervision had failed, despite the youngster reporting to the office fairly regularly, because the:

> Difficulty is that the parental relationship is the source of the problem, but the parents resist social work involvement.

Based on this small sample and some information gleaned from our 'care' sample subject to community supervision, we can tentatively conclude that the two agencies organize and deliver community supervision somewhat differently. Countyside probation officers tended to operate an office-based pattern of supervision, involving some degree of regularity for the young client. City social workers were more eclectic and if anything favoured a more 'home-based', family-centred approach which tended to be less disciplined in terms of regular contact. Each approach has its merits and limitations. The office-based, individualized 'casework' model, while setting clear boundaries between the youngster's problems and the functioning of his family, clearly espouses the notion of juvenile culpability and also avoids social work 'trespass' into sensitive areas of the youngster's family life, which can bring resentment. However, it runs the risk of over-concentration on the youngster as 'the problem' when there may be some tie-up between his or her offending and the family or neighbourhood itself. It is tremendously convenient and 'efficient' for the probation officer of course and also probably more in keeping with Countyside court's expectations.

By contrast, the family-centred approach is more likely to pick up a range of issues arguably related to offending but certainly related to a youngster's needs or interest. Our own interview visits, for instance, led us into the midst of major family rifts, rows and crises which were simply unknown to the probation officer supervising the juvenile.

We noted in the previous chapter that some parents and youngsters tended to view the social workers' focus on the 'child-in-the-family' as unnecessary and unwanted interference in the private affairs of the family; but, given the small numbers in our follow-up sample, we are not in a position to comment authoritatively on the extent of such family-centredness in general in social workers' approach to youngsters' problems. However, in three out of the five cases, the social workers admitted that their main relationship was with the parents, particularly the mother, and that the youngster was seen only as part of a regular pattern of home visits, whose purpose was to see the parents. Although there might well be good reasons for concentrating on the family, this shift of focus away from the juvenile to the parents seems to explain why many of the youngsters did not see their relationship with the social worker as important or significant. From their point of view the social worker was in their home to see their parents and was not there primarily to do anything with them, or apparently for them. Perhaps the social workers, by concentrating on the 'child-in-the-family' are, albeit inadvertently, tending to undervalue the youngster in his or her own right.

SUMMARY AND DISCUSSION

The differences in the delivery of social work is another facet of the diversity in the production of juvenile justice. Here there is diversity not only in terms of which social work agency is used to respond to juveniles in trouble with the law, but also in the form which organizations like probation and social services take at a local level. Such diversity makes comparisons difficult and our conclusions are thus tentative.

Social workers are not court specialists like their colleagues in probation. The service which they provide to the courts is just one of many roles they are called upon to perform in relation to a variety of different client groups. Consequently, for many of them, their attendance at court is infrequent and they do not develop the sense of 'belonging' in the court setting, which is much more characteristic of probation officers. As a result they more often seem to share the sense of discomfort, anxiety and reluctance to assert themselves in the criminal court, which has been expressed by many of the youngsters and parents in our sample.

Social workers and probation officers are very aware that they represent the 'welfare' component of juvenile justice, not least because of the tension they experience between their own and other court 'teams'. They feel on the defensive in the juvenile court and consequently would like to see their own position strengthened vis-a-vis the police, solicitors and magistrates. Yet the joint social work sample seemed to have little idea about how the system could be restructured and so tended to perceive change in terms of minor tinkering with the present system.

The social work performance in and around both court systems was markedly passive. During the hearing itself both groups of social workers were either absent or marginal to proceedings. Even in areas where a vacuum exists — in preparing families for the court experience — the social workers and probation officers showed little enterprise. Their social enquiry work was also characterized by inconsistency, particularly in relation to discussing and showing the reports to parents and juveniles — and this despite these social workers' belief that they had a greater empathy with the court's customers than other full-time workers.

Whilst City social workers worked in a system which rarely challenged their professional credibility or tactical ability, Countryside probation officers were enmeshed in a highly punitive regime which

highlighted their vulnerability and lack of overall strategy. Their prag-
matic and indivualized response to the Countyside regime involved
their 'internalizing' the shortened tariff and the 'TDA policy' and hence
offering very little resistance to punitive sentencing. In both courts the
social work performance reflected the in-court regime rather than
created or manipulated it, with social workers having real influence
only in terms of the making and administration of '7 (7)' care orders,
supervision orders and to a lesser extent, DC licences.

In practice, we have suggested that this influence is used differently
by the two agencies. Countyside probation officers tend to operate an
office-based, individualized casework approach to community supervision, whilst City social workers appeared to adopt a less structured,
home-focused, family-casework approach. There are strengths and
weaknesses in each approach and both show that the social work 'self'
is or has to be regarded as the key resource. In the end, the social work
'welfare' role in juvenile criminal proceedings is a small part of a system
which is essentially about the social control of working-class youth.
Social workers and probation officers have almost no *de jure* power in
the system and their function can be totally undermined by local magistrates. Indeed the area where they do have some control, in '7 (7)' care
orders, is being cut back at present (see Home Office, 1980b) and the
area where their supervisory role will be in greater demand, via DC
licence, is hardly a celebration of their professional ideology.

8

Perceptions of Social Work Supervision

INTRODUCTION

We have stressed throughout, by the qualitative nature of our research, our concern to contextualize the views of adolescents and their parents subject to the juvenile justice process. This chapter, focusing in depth on the passage of a handful of adolescents through criminal proceedings in our two courts attempts to draw these perspectives together. We will also look at the social worker's task and the ways in which social workers, like their clients, are trapped within an organizational structure which limits and curbs their abilities to 'advise, assist and befriend' (see Hugman, 1980). We have shown that many who campaigned for the 1969 Act saw it as a vehicle for increasing the part played by welfare professionals in our juvenile justice system with the supervision order becoming a key, imaginative disposal available to the bench. Yet the use of community supervision, and hence the part played by social workers and probation officers, has not risen significantly with the partial implementation of this Act. We found, in practice, these welfare professionals did not play a significant part in the lives of many working-class families who met and talked with us about their experiences of criminal proceedings. Rather, clients' impressions were of a peripheral figure, whose brief task was limited to the preparation of a court report and who was not routinely present in the courtroom. This low-key involvement, with social workers and probation officers undertaking further work with adolescents only at the discretion of local magistrates' sentencing, contrasts sharply with the experiences of families subject to care proceedings as we detail in the following chapters.

145

'JIM'

Jim lives with his parents and youngest sister in a terraced council house built on a large out-of-town estate with a considerable reputation for delinquency. Jim's parents, both in their late 40s, are in full-time work, with Mr G employed as a skilled process worker and Mrs G as a factory worker. Jim himself had left school a few months ago without any qualifications and, after a long search, was taken on as a storekeeper at a local factory.

Jim has two previous appearances before City's juvenile bench. A year ago he was charged with 'disorderly behaviour' and on that occasion the case against him was dismissed. He came to notice again some seven months later, accused of taking a car (TDA), when City's magistrates decided to impose fines totalling £60, together with a licence endorsement. The current offence, the subject of our interest, followed within the space of a few months. Again he was involved in a TDA incident with another lad and, as they skidded round the estate at twilight with the police in pursuit — a familiar sight in the neighbourhood — Jim lost control of the stolen car which mounted the pavement, hitting and seriously injuring an elderly pedestrian. He was arrested on the spot, taken to the nearest police station and charged, and, with his parents away on holiday, he spent the night in police custody. Jim appeared alone before City's juvenile bench the following day: he was remanded to the care of the local authority pending his parents' return from holiday. Two more juvenile court appearances followed at weekly intervals — Jim pleaded guilty to the offence and the bench adjourned his case for legal representation and reports. He was granted bail on condition he kept to a curfew. On his final appearance, some six weeks after the incident, the bench sent Jim and his co-defendant to detention centre on the basis of its being a very serious offence.

Before his case was finally dealt with, Jim says he saw a social worker twice at his home. He contends the social worker 'just started asking questions' and at first he didn't realize she was gathering information for a report. As he sees it, the social worker had the upper hand during these brief interviews.

Just said I'm putting you down and that's it — she wasn't concerned — was a waste of money.

Jim's view was endorsed by his father, a politically aware man with left-wing views, who felt SERs a waste of public money and suggested parents should routinely give a verbal account of their home circumstances to the bench, cutting out the need for a written welfare assessment. Certainly, Jim himself felt the social worker's recommendation influential:

> They can influence the court because the court doesn't come round to your house — she does, if says recommend DC, they take it into account.

He also reckoned the preparation and handing in of reports was the sum total of the social worker's task in the juvenile justice process since he noticed his social worker 'never even got up' throughout the proceedings.

Jim's social worker, in turn, told us that the car accident had generated a good deal of local controversy and moral outrage: the injured pensioner, who seemed likely to lose a leg as the result of her ordeal, was also a client with the social services department and this consideration together with the 'serious', albeit unpremeditated, nature of Jim's offence made it 'hard to be objective'. The social worker felt the unusual gravity and consequences of this offence were such that she could not let Jim's best interests, his 'social needs', take precedence over considerations of 'justice' and punishment: in short, she believed he should be taught a lesson and put away. Accordingly, she describes Jim in her report as a 'pleasant' and 'cooperative' lad with 'no behavioural problems' but goes on to recommend 'a period of custodial sentence' since 'he does not appreciate the true significance of his actions and the extreme seriousness of the offence'. Jim's social worker added that both the magistrates and the police expected her to make a high-tariff recommendation for this 'serious' offence. She argued that the bench would not have followed a less punitive recommendation anyway and it would merely have damaged her credibility with these courtroom colleagues not to recommend a custodial sentence:

> The arresting officer in Jim's case said straight out 'I don't like social workers' but then he saw I was taking it seriously and was not going to recommend a conditional discharge.

Jim's social worker went on to describe further constraints making her task with young offenders a difficult and pressurized one. A woman in her mid-twenties, she had worked as an unqualified social worker for some four years, taking home little more than she had as an office junior. Now, with public spending cuts, she sees her chances of seconded social work training slipping away. She is neither graded nor paid to take on statutory cases like Jim's, but staff freezes increasingly put this kind of work her way and she feels she has 'no choice'. She is worried that she lacks sufficient time to prepare her SERs thoroughly and inadequate typing facilities merely add to her frustrations. Nor is she helped by office organization: for, with social work teams split into 'in-take' and 'long-term' groups, continuity of work, with young offenders previously unknown to her department, goes by the board. For these adolescents the organizational structure of her own office dictates that an in-take team member prepares an SER and a long-term worker then assumes responsibility should a statutory supervision order result. In Jim's case, agency continuity will be broken too, for, by local agreement, the probation service takes over 'licence' work with 16 year olds returning from detention centre:

> Jim will go to probation because of his age. I'm in in-take so he would go to another social worker anyway.

When we saw Jim again, he was on DC licence to the probation service, reporting fortnightly to the local office. Looking back on his juvenile court appearance, he felt City's magistrate had sentenced him leniently; he appreciated his 'joy-riding' had resulted in serious consequences and fully expected the bench to make a Borstal recommendation. Yet what he had not bargained for was the havoc a custodial sentence had brought to his life. For his six weeks short, sharp, shock stint, also lost him his job and on his return we met a disillusioned, unemployed youth who had once said he'd never exist on social security payments. He told us of his fruitless search for work and his lack of money. He said that his daily moping about at home had caused friction with his hard-working father. We found him staying with friends in a delapidated, walk-up block of flats a few streets away from his home. As he described family rows, we asked Jim whether he had told his probation officer about his home circumstances. He shrugged in a non-commital way, suggesting there was 'no point'. Since his probation officer had never visited his family home or talked with his parents, he felt she could offer little advice. He described his office reporting routine:

> Has no conversation with you — doesn't talk about *you* really. Always first asks 'How are you getting on at home' and asks me if

I'm working. ... If she's in a hurry, that's it — if not in a hurry she'll spread out the questions a bit. ... She's all right, but to her it's just a matter of 'I've got to see him' ... she wants to get it over ... I don't see any point to it.

Jim's story and the repercussions of his juvenile court appearance will continue. Perhaps, as he gets to know his probation officer, his confidence in her will grow and, on reflection, his assessment of the DC licence period may become less negative.

'SANDRA'

Sandra, also 16, lives with her parents, her brothers and a sister in a third-floor tenement block situated in another poor part of City. Her father, sometime labourer, has now been off work for several months and, given his failing health and the region's high rates of unemployment, he is unlikely to find work again. Sandra's parents manage on state benefits whilst, without any qualifications, her own future is by no means secure.

Sandra, unlike many girls we saw go before City's juvenile bench, has a long record of shoplifting. Her current appearance, on a charge of stealing baby clothes, is her eighth consecutive juvenile court appearance in two years. City's magistrates have fined her on a number of previous occasions and she is currently subject to a supervision order with a social worker who has known her and her family for about four years.

Sandra argues that her long criminal record in part reflects a battle of wills between adolescents and the police fought out on City's streets, both her brothers have been in trouble with the law and, as a known face, she reckons the police are particularly vigilant towards her and not above manipulating evidence in court. Thus, like many youngsters we met, Sandra sees her record as a distortion of her real offences, amplified and redefined by police methods. Sandra's mother offers a less acrimonious explanation: she thinks her daughter's criminal record is part and parcel of living in a poor, decaying area where juvenile delinquency is the norm:

Her father gives her hidings but that's not the way: it does no good. She's *done well* keeping out of trouble for this time [seven months] — she was in court every week before that. She knows she'll get sent away next time. I keep drumming it into her . . . if she robs again, she'll go away. She doesn't know what it's like to have it rough, she's no idea.

At the final hearing for this latest offence, Sandra made a guilty plea and her social worker duly prepared an SER. But the hearing coincided with his annual leave so he did not attend court. Neither Sandra nor her mother were aware of his holiday arrangements and put his absence down to a lack of real concern. To her mother's way of thinking:

She needs someone to help her. . . . He never even turned up in court this last time. I think he should have been there like before.

On the day, City's magistrates, after much conferring, decided to impose a further fine to the tune of £70 with the senior magistrate delivering a stern, final warning to Sandra. Both mother and daughter felt this a favourable outcome for, like most other families we talked with, they accepted the principle of full-tariff sentencing and realized a custodial sentence was due. Taking into account Sandra's antecedents, committed in rapid succession, they fully expected the bench to make a Borstal recommendation this time. In fact, Sandra braced herself for a custodial sentence by ensuring that her mother took charge of her jewellery for safekeeping before she entered the courtroom. As it turned out, she agreed with her mother that, because she had a new factory job and a medical report detailing a minor heart condition, she may have been saved from custody.

MOTHER: I thought was fair. Well, I thought she might go down but with the medical note that must have made the difference . . . a big fine, *she* has to pay was fair.

Yet, this family, while more than satisfied with the bench's final decision, went on to assess their social worker's part throughout the proceedings in a less favourable light. Both Sandra and her mother took issue with his SER and the quality of supervision offered.

First, both had seen the report, via their solicitor, and, when we met them on separate occasions, they told us they were perplexed by the social worker's written conclusions. They argued in particular that the report's contention that 'supervision wasn't working' amounted to an empty, foolish statement since, to their way of thinking, the social worker had never really got to know Sandra. They claimed he had never offered her a programme of regular interviews and Sandra interpreted this lack of contact as a lack of effort and concern:

> He said supervision wasn't working in the report but I don't see him. I get the feeling he doesn't like me − he never comes down to see me − he never says anything when I go to the office.

Similarly her mother, who accepted this social worker had no easy task with Sandra, commented:

> I think she needs someone to help her but he only comes down when she gets into trouble.

From the social worker's point of view too, Sandra had proved a difficult youngster to work with. He told us over the past three years he had been called on to prepare a total of nine reports for her and now felt hard-pushed to justify a non-custodial recommendation. His report outlines the family's 'cramped' accommodation, Mr D's 'generally poor physical conditon' and Sandra's own 'serious heart condition'. He points out that Sandra has found herself a job packing shampoo − 'I understand that her employer thinks highly of her and is anxious that she should remain.' But he does not go on to make any specific recommendations to the bench. He told us this time he had deliberately left his report 'open', pointing out Sandra's failure to respond to supervision, and leaving it for the magistrates to reach their decision. He felt that by not spelling out any recommendation for a custodial sentence, Sandra might perhaps be given yet another chance. But, should she offend again, he would be 'forced' to come clean with a high-tariff recommendation. In the event, he said he would probably have to suggest a care order, a disposal which he argued would prove 'less destructive than Borstal: Borstal would destroy Sandra'. Perhaps his speculation, as a middle-aged man with children of his own, also reflects a paternal concern for his teenage girl client. Certainly, as an experienced social worker with several years of juvenile court work behind him, he found Sandra's repeated offences caused him some embarrassment with his City courtroom colleagues. Time and again the buck seemed to stop with him and sometimes even he despaired of Sandra − 'and the social worker is usually the last to give up'.

Second, from their experience of the supervision order in practice, both Sandra and her mother concluded this social worker was 'not really doing anything to help'. Since he usually called at their home when Sandra was out, he seldom saw his young client, who took it that he just couldn't be bothered with her. Her mother, trying to bring up four teenage children on a fixed income, told us she appreciated the social worker's visits but at the same time found his efforts with Sandra sadly lacking. She recalled how another social worker had taken the trouble to arrange camping holidays for her son, providing him with alternatives to delinquent activities. Again she contrasted the present social worker's approach with that of a student social worker, a young woman who had been able to give Sandra more attention: over a couple of months she had taken Sandra out horse-riding and seemingly made a real effort to get to know her. Unlike Sandra's present social worker, of course, student social workers have very restricted caseloads with ample time off for study and reflection. They are attached to local offices for a number of weeks and are not as yet worn out with years of high bombardment in an inner-city area. In any case, Sandra's social worker told us that he did not regard her alone as his client, rather, after several regular interviews with her, he assessed his work should focus on her family as a whole and, with her brother also subject to a supervision order, family visits would make the most efficient use of his limited time.

'FARIDA'

Another girl's case, that of Farida, demonstrates further a social worker's reluctance to step up the degree of state intervention into a young offender's life. Farida is 13 and lives with her mother, stepfather and four step-sisters in a back-to-back terraced house in City's docklands area. When we met her she was subject to a supervision order for a second offence of shoplifting: together with another girl, she had been caught stealing chocolates from a local supermarket. Farida's mother is a strict Muslim and doesn't approve of her daughter going out — hence Farida's tastes for fashionable clothes and discos are anathema to her. The result is constant friction between mother and daughter. Tearfully, Farida told us that she finds her mother's discipline unduly harsh and had asked her social worker to receive her into care:

I asked to go into care but she's never done anything about it.

Her mother, unaware of Farida's request, has no time for social workers. She sees Farida's social worker as an unnecessary interference in her family and a threat to her duties as a mother:

> I don't like social workers ... they don't take any notice of the mother. I know my daughter better than a social worker ... punishment is a mother's duty. I said to the social worker if I or every mother done what I do and beat them when they do wrong in the proper way and keep her in, you people would be out of business. I beat her with a little stick: I say 'school' every day.

Farida's social worker, in turn, is well-acquainted with the family rows and Farida's unhappiness. She is conscious too that a care order and Farida's removal from home could sour mother—daughter relations for ever. After careful assessment, Farida's social worker decided the supervision order would offer some structured support to both Farida and her mother. She was reluctant to recommend a '7 (7)' care order, since this disposal is a controversial one in criminal proceedings and, for a girl of 13, could stretch out for several years. She knew also that voluntary care would prove quite unacceptable to Farida's mother. Also she dislikes work in care proceedings and feels she has insufficient evidence to bring a watertight case:

> When we initiate care proceedings, we go into it in more depth — have to examine if we have a good case for getting it and it is sometimes hard to prove ... because of the '69 Act we have to be involved in these cases but I don't like this aspect of the work ... supervision order ends in September or October but because of the home problems think I'll be seeing her beyond then.

This supervision order has not been easy to operate; certainly the social worker has been unable to please both parent and child. Farida's mother firmly believes the social worker has failed to help her daughter: rather, she told us, the social worker has undermined her authority, adding to her difficulties of bringing up a large family in a poor and vandalized environment:

> Farida was under a social worker and they were taking her to restaurants, pictures ... doing a good deed for a wrong deed. ... To tell you the truth, I am blaming the social worker when Farida was first in trouble. They gave me the wrong advice when I

was doing the right thing: they told me I was cruel to keep her in and wrong to beat her but Farida is a hard child.

These embittered comments are irreconcilable with the views of Farida's social worker, who said she had taken pains to explain her work to Farida and her mother. Farida herself rates her social worker very highly — she even asked the research team to make her feelings plain to her social worker:

Think she's helped me. When Mum wouldn't let me out, used to talk to my mum so she let me out once a week.

This triangle of conflicting evaluations is a clear-cut one, with Farida, her mother and her social worker expressing their views forcefully and unambiguously. There is no easy way out of such conflict. The actors are locked into a situation which will not be easily or quickly resolved. Farida may yet end up in care.

ONE PROBATION OFFICER, TWO 'CLIENTS'

Mick and Ricky were both subject to DC licence supervision. They were allocated to the same probation officer. We saw both juveniles and the probation officer twice over a four-month period. Mick was keeping his probation officer at arm's length. He felt that he had already served out his punishment in detention centre and resented this 'second sentence' of compulsory supervision (see Ericson, 1976). He complies nominally with the licence by reporting, as stipulated by his probation officer, and thus resists any return to custody for breaching the order, but he maintains an aloof and defensive silence throughout such meetings. Mick's wall of silence buffers against any would-be adult do-gooders. It extended to our research project when, despite wanting to take part, he kept his replies to an absolute minimum:

M (*of PO*): Don't like her.

HP: Why?

M: Just don't.

HP: What do you talk about?

M: Not much. She asks me how I'm getting on and about my family and that.

HP: And about offences?

M: Yeah.

Mick's probation officer is at a loss, finding herself powerless to break down his wall of silence:

> He's never missed an appointment, he just sits there. The only words he's ever said are 'Yes', 'No' and 'What do you mean?' He won't respond at all. Sits there looking at the floor. . . . I asked a senior colleague about it and he said you occasionally get these cases. They just keep appointments and refuse to do anything else. . . . He refused group supervision − just wanted to carry on reporting. And now he's got another offence in the pipeline my senior insists I have to keep the licence on.

Had she called at Mick's house and seen his widowed father, this probation officer might have noted the family's immense poverty and the tensions between father and son. Whilst we were there on a second visit, for example, Mick's father swore at him and belted him over the head. But an insight into Mick's home life may not have made his probation officer's task any easier or any more pleasant. She would know the social services department had already failed with a recommendation for a care order on Mick's first offence. A similar recommendation from this probation officer, unfamiliar with placement resources, might meet with the same fate whilst a year or more in a community school, sentenced to care, could turn this lad into an even more bitter and resentful young adult. Mick's home situation was extremely bad. Any typical social work assessment would have produced a very high social-need score. Yet the criminal juvenile justice system is not in practice concerned with this issue. The fine words of the white papers on the 1960s do not impact greatly on the production of juvenile justice. Indeed given Countyside's punitive attitudes, Mick's probation officer accepted the inevitable. Mick has recently started a Borstal sentence. His delinquency is the main issue.

Ricky too was initially suspicious of this same probation officer. Gradually, however, his views of her became much more positive. For him the regular chats with the officer slipped by without tension. He saw his supervisor as a helpful, adult friend, summing up his supervision in a fuller and more positive way than the probation officer herself. She told us she had adopted a casework approach. She had structured her interviews with Ricky so as to get him thinking about himself, his friends and his future work. She felt Ricky probably pictured her as an authority figure:

> When he came to see me, he made use of the sessions but he also responded to authority.

Ricky said he had found his probation officer helpful but he seemed to most value her practical advice, including a referral to prospective employers. He didn't mention anything about gaining insight into his own strengths and weaknesses. He reckoned his contact with a caring professional meant 'more people looking out for me now' and, above all, it was the probation officer herself and her friendship which he had come to esteem. He did not, as others in our sample did, long for her to 'lay off' and end the licence. At our first meeting Ricky said he found his probation officer 'OK'. Later he couldn't speak highly enough of her:

> Time just flew over – she was like friendly tho' knew she was still a probation officer . . . trying to help me out and keep me out . . . not nosey, actually trying to help me.

Just as a similar approach by the same officer can produce totally different responses in supervised juveniles so the same juvenile must face different definitions of supervision as one City boy, Neil, found. We originally included Neil in our care sample, noting his scheduled juvenile court appearance on grounds of non-school attendance. But, in the interim, Neil panicked and ran away from home: the police caught him stealing in a neighboring area and brought him before a juvenile court there. He was remanded in care to a secure establishment, a salutary experience which gave him an unwelcome taste of being 'in care'. Neil's case was then remitted to City juvenile court where the bench dealt with this offence, his first, by placing him on a supervision order for two years. The senior magistrate explained to Neil that the decision, a middle-range disposal for a first offence, had been made because of his persistent truancy. Then Neil was taken across to the care-proceedings court where this rationale and the consequences of failing to attend school regularly were spelt out to him again. When we met him, the magistrates' message was clear in his mind:

> If I go to school, they'll drop things but if I'm off school again, they'll take me back to court.

Yet this consistent reasoning, drummed in by two different sets of magistrates, presiding over both criminal and care proceedings, was not followed up by Neil's supervising officers, for, as his case was passed on from an in-take to a long-term social worker, the purpose of the order was re-interpreted. Thus the first social worker led Neil to believe that once he left school the order would be discharged. Neil understood this social worker's task and valued his help throughout the court proceedings. He told us this social worker was 'for' him — 'reckon he's all right . . . just make sure that you keep on at school.' However, the second social worker chose to relegate this task and introduced some new casework aims: he preferred to turn a blind eye to Neil's continued truancy, arguing the lad was coming up to his school-leaving date. He, in turn, told us he planned to continue the order to see how Neil 'matures' and settles into some kind of job. This social worker saw his own job as helping Neil:

> To gain more self-confidence and self-esteem and to try and help
> him mature with regard to his self-centred attitudes.

Thus the criteria for discharging the supervision order had shifted with a change of social worker. When we met Neil he could draw on his contact with these different social workers but, like other adolescents who talked with us, he did not feel their various idiosyncrasies and changes in plan harassed him unduly. Unlike his Countyside contemporaries, with probation officers who expected regular office reporting, none of Neil's social workers stipulated frequent interviews: all in all, the experience had 'not bothered' him.

DISCUSSION

We have shown how the juvenile court can use the local social services and probation departments by deciding in a small minority of cases to place young offenders under their supervision. Although magistrates may have particular goals in mind, we have illustrated how it is left to individual officers to carry out their duties as they themselves think fit. The supervisor's legislative brief is a permissive one to 'advise, assist and befriend' and, whilst the court can attach conditions, and although they are accountable to senior advisers, the 'front-line' nature of their work allows each officer some scope to plan privately the content of their work with adolescents referred to them. We have also shown in chapter 6 that for working-class families the nature of statutory supervision can vary both between local agencies and between individual workers with their perceptions influenced by an officer's own social-class background gender, personality and training.

Where adolescents, their parents or their social workers gave us different or conflicting accounts, we have tried to let their respective viewpoints speak for themselves, rather than champion any particular side of these triangles. And, had we taken these threefold viewpoints in isolation, our conclusions might be easier to draw. What is clear, however, is that there is no agreed agenda amongst social workers and probation officers undertaking community supervision. For, as we have shown in chapter 7, these various officers do not have generalized goals and hence they often share in their clients' confusions and frustrations. They are the symbols of help and welfare in a system which is fundamentally about routine social control and punishment and they become a part of that structure, particularly when they prepare SERs for recidivism and serious offences and when they take on DC licence supervision.

We have shown by implication that social workers and probation officers can have little impact on the lives of poor working-class families living in a depressed region which offers adolescents poor schooling, few job opportunities and little social justice generally. When these youngsters try to steal some of the material advantages they have been systematically denied, the police take strong action. As the juvenile justice process is set in motion, welfare workers are not routinely consulted: they will only be brought into the picture if an adolescent is already on their books or, more commonly, if the bench requests an SER. This document may be scripted from a couple of brief family interviews: it is commissioned for the court, not for the youngster, and its author is governed as much by the local court's concern with 'justice' and punishment as by professional considerations of help and treatment. We have shown how Mick's probation officer, for example, was faced with a sullen adolescent, serving out his 'second sentence' of DC licence with a court summons for further thefts. She is bewildered about what to recommend again and, whilst she lacks complete knowledge of the lad's tragic home circumstances, she is aware welfare considerations play little part in Countyside juvenile court's sentencing preference. Borstal becomes inevitable. For adolescents like Mick, it seems, the promise of social justice and compensatory programmes held out by the reports and white papers of the 1960s are but empty rhetoric. And even where a social worker can utilize her assessment of the 'problem' the solution may well remain elusive as Farida's social worker realized.

The experience of receiving statutory social work supervision, via criminal proceedings, is very mixed. We can draw no black and white conclusions from our data, but merely illustrate what a complex grey area it is and will probably remain. Clearly local social work agencies and their officers can place different emphasis on the supervisory task, but essentially, measured by whatever usual criteria, 'success' comes against the odds and in an idiosyncratic form, since the very meaning of social work intervention wedged into a juvenile justice system geared towards routine punishment and social control remains problematic.

In the face of so many constraints the remarkable feature of our findings is that overall so many clients remain 'neutral' or actually like their social workers and probation officers — whether or not they feel 'helped'.

9

City's Welfare Justice

BEHIND THE CARE STATISTICS

City's 'care' court sits two or three times a week. The lists for each session are small, reflecting the fact that only about 200 cases are dealt with each year. However although the bustle of criminal proceedings is not repeated, such apparent calm should not be misinterpreted. For whilst in City, if not Countyside, only 10 per cent of criminal cases will lead to custodial or institutional disposals no less than two-thirds of those children and adolescents proceeded with in care cases will receive care orders, usually involving some period of institutional care which, for the majority, will be longer than custodial punishments. Of the remainder, about 15 per cent will be the subject of supervision orders and about 20 per cent of cases which get as far as an interim care order (i.e. enter the courtroom proper) will be allowed to 'lapse' out of statutory jurisdiction or be withdrawn or adjourned *sine die*.

Table 9.1 provides a detailed picture of the position of statutory care orders made via the 1969 Act for City and for England. The significance of care orders '7 (7)' made in criminal proceedings is quite obvious and, as we shall show, the integration of criminal and care proceedings is considerable, through the vehicle of the '7 (7)' order. The annual 'build-up' of all care orders made under the Act and recorded in table 9.1 accounts for just under half of all children in care in England (excluding interim care orders). City had a grand total of 2,000 children in care at the end of 1979. Consistent with the national picture, just under half of these were 'statutory' under the 1969 Act. A similar proportion, over 40 per cent, were received into care voluntarily under Section 1 of the 1948 Children Act (now incorporated into the 1980 Child Care Act). The remainder came into care via various matrimonial proceedings and the assumption of parental rights under Section 2 of the 1948 Act.

TABLE 9.1 CHILDREN WHO CAME INTO CARE IN ENGLAND (12 MONTHS ENDED MARCH 1978) AND CITY (1979) BY AGE AND SEX VIA CHILDREN AND YOUNG PERSONS' ACT 1969.

Legal states of care order	Boys (England)		Boys (City)		Girls (England)		Girls (City)	
Age	0–9	10–17	0–9	10–17	0–9	10–17	0–9	10–17
Neglect, ill-treatment 1(2) (a), (b), (bb)	1 010	356	37	9	823	401	26	9
Moral danger 1(2) (c)	17	39	0	1	14	170	0	1
Beyond parental control 1(2) (d)	64	242	0	8	16	289	0	10
Non-school attendance 1(2) (e)	59	593	0	7	27	477	0	7
Offence/care 1(2) (f)	–	475	–	0	–	110	–	0
Sub-total	(140)	(1 349)	(0)	(16)	(57)	(1 046)	(0)	(18)
Offence/criminal 7(7)	–	3 025	–	62	–	626	–	12
Variation to care order 15(1)	32	247	1	5	10	140	0	4
Total	1 182	4 977	38	92	890	2 213	26	35

Of these 2,000 children and adolescents, some 800 were in residential care (including those on interim care orders usually in observation and assessment centres) and a similar number were with approved foster parents, the remainder being 'placed' with a parent, relative or guardian. This total 'in-care' figure, as one might expect, given City's socio-economic status, is 14 per 1,000 of population, twice the national average. The care total is 25 per cent higher than it was a decade ago, despite the at risk population declining by nearly 2 per cent per year during the same period. It is also worth noting that despite this high figure it is widely recognized locally that the remaining strength of the extended family in the City's inner area and the ability of poor families to cope independently through this network, despite tremendous difficulties, probably keeps this figure down, when compared with many other urban areas in which extended family networks have been more severely disrupted by urban 'renewal'.

In this study, concerned with the statutory care and control of adolescents, we will be limiting our focus, through our sample,[6] to 10–17 year olds processed via the 1969 Act. Further, we have largely restricted our discourse to *status* misdemeanours (see table 9.1) or trouble. In a sense all the primary conditions which produce statutory care proceedings are related to the juvenile status of those taken before the court — in that a care order involving potentially long periods of institutional living ceases automatically with birthdays coinciding with the end of adolescence. Thus, whilst offending is not defined behaviour exclusive to juveniles, the making of a care order which is, within the 10–18 year old bracket, 'indeterminate' is a power given to the juvenile court which has no equivalent in the adult criminal justice system. Moreover Sections 1(2) (c), (d) and (e) owe their very existence to the creation of childhood. By definition, as a juvenile reaches a specific birthday, then he or she can no longer be legally deemed in moral danger, beyond parental control or a 'non-school attender'. It should be noted that the age–sex criteria we illustrate in table 9.1 for England and City are not normally published at all and as a consequence the age and gender 'bias' in the operation of care proceedings is rarely discussed rationally.

In this and the coming chapters we shall offer an analysis of how City social services and City care court select and process adolescents deemed in need of care and control. Before this, we must introduce two issues which we will define and demonstrate to be key social facts. First, as initially revealing as the hidden statistics appear to be, their meaning is far from obvious. The legal status attached to a care order, as shown in table 9.1, is something of a facade. This official label does not necessarily elucidate the real reasons *why* a care order has been sought and granted. The advocates of Justice for Children, with an emphasis on legal rights and judicial decision-making about balancing the 'best interests of the child' and the civil rights and liberties of the parent and or youngster, have made an impressive case against the use of the '7 (7)' care order in particular. Given that these orders are made in criminal proceedings upon the finding of guilt, their severity vis-a-vis the minor criminal records of the young subjects is clearly totally inconsistent with the principles of justice, especially the notion of proportionality. Although not as devastating as some other analyses of the local use of '7, 7' orders, an external assessment for City social services of a sample of 180 of their '7 (7)' care orders showed that 70 per cent were made on juveniles having less than three previous convictions, almost all property offences or police-defined infractions.

However, if it is accepted — as we will demonstrate it should be — that the making of a '7 (7)' order, on the recommendation of a social worker is, from the social service department's point of view, not about punishing him or her for a misdemeanour but intervening as a result of an assessment about the range of needs and problems in the juvenile's life, including sometimes the fact that the youngster's parents don't want their son or daughter at home, then '7 (7)' orders must be seen in a radically different way — as vehicles carrying hidden agendas. This same process often occurs with education care proceedings because the Section 1(2) (e), non-school attendance clause, usually carries cases through the court successfully — as truancy is easy to 'prove'. Indeed if regular non-school attendance were laid against City's 50,000 secondary school children and their repeated, unacceptable absence used also as proof that they were also in need of care and control, as it often is in court, the numbers of adolescents in care would be legion. The number of adolescents in care for non-school attendance is no reflection of the reality of truancy nor are those in care with that legal status attachment there simply because of their refusal to go to school. They are selected for particular reasons.

This 'misuse' of the legislation, for example the '7 (7)' order, should therefore not be seen in terms of vindictive retribution lurking in social workers but the consequence of the adolescent's problems (which as we will see he or she does usually acknowledge), the inadequacy of the community-based child care *system* to cope with and solve these prob-

lems and of course the suitability of the social work judgement to
proceed with statutory intervention.

The social workers' and magistrates' judgements about a youngster's
best interests are partly moral or value judgements since, as the present
legislation itself accepts, such judgements can only be made 'on the
balance of probabilities'. Those of us who debate the efficiency of the
present system of statutory child care should be aware that we too are
trading in moral judgements. This is as true for liberal reformers who
put their faith in legalistic solutions to the dilemmas involved (Morris
et al., 1980) as it is for the social work profession with its own predi-
lections about 'at risk' working-class families.

Once this second issue is accepted — that care proceedings involve
moral judgements — and again we hope to demonstrate the inevitable
recourse to these judgements in statutory child care, it becomes clear
that the present important debate initiated by the Justice for Children
lobby needs to be shifted back in the care process to the point of
referral and not least to what parents and youngsters think and feel
about outside intervention. Once this is done the 'solutions' at present
being offered by this lobby will, we contend, have to be returned to the
drawing-board.

First in this chapter we shall look at the nature of decision-making
involved in a care case 'going all the way' to court. From the cases we
observed it is clear that the highly subjective nature of the law in care
proceedings means that local officials and court 'teams' have to develop
certain operational rules and mechanisms to make the system work
efficiently. In City the style which has developed over the years has
become increasingly routine and increasingly consensual to the extent
that magistrates, defence lawyers and clerks, all potentially officials
who can challenge the local authority's care proceedings, in practice
usually facilitate, occasionally modify, but rarely challenge the cases
the local authority takes to court. In short, all local officials appear to
accept as a general rule that the local authority's use of statutory care
proceedings is indeed 'for the best'. Consequently they off-load the
moral dilemmas and value judgements to be made on to social workers.
This places the social worker in a very powerful position.

MAIN ROUTES TO THE 'CARE COURT'

Care as a last resort

There are many similarities between the way in which potential statutory 'care' cases and criminal cases are sifted and sent on their way to

court. On both 'sides' of juvenile justice, officials use the considerable discretion vested in them by the law. This discretion is mediated by their own agency's ideological and organizational goals. For both types of proceedings, police and social services (and education department) record 'intelligence' about children, presenting it 'against' those they do push in and storing it 'against' those they do not, for future use. The social welfare equivalent of the police machinery being the 'at risk' register, case files and school attendance registers.

However, there are some crucial differences also, for, while non-accidental injury and neglect cases '1(2) (a) and (b)' are increasingly 'steered' by formal procedures, for the other primary conditions the issues are even more subjective and the procedures more ad hoc. First it should be said that 'trouble' between parents and teenage children is normal. The large family case loads carried by area social services teams and voluntary agencies bear witness to this. And even when that trouble cannot be contained within the nuclear family or with the support of the extended family — 'go and stay with your auntie for a few days' — it can often, for working-class families, be sorted out informally with the help of the local welfare agencies.

Indeed the local authority (LA), the local state, through community health officials, social workers, education and 'child guidance' workers, is basically geared up to cope informally and voluntarily with family problems and 'problem families'. In short the goal to *prevent* children and adolescents or parents being taken to the care court is primary, the responsibility through law to take over parental rights, to remove children, is only apparent when routine work fails or when a real crisis or emergency arises. This is borne out by the relatively small number of youngsters who are the subject of care proceedings, compared with the at risk population. Indeed, even of those cases that do go to court, many have been 'held' as voluntary cases. In our sample half of the cases that finally went to court had been 'known' to the department for some time and in half of these cases for over two years. Within our sample, case conferences had led to no further action, place of safety orders had been allowed to lapse, voluntary care measures tried and failed, and in 'genuine' education cases several 'warnings' had been tried prior to 'prosecution'. Whilst such reluctance to initiate proceedings has clearly not been the order of the day with non-accidental injury cases (see Geach, 1980) we should be clear that the 'push-in' is *not* a natural tendency in the professional ideology dominating social welfare, as with the police faced with alleged delinquency.

However, once an LA official (or the police) decides to take a place of safety order with the signed authority of a JP, and calls a case conference of 'interested' local agencies, there is, as we have shown statistically, a strong tendency for the case to go all the way, the exception being a 'genuine' non-school attendance case, which we will deal with shortly. In a sense therefore, when we rule out the highly regulated ill-treatment or neglect cases, the decision to call a case conference or to actually go for care proceedings without one, is made at the district or area social services level by a social worker in consultation with his senior. In retrospect our research did not pay sufficient attention to this point of negotiation and we wish to identify it as an area requiring further investigation. The information we did gain from social workers suggests that, over and above the 'risk' and 'need' factors one would expect them to be concerned with, there were other organizational influences. The lack of availability of voluntary care facilities was clearly relevant. Statutory proceedings are given high priority and so unlock the door to scarce residential resources. And within this constraint of suitable placements, more than one social worker admitted that the availability of places in a 'suitable' observation and assessment centre was a major consideration:

> I [City social worker] would simply not have taken proceedings
> if I'd had to send her to Rampton House. That would have been
> infinitely more destructive than the pressures at home.

Three-quarters of our sample cases went to court after a case conference. Apart from one police place of safety order and the 'genuine' non-school attendance cases, these were all initiated by social services. Once this decision is made, the 'control' of the case moves slightly away from the social worker and his senior. Indeed in a minority of cases the conference decision to go for care was opposed by the social worker. The case conference represents the considered opinion of the local state welfare machinery; it is normally a multi-departmental decision. Thus once the conference decides to go for care proceedings there is very little turning back. The social worker, sometimes partnered by the education welfare officer (EWO), becomes the *key* worker, the representative of the local authority and, as we shall see, for the families involved *is* the local (welfare) state. The exception to this occurs when the case conference can encourage or pressurize the police to prosecute an adolescent for an offence, often very petty, with the aim of, through the social enquiry report (SER), securing a '7 (7)' care order. This decision will be made when the conference feels that a care order would be in the child's best interests but either has insufficient evidence to prove this or wishes to avoid both a messy case and, as we shall see, the dreaded confrontation with the family in the care court. Proving an offence involves less emotive input than 'moral danger' or 'beyond parental control'. This practice is a gross misuse of the relevant legislation and the fact that the correct offence clause '1(2) (f)', which would involve care proceedings and the 'beyond care and control' test, is just not used in City care court must be seen as confirmation of this misuse. However, the reasons for this official deviation are comprehensible and, as we will show in this and the coming chapter, are often reasonable given the difficulties and uncertainties inherent in some situations, though unacceptable in terms of natural justice for children and their parents.

Similarly the case conference initially called for a quite specific reason — for instance a teenage girl found wandering the streets in the early hours, a boy threatening his mother with violence, may also 'dig up' quite diverse 'social needs' or 'serious problems' for the adolescent. Most often and most easily it will 'discover' truancy. It is on these occasions, when this easy primary condition can be made, that a care case for an adolescent will begin to be shaped up as a '1(2) (e)' non-school attendance case and the real agenda hidden. We are thus making a distinction between 'genuine' education cases where truancy is the central reason and those where the legal status '1(2) (e)' is merely a vehicle which fails to describe the real reasons for proceedings.

Shaping up the care case

Once it has been decided by the field social worker and his or her district colleagues that a case will go all the way, the arena shifts from the district office to City's social services headquarters. The key social worker moves with the case, coordinating its passage to court. In consultation with the legal team — a City solicitor, who acts as prosecutor in care proceedings, senior child care officials, one of whom may well have chaired any case conference, and the senior court social worker — the case will begin to be 'shaped up'. Once a case has come this far it is rarely turned back. As one of the legal team put it when asked if he felt that all the proceedings that went to court were appropriate:

Yes, because when we get them they're already solid. There's been a lot of discussion at district.

By 'solid', this person meant genuine. He judged solidity in social work
terms, rather than legal terms. Thus he and some of his colleagues saw
no inconsistency in saying a case was solid and then spelling out the key
task of the legal team as being to decide, through informal discussions
with the district office involved and other agencies, how best to shape
the evidence to fit a particular clause and so satisfy the court. The legal
team accepted:

> We've often got slim cases. A lot of suspicion . . . bits and pieces.
> Here we try to find the safest clause to try for care.

In a city with high truancy rates and high levels of petty delinquency,
the safest clauses will often be '1(2) (e)' and '7 (7)' through the criminal
court. Although making the strongest case with the available evidence is
the legal team's key objective, 'seeking agreement' with the subjects of
the proceedings is potentially as important. This invariably occurs
through the adolescent's solicitor or barrister (all our sample and almost all the observed cases were legally represented). 'Agreement' is,
according to the *Oxford* dictionary, a legal contract or a mutual understanding. When the LA legal team, including the key social worker,
tries to seek agreement it is essentially trying to reach a contract with
the defence. The social worker must also bear this in mind in her
negotiations with the family but she, as we shall see, is aware that
mutual understanding is another matter. In the next chapter we will
show that although most parents and adolescents did accept that there
was a 'problem' which had quite legitimately or at least inevitably
become a matter for the LA, what they regarded as appropriate and
reasonable action remained problematic throughout their passage
through the care process. Hence mutual understanding was not a
realistic objective in most cases and client compliance became the main
goal in shaping up the case. This should be remembered when we focus
upon the 'agreements' routinely announced in the care court.

Seeking agreement about the nature of the legal proceedings and the
anticipated outcome is, in functional terms, vital for the care court to
operate smoothly. City's care court does run smoothly and without
regular drama, conflict and outrage between prosecution and defence.
These are not glib words: consider for a moment the significance for a
parent of having one's child taken away and being implicitly or explicitly
condemned as unreasonable or inadequate. The care court, as we will
shortly show, is a potentially dangerous place for local state officials
who must challenge parents on such emotive issues.

The onerous task of taking a case all the way is thus made infinitely easier if the defence solicitor will agree to the general nature of the LA case. The fact that a high-level of agreement was reached between the legal team and the defence solicitor or barrister in the majority of City cases we observed does not, however, mean that there was necessarily mutual understanding between families and local authority. Nor should it be seen as necessarily a consequence of inadequate legal representation. The defence lawyer in care proceedings is in a very difficult position. He is officially the youngster's representative, yet in practice is often engaged and instructed by the parents (see Morris *et al.*, 1980). Sometimes parents and their children are themselves in conflict. Furthermore the defence lawyer is not above the case. He too accepts the view that care proceedings are normally in the child's best interests. He may wish to challenge various pieces of evidence and negotiate over the likely legal outcome (i.e. care order or supervision order) and the practical outcome (e.g. whether care order will rapidly become 'home on trial') but statistically in City he will rarely challenge the case itself. From City legal team's point of view, it is ideal if these negotiations occur before the court hearing, and so in preparing their case and shaping it up:

> We get on with the back room deals with the solicitor for the child. Some things he'll agree, some he won't. This is where the game begins.

One legal team member, an old hand, felt that defence solicitors were essentially an extension of his team not the defence's:

> He knows the local authority is taking proceedings for the child's sake, yet the parents who got him expect him to get them off, get them home. Sometimes he doesn't know what the hell to do and we just push it. Sometimes he sees the parent's a pig and he must think that the child's better off in care.

The dilemmas faced by the defence solicitors were confirmed in our interviews with several of them. They felt that their role was genuinely perplexing. One lawyer could recall having only two cases in which the parents' and the child's interests really coincided. He actually makes a point of interviewing the youngsters and their parents separately in preparing his case. For another court regular, well known for his forthright defence of juveniles in criminal proceedings, care cases clouded up his goals and ideals. He felt that his role in care proceedings was, in practice, reduced to diplomacy and arbitration: he would explain the kid to the parents, the parents to the kid and the social worker to everyone. He felt the LAs applications were invariably in the child's best interests and so saw his job as persuading parents that proceedings, and usually a care order, was for the best but at the same time he tried to protect their self-esteem, shielding them from the discussion, in open court, of potentially degrading information and generally trying to smooth things out. We observed this to be the case generally in City's care court. It is clearly not an inevitable style of operation but one which has developed locally.

'Shaping up' a case, then, is a complex business and more importantly a crucial stage of the care process, hidden from the courtroom. As we shall see, agreement or compliance is reached in the majority of cases before they reach the substantive care hearing. How they are finally presented, and indeed under which primary condition, is a far more devious business than the statistics imply. Similarly the legal and the practical outcomes are generally known *before* the hearing and indeed transmitted to the family via the social worker or family solicitor. Obviously this is only a general rule: some cases are genuinely contested and others require refereeing. On these occasions the courtroom is really where judgements are made. However, in the majority of cases, the court merely confirms and legitimates that the shaping-up of the case by the legal team is acceptable within the legal framework.

Finally it is important to put a temporal dimension on these out of court negotiations from the initiation of care proceedings to the full hearing. The norm during our period of observation, and confirmed by records' analysis, for a care case to reach a substantive hearing was more than two months. In most cases the adolescent was in residential care on a place of safety or interim care order during this period. This may be convenient for the officials but, as we shall see, was not usually well received by parents and some youngsters.

Education care proceedings

'Genuine' non-school attendance cases, that is those cases where truancy is the real focus rather than the format for pushing through a hidden agenda, are regarded by most education welfare officials, and certainly those who are attached to the LA solicitor to make up the legal team for '1(2) (e)' cases, as products of failed negotiation. For before an education case goes all the way it will have been subjected to numerous promises, threats and 'warning shots' in attempts to 'cool it out'. The formal procedures are such that in every case there will be several attempts to persuade a youngster to return to school or his parents to make him/her do so.

In theory the first formal procedure, after some verbal warnings, is for the EWO to make a home visit and assess whether the bad attendance is due to the parents not carrying out their statutory responsibility to ensure that their child attends school regularly or whether the problem lies with the youngster. If the initial assessment involves deciding against the parents, they are prosecuted under Sections 37 and 39 of the 1944 Education Act. City prosecutes 300–400 parents a year. Ironically, if this fails, the focus is shifted to the adolescent, since in most 'genuine' cases which go to the care court the parents have been previously prosecuted.

Once the focus is upon the adolescent, a new series of warnings will be given, punctuated by a case conference. It is our *impression,* based mainly on our group work cases with girls not going to school and discussions with some education officials, that even for 'genuine' non-school attendance cases stemming from the education department's 'route', two further inputs were at work, which affected whether they went all the way to court and whether they were dealt with by a care order or not. The first concerns the discretion allowed to EWOs about which cases they push in (they have no procedural guidelines) and the power of head teachers. Although we cannot publish the figures for City, the same differential truancy rates between secondary schools noted elsewhere hold (Reynolds, 1976). Yet these rates are not reflected in the cases pushed in. Instead certain head teachers and EWOs produce 'purges', whereby several cases from one school will be proceeded against as a public statement to all its truants in an attempt to reduce non-school attendance throughout a particular year band. Just as the police prosecutions departments knew of sub-divisional inconsistencies, the education legal team were aware that two or three schools produced a disproportionate number of prosecutions and proceedings, but all felt obliged to accept this without comment. These cases would often be dealt with by making a supervision order.

The second undeclared input concerns the 'discovery' of further problems about adolescents during the warning and cajoling sequence. This process usually involves the EWO during his home visits and discussions with the school being told or imputing that the adolescent, as

well as being a truant, is also delinquent, 'cheeky', 'truculent' or uncooperative with teachers or parents. If the formula, 'truancy plus
further problems' is 'discovered' and, particularly if the subject is
female, there is a strong tendency for a case conference to be called and
the agenda formally extended. We can see the consequences of this
process when we look at the written evidence presented to the court,
which we will illustrate in the next section. 'Genuine' non-school
attendance cases then usually only go all the way *and* include a care
order recommendation if they fit the 'truancy plus' formula. Logistically
they *must* do so, not simply to prove an adolescent is beyond care and
control, but because if non-school attendance — say at a rate of 40 per
cent absence per term for a child — was to become the sole issue then
the push-in would be immense and an official 'crisis' about City schooling precipitated. All the officials 'playing the game' know this — but
they obviously don't say so. It is not in their interests to publicly admit
that 'we give up with the final-year kids and concentrate on the third
year' or that once a case has been through court the chances of any
'decent' City secondary school taking the youngster involved on to
their rolls is minimal.

THE STAGING OF WELFARE JUSTICE

Courtroom communication

Two or three afternoons a week, number 2 court, which has bristled all
morning with criminal cases, becomes a quieter and more measured
tribunal. Each afternoon session will see between five and ten cases
listed. Up to half the list will be swiftly dealt with, involving the making
or remaking of an interim care order. Perhaps a sulky teenager will
enter next and sit through the 20 minutes it takes for a full care order
to be made. Then the adolescent non-school attender will be ushered in,
his case being followed by a more dramatic case of ill-treatment to a
five year old. This diverse pattern of cases was typical of most sessions
and illustrates the wide and detailed knowledge of child care that the
court implicitly expects magistrates to make judgements on. The main
exception to this pattern was the monthly session to deal exclusively
with education proceedings when non-school attenders queue to stand
before the magistrates, who themselves, not insignificantly, are often
head teachers taking an afternoon off school!
    There are two further remarkable features of the care courts, which

distinguish them from other proceedings. First, rather than communication being directed by the clerk on behalf of the magistrates, the proceedings are directed by the prosecution solicitor on behalf of the local authority and since, as we have implied, he has already usually reached a level of agreement with the defence solicitors, the flow of communication is basically cross-court. Second, the reading material, the piles of documents, which the onlooker never gains sight of, is the medium for the communication of key evidence and recommendation. This evidence is read in silence and not much discussed in open court. 'Due process' is thus partly absent from the courtroom discourse, being substituted by justice being eventually merely said to be done or alternatively justice simply being read to be done. These modes of communication flow from the fact that cases are already in a negotiated or agreed form and from the ethos shared by all court officials – an ethos that accepts, in general, that the local authority brings cases to court only when it is necessary and consistent with what is right for the child or adolescent, or at very least with what is expected by society.

The key official in the courtroom, therefore, is the prosecution solicitor representing the local authority and his most important assistant is the fieldwork social worker – and sometimes the EWO. The clerks in City's care court generally keep a low profile. They set the scene for each case and then hand over the floor to the LA solicitor, intervening only when confusion or 'difficulty' occurs, when precedural rules not normally manipulated are clearly breached, or when a case, or part of it, is genuinely contested:

CLERK: It would appear that the legal aid forms have been lost. In the circumstances I suggest that rather than adjourn the case your worships grant Mr Grieves [solicitor] legal aid and so allow the case to continue.

MAGISTRATE: We can do this?

CLERK: It is in your powers to do so.

And where a procedural rule is breached:

CLERK: These reports are not evidence Mr Edwards [social worker]. I hope you are going to produce some evidence on the 15th.

The clerks also encouraged certain operational and informal rules. Whilst not as clearly visible as the rules in criminal proceedings, certain customs were observed. For example, a clerk advised his magistrates *not* to make a warrant for a youth who had failed to turn up in court but issue a warning that should the youth fail to turn up next time then a warrant would be made. This 'softly, softly' approach is, we shall see, consistent with 'seeking agreement' and avoiding unnecessary confrontations.

The magistrates' role in City care court was also more subdued and even peripheral compared with criminal proceedings. There are many reasons for this and some exceptions to it. Obviously the pre-arranged nature of much of the work is a crucial factor, as is the lay status of magistrates, emphasized in such a complex and esoteric arena typified by 'expert' witnesses and lengthy jargonized reports. Most magistrates appeared to have the self-poise to accept this, intervening only when they really saw reason to do so. A few magistrates found this enforced passivity threatening and clearly in our view deliberately asserted themselves from time to time to satisfy their own needs. However, there were some cases we observed which needed a neutral referee and on these occasions the bench would become active. Finally the court actually expected the magistrates to make certain moral judgements and statements about the past and future behaviour of adolescents and parents.

The other court officials, particularly the lawyers, were aware that they, rather than the magistrates, were running the show, and so would go out of their way to give the bench a symbolic status rather like that given to the monarchy. Court officials would repeatedly ask witnesses, who knew the ropes anyway, to 'address the magistrates'. Lawyers would quite excessively seek 'permission' to present evidence or reports from the bench. Proceedings would be punctuated with 'If your worships would kindly look at Document C', 'would bear with me a second' — and so on.

If magistrates are less prominent in care proceedings than in criminal proceedings the social workers ascended in prominence. Social workers who did not routinely accompany their SERs in criminal proceedings, and even less often addressed the court, were invariably present in care proceedings. Indeed during our observation period not only were the social workers always present but more often than not so were their seniors. Although only occasionally called upon to give extensive 'verbals' and only rarely seriously cross-examined, the social worker's

presence in the witness box and as the presenter of much documentation gave him/her the status of a key official.

Before moving on to the generalizable aspects of City care court, we
must discuss one more goal shared by all officials, a goal learnt from
bitter experience and reinforced by the same. This goal was to at all
costs try to avoid one type of communication – the *'dreaded performance'*. Despite the apparent calm, care proceedings are tense. The
concerted efforts to get everything agreed before the appointed hour,
the fact that the proceedings invariably start late and the reluctance of
the officials to get involved in any depth of discussion with either children or parents must, in part, be seen on this backcloth of tension. The
experts, the regulars, particularly the lawyers, the social services court
officers, the clerks and the relatively small number of magistrates who
sit in care proceedings, all feel this tension. They feel it because they
have experienced the ugly or embarrassing moments when stage
management has collapsed and unscripted and uncensored performances have come from the centre of the stage. Such incidents may involve
only bitter comments, usually by parents: 'The whole thing's ridicu-
lous', or 'These reports are definitely not true'. However, they may en-
tail more articulate or sustained criticisms. The father who lost his
temper with the court performance on several occasions and accused a
probation officer of lying got the court into some real difficulty. The
final straw was when the magistrate at the conclusion of the case (a care
order being made) asked the boy to comment. The boy stared him in
the eye, tapped his finger to his own head and retorted:

Why should I tell you, you think I'm thick.

The court quietly tries to forget such incidents. The clerk, between
cases, tries to project the difficulty back to the family:

CLERK: You can see where he gets it from, sir.
MAGISTRATE: Yes, it's not surprising when you see the father.

Yet, despite attempts to smooth over the aftermath of an unscripted
performance, care court officials are affected. Magistrates we spoke to
admitted they didn't like sitting in care proceedings because of the
responsibility and significance of the decisions. Ushers recall horrific
events where violence has broken out or pandemonium set in. No one

likes the tearful angry mother crashing out of the wrong door shouting: 'You fuckin' bastards, what do you care?'

The dreaded performances are rare but not so rare that the last one is forgotten. The desire to avoid a case 'blowing out' in open court, to avoid the unnecessary washing of dirty linen or slinging of mud is a major incentive for all officials, not least defence lawyers, to 'seek agreement' and predict and even announce the likely outcome of proceedings *before* the hearing takes place and as we have said 'hide' the real agenda usually in written reports.

The analysis which follows is based on the contention that there is a spectrum of outcome predictability in care cases and that in City care courts the majority of cases which enter the courtroom are 'water-tight' and the outcome almost totally predictable in favour of the local authority. Next comes another large band of cases where the final outcome will be in favour of the LA but where the exact details of either the evidence or the disposal (e.g. care order or supervision order or adjourned *sine die*) are still to be negotiated. Finally, there are a small number of cases that are genuinely contested and which need judging in the real sense. None of our sample cases and very few of the observed cases were contested and so we will limit our analysis to the first two overlapping categories which represent the 'everyday' reality of City care proceedings.

Announced agreements

The invariably late start for City's care proceedings, scheduled for 2 p.m., is not a symptom of lunchtime drinking; key officials arrive well before 2 p.m. In a sense the proceedings start early, as the officials will be seen huddled together or pacing around industriously putting the final touches to their scripts for the 'public' performance. Indeed, so crucial are these last-minute touches that interruptions such as the mere arrival of the magistrates are rejected:

USHER (*to group of officials standing in courtroom*): The Newtons have arrived by the way.

L.A. PROSECUTOR (*to clerk*): Who's on the bench today?

CLERK (*shrugging*): Don't know.

USHER (*returning through magistrates' door*): Are you ready, Mr Kelvin?

CHORUS: No.

The usher backs out and is heard enticing the magistrates back into their retiring room with soothing noises 'Won't be long, now' etc.

Once proceedings begin and interims have been routinely dealt with, the clerk will introduce the first substantive hearing, the style of the day will quickly be confirmed either by the clerk himself:

> CLERK: I believe in this case a certain course of action has been agreed. Is this right?

or by the LA solicitor who early in a case, as with 'Tricia' and her non-school attendance, will sketch out the details of a previously agreed outcome:

> L.A. PROSECUTOR: The local authority in this particular case thinks that a supervision order is adequate ... I hasten to say that as far as my friend [defence solicitor] and I are concerned these are all agreed documents ... Mr Eaves (social worker) will present reports.

Later the defence announces:

> DEFENCE SOLICITOR: There is no objection to an order being made.

After the magistrates have 'agreed the primary condition' the SER is presented and read by the officials, but not by Tricia or her parents. The LA solicitor points out that the family have welcomed social work assistance and then with the report in his hand makes it do the work of confirming the family's compliance:

> L.A. PROSECUTOR: Since Tricia has been in care ... parents now more frank with each other ... won't leave things to fester now ... realize their mistakes ... and will take steps to avoid it again ... parents want her home ... If the court agrees, this is what will happen ... Tricia herself realizes ... if she complies ... if she goes to school ... she will have a happier home life.

Or again, for an adolescent girl deemed beyond care and control, the LA solicitor stresses that:

L.A. PROSECUTOR: The case is agreed by those representing Marie. On that basis I will put the reports before you ... that seems the most civilized way of doing things.

This prior agreement had also allowed the appearance of witnesses to be waived. No reports were shown to the mother or Marie and after reading the evidence, finding the primary condition proven and reading the SER, the bench declined to talk to the social worker as it was 'not necessary' and turned to look at the girl's solicitor. He confirmed compliance:

DEFENCE SOLICITOR: The reports are there. The content is quite clear. On behalf of Marie herself, I do not oppose the order.

The magistrates then looked at Marie:

MAGISTRATE: Stand up please. We are making an order placing you in the care of the local authority. This means. ...

The case was over without the family's problem being discussed in open court. Such announced agreements, and thus rapidly concluded hearings, dominated care proceedings during our observation period. We will show in the next chapter that what the court announced as an agreement was for parents and children an acceptance of the legal outcome rather more often than the coming together of all parties in mutual understanding. Even cases in which the relationships between the social worker and both parents and child were excellent the *manner* in which intervention occurred, help given or control exerted, still upset or angered families. One function of the defence solicitor is clearly to air these criticisms as well as to announce agreement:

DEFENCE SOLICITOR: We want to work hand in hand with the local authority and, whilst we would have preferred *voluntary* reception into care, Mrs Mount, although she dearly wants Carol back, will leave it in the hands of Mr Eccles [social worker], whose judgement she respects.

Such a statement takes us into the overlap on our spectrum, as we move on to deal with those cases in which, although some agreement has been reached before the substantive hearing, it is not complete and indeed may never be. However, despite this, the parents and/or adolescent accept — that is defer to the advice of social workers — or more usually defence lawyer, that the case will be proven anyway and that things would be made worse if they were obstructive or difficult. In these cases there is a contest of sorts, although it is within a framework of inevitability. For the defence it is a matter of gaining dignity or refuting stigma, of challenging particulars and getting informal agreements about the practicalities of the outcome, particularly when a care order will be made. Finally, all this must be done very carefully as this range of cases is more likely to involve parental anger and resentment and therefore the possibility of the 'dreaded performance'.

Negotiated outcomes and ritual resistance

The range of cases we have in mind under this heading are still essentially 'agreed' in that outcome predictability is high. A supervision order, rather than a care order, may already have been conceded by the local authority prior to the substantive hearing. However the defence solicitor would still like it known, and asks the court to confirm, that his young client does not have a criminal record and so:

> DEFENCE SOLICITOR: Supervision seems a sensible application. Clearly this is not a case to warrant a care order . . . which we would oppose, but yes, it may well warrant a supervision order and Mr Welt would welcome some support.

There are, then, cases which arguably could have been 'voluntary' and the defence tries to make this point, thereby destigmatizing and normalizing the family. And if a care order is 'inevitable' but the family can still be seen as blameless, the defence lawyer will still negotiate on this subjective level.

Less impressive representation occurred as often, however, with defence lawyers going through the motions by offering ritual resistance to the local authority cases. The very same sign language which we noted in criminal proceedings was sometimes used. Thus, in the case of a care order being asked for 'against' an adolescent girl, the defence lawyer sends his double message, informing the court that he privately accepts the prosecution case:

DEFENCE SOLICITOR: I do have instructions from my client that she opposes the application so I do so.

Yet this lawyer did not in practice really do so and indeed, given the nature of the case, he would have startled the court had he so done.

Where a care order is 'inevitable', negotiations focus upon agreeing the practical consequences of this outcome. These deals may be made just before a subject enters, as with the solicitor who addresses the court before his client comes in, saying that he will agree to a care order if it is informally agreed in court by the local authority that the boy will be allowed home to live with his brother and sister-in-law. Clearly such deals are strictly outside the court's jurisdiction but when such promises will seal the case and obtain agreement or compliance such unofficial bargains will be struck, the onus being on the social worker to carry them through:

GIRL (*on interim order*): I only want to know if I'll be going home on the 21st.

MAGISTRATE: Well, it really depends on the magistrates on the day.

CLERK (*quickly intervening*): I think everybody expects you to go home . . . I'm sure. . . .

These unofficial concessions (for strictly the details of a care order are made post-hearing by a case conference on behalf of the local authority) were regularly sought by the defence and usually 'granted' by the court — all officials being aware of the need to give the defence lawyer some 'reward' or reassurance to help him keep his party sweet or at least less bitter and more prepared, the worry of the unknown having been removed, to comply with the legal outcome and not turn in a 'dreaded performance'.

No contest

The fact that so few care cases are fully contested should not be seen simply as criticism of the legal profession. As we have shown, the defence lawyer has a problematic role and status in care proceedings. Furthermore, without seeking independent 'expert' evidence, for instance by having an independent SER prepared, the defence lawyer obviously has some difficulty arguing against the local authority case.

The 'prosecution' for one case, will often present reports from social worker, residential establishment, health visitor, school and educational psychologists. Each of these 'experts' is also capable of responding to verbal questions about written judgements with further jargon. A father questioning the social worker about his daughter's difficulties can be told:

SOCIAL WORKER: Jane is a disturbed child with a range of behaviour problems.

The education psychologist will counter a point with:

PSYCHOLOGIST: Well, the distraction tests would seem to indicate that he. ...

The experts are not easy to challenge and the LA solicitor can, if necessary, usually build up his expert witness:

L.A. PROSECUTOR: Will you tell the court how long you have been a social worker?

SOCIAL WORKER: Five years.

L.A. SOLICITOR: And is it correct that before that you were a house father in a community home for two years?

SOCIAL WORKER: It is.

Most important of all, however, is the subjective belief that the court team shares — that cases do not come all the way for nothing and particularly that adolescents stand before them because either they or their parents, or both, are in some way responsible for the proceedings having had to be initiated. This leads in practice to the primary clause proving the secondary. This is classically illustrated with non-school attendance, when the school system, the limited choice available, the lack of special facilities, are never on the courts' agenda — only the family is blamed. Parents are in an invidious position. If they admit that they have tried unsuccessfully to get their child to school, the child is in need of care and control which the parent has been unable to exercise. If they claim that they haven't yet tried as hard as they might to get the child to school then, given the previous warnings they have had, the child is in need of care and control since the parent has been negligent or unwilling to exercise adequate control. A haggard, lone parent is quizzed:

> L.A. SOLICITOR: Do you think you have tried to get Sharon to go to school?
>
> MOTHER: Well ... with problems with school uniform ... when you've got seven children ... it gets difficult.
>
> L.A. SOLICITOR: So, despite your attempts to get her to school, you have not succeeded. You have done your best to get her to school, haven't you?
>
> MOTHER: You can't blame her for fifteen years for not doing what I tell her. When I was in hospital Sharon did everything.

Finally we should make the point that the dominant 'seeking agreement' style of City court tends to badly confuse 'due process'. We were never able to identify a consistent procedural approach in the care court. On many occasions evidence was not properly presented; the distinction between statements of evidence and the presentation of reports was blurred and the division of the proceedings between finding the primary and secondary conditions satisfied was, for the onlooker if not the officials, often totally absent. On one occasion, for example, the senior magistrate announced:

> The order's made but we'd still like to see the report.

We gained the impression that the court officials themselves were not always clear as to what the correct procedural rules were and thus the judicial style of proceedings varied from session to session.

JUDGING FAMILIES

Occasional lectures

Care proceedings are overtly and necessarily concerned with making moral judgements about parents and children. Once the principle of state intervention in the family and 'preventative' intervention has become legitimated, the judgemental nature of care proceedings becomes inevitable. The recognition of this is clear in the statutory instructions to the magistrates that they should decide whether the local state should take over parental rights or supervise child-rearing 'on the balance of probabilities' that it would be in the child's best interests. On occasions this is a very difficult and painful task although most often, as we have shown, the decision is already taken in the agreed package passed through the court having been delegated to the social worker.

Court officials will also make subjective and moral judgements about cases, as do researchers sitting at the back. We cannot help having such feelings. However, in care proceedings there is something of an expectation that in certain cases magistrates will express opinions about culpability. Very often these expectations are related to the future rather than the past. The bench will be 'cued', if necessary by the clerk or the prosecution. Non-school attenders are the most likely recipients:

> I would be grateful if your worships would emphasize to Tony the consequences which will follow if he does not attend school regularly.

Non-school attendance cases provoke the most comment from the magistrates and, in keeping with our findings in criminal proceedings, take the form of a lecture about the virtues of education for getting on and settling down, the focus being invariably on the child and the family. Speaking generally about adolescents in care proceedings a well-seasoned usher whispered to one of us sagely:

> Nearly all our customers hate school. It's one of the requirements.

Hating school, however, cuts no ice with the court. In keeping with the numerous attempts to get a juvenile back to school without a care order magistrates would, when using the supervision order or adjournment *sine die,* invariably fire the final 'final warning':

> MAGISTRATE: With a care order you can be taken ... to a boarding school! No doubt you have your own reasons for not going to school ... if you don't complete your education, you won't be able to get a proper job ... buy clothes, go away on holiday. You may be unhappy and have your own little reasons and you can discuss these

> with your parents. A lot of people in this room
> don't like going to work and would rather stay
> at home and look after their gardens but they
> have to. . . .

And for boys a similar lecture would be given, with references to expectations of manhood:

> MAGISTRATE: Do you want an apprenticeship . . . I've got lots
> of lads who come to me [as employer]. If you
> don't go to school you get into trouble and end
> up in detention centre or Borstal. If you ignore
> your mates, stay out of trouble then you can
> get a good job . . . and buy . . . and then get a
> motor bike.

After such lectures the supervision order has to be sold carefully, especially for girls where 'social need' has been implied by the written evidence:

> MAGISTRATE: I don't want you to see the social worker as a
> school teacher or a headmaster. He's there to
> help you . . . you must help your mother . . .
> you're a young lady . . . we would like to see
> you having a good job.

If the court has to be cruel to be kind it doesn't like being misunderstood. At an interim hearing the local authority announced that in another month, at the substantive hearing, it would be asking for a supervision order but in the meantime wanted Tricia to remain in care to catch up on her education. The father pointed out that his daughter had been in care for two months already:

> FATHER: Surely that's punishment enough.

The senior magistrate was shocked:

> SENIOR MAGISTRATE: Mr Kole. This is *not* to be considered a
> punishment. No, it's not a punishment. She's
> receiving *care* from the local authority.

On another occasion, after receiving his lecture, a boy was asked to leave the court while the mother was made to stand before the bench.

It had already been established that the woman went to work at 6 a.m. and that that this was her 'excuse' for her son not going to school. The mother was told:

MAGISTRATE: You selfishly have been putting your money before your son . . . I have never come across a life of such sheer selfishness . . . leaving an 11 year old boy to feed and clothe himself [*continues and finishes*] . . . Anyway . . . you . . . start thinking of looking after your boy or you could lose all your family . . . and make sure you cooperate with the social services.

Non-school attendance cases, then, produced the harshest moral judgements although all the 'status' clauses, because they involve dealing with adolescents and therefore culpability, might receive warnings and advice about the necessity of rapidly becoming a model teenager:

MAGISTRATES: This lady sitting next to me and I have great powers . . . from now on you do as the gentleman at the back says . . . if you make me use these powers, you'll really jump.

You and your mother will have the guidance and assistance of a supervising officer. You must obey him, you must obey your mother and you must keep good hours.

These verbal demands are, we must emphasize, expected of the bench, for if they do not make them, the clerk will often make the 'reinforcement' himself or the LA solicitor will ask for a stern warning.

Overall, however, care proceedings produced much less verbal comment from the bench. Particularly when full care orders were made, and this is in the majority of cases, we should emphasize that court officials made little verbal 'judgement'. Indeed the reluctance of magistrates to get involved in the moral, ethical and cultural machinations connected with 'status' care proceedings was considerable. We observed several sessions in which they would make no comments whatsoever, except to utter the legally required phrases, as several cases passed before them. 'Silence' is obviously hard to illustrate and we can therefore only emphasize the point.

Court officials in City clearly preferred not to have to face squarely the moral dilemmas inherent in their function. They preferred not to disturb the hornets' nest. They welcomed the tip-off from the LA solicitor, who points out before a case enters that the girl's defence lawyer has no objections to a care order being made but notes:

> L.A. PROSECUTOR: The court is placed in an embarrassing situation because the parents do ... so rather than embarrass the girl I've agreed with my learned friend to make this known to you now.

In fact the embarrassment to be avoided was the court's. Magistrates learn not to dig into the unknown or the unrecorded. They prefer to be able to make positive comments or, as they did routinely, show kindness to small children, victims of adults, or to parents trying their very best but simply not having the equipment to cope.

It would be foolish to expect care proceedings to operate without moral judgements. The issue must be — as it is for criminal proceedings — with what ideological and theoretical constructs are such judgements made? In City's care proceedings the crucial judgements about child-rearing, culpability and the causes of the problem came from the social services and education officials and predominantly in written form. Because of this mode of communication and because so much of it was 'agreed' by the defence solicitor or not resisted by parents or child, even if they saw the reports, 'judging families' was a very clandestine business.

Written judgements

We shall deal here with written reports, namely SERs, only in terms of locating their function in the staging of welfare justice. From this perspective our analysis of reports relating to our sample cases indicates two key qualities — they were *persuasive* and they were predominantly *family focused.*

The reports we analysed were usually over 400 words long, complex and, in terms of their intended impact upon the magistrates, seemed, and clearly were, highly persuasive. The social workers we interviewed confirmed that their care reports were indeed 'superior' pieces of work in terms of the time and effort they took compared with SERs for criminal proceedings. Furthermore, most sample cases had 'files' on them and/or case conference material available with which to embellish reports. The amount of contact time between the subject family and the report writer was also greater than for routine criminal reports. This greater range and 'quality' of material plus the 'key worker' status of the social worker encouraged authoritative report writing. The 'experts' in these reports have no intention, as in criminal cases, of leaving key decisions to the lay bench. The reports spell out the dangers, the grave risks if a care order is not made:

> In the light of the most recent events plus both parents requesting a care order I . . . request . . . to grant a care order. I am quite willing to rehabilitate Elaine 'home on trial' but with the care order the framework will be there so that she can be returned to care whenever the parents find they cannot cope and Elaine herself will then not feel she has to run away to get away from the stress in the home.

Or for another girl the 'packaged' reports conclude:

> When the strands of Diane's record of stealing, her school record and her relationship with Mr X are put together, the general picture is of a girl who has lacked an overall, consistent discipline for some time.

And since the parents 'tolerate behaviour within the family which is considered unacceptable by wider society' a care order is required.

Which bench will argue, which court will take the chance of taking risks with adolescent girls billed, as these two were, in the first case as 'aggressive, disobedient . . . going missing, sleeping rough' and in the second as sexually permissive 'immature physically and socially and educationally functioning at a very low level'?

The persuasiveness of care reports was almost always built up around the deviant behaviour of either the adolescents, their parents, or both. After the usual preliminaries about 'three-bedroom council houses', 'father unemployed', 'a run down area', the focus of the social need was narrow and turned upon family disfunction:

> Mr P is a very dominant and demanding person in the home though when Julie is in care he wishes to be seen as caring and indeed presents as paternal. . . . Mrs P presents as totally dominated . . . giving in to any demands for the sake of peace.

Tends to stick very much to his mother's apron strings and is very rarely far from her side ... it is obvious that the split in his parent's marriage left him feeling rather insecure and a little confused. His clinging behaviour towards his mother may be a symptom of this and is certainly not very healthy for a young man in his teens.

It would be all too easy to launch into detailed attacks upon the nature of the social enquiry reports we analysed. That has been done elsewhere and in a more appropriate setting (Bean, 1975). However, given the state of social science knowledge and the fact that care reports are inevitably dealing in value judgements, we will restrict ourselves to some brief general comments. Clearly these written judgements are contentious. First, they are highly selective and rapidly constructed cameos latching on to small parts of a family's history. As we shall see in the next chapter, although not always seen by the families involved, when they are read they are often privately challenged, rather than publicly in open court, by parents. Second, and in this they share the essential criticism of the whole juvenile justice system which is the concern of this book, they are extremely narrowly focused, rarely locating the 'problem' in a social structural framework.

Yet such reports are, in a sense, not intended to tell it how it is. They are designed to produce results, to get a desired outcome. They very often deal with the 'hidden agenda', the real issues as the social worker sees them which are not discussed in open court. Nor is the bench going to ask Mr Goyle if he agrees with the social worker's written contention that:

He keeps his children in night clothes in the bedroom for days when they get on his nerves.

or read out aloud, the social worker's opinion that the youth before them:

Has emerged as a very devious boy who will neither accept nor recognize any form of authority. He has a total contempt of any attempt by adults to guide or advise him.

It will, if possible, accept the case on the non-school attendance billing it comes to court with.

The care court then is not keen to challenge these written judgements. They are complex, highly personal and full of explosive judgements about both children and parents. The reluctance of City court officials to show reports to parents (adolescents hardly ever see them), except if procedural rules really require it, is understandable, though not necessarily acceptable in the circumstances. The court officials *are persuaded* they would rather not check up that:

> She comes over as a girl . . . in times of stress [who] is totally out of control of her emotions.

We are not suggesting here that these written judgements are wildly inaccurate – our judgement is no better than the social workers' – but they are narrowly focused and they are constructed 'to get the order' on the grounds that this is for the best. The real reasons for statutory intervention, then, are more likely to be found in these typed pages than spoken in court or identified by the legal status of a particular case. The reasons why a case 'goes all the way' cannot be fully comprehended without analysis of these written judgements. They stir in the component parts or come up with a care formula which usually produces a compelling picture about what's best for the young subject.

AFTER COURT

The care passage is complex and becomes increasingly so after the substantive hearing, with a further fanning out of routes. What is clear is that, with the exception of non-school attendance cases (disposed in recent years by about 30 per cent receiving supervision orders, 40 per cent care orders and 30 per cent adjourned or withdrawn), it is unlikely that intervention will cease immediately. For the other 'status' clauses, including those hidden via '7 (7)' orders, the vast majority of cases will end in care orders, with about 15 per cent involving supervision orders.

Of our 21 cases, two-thirds received care orders, four supervision orders and three adjournments *sine die*. Of the 14 who received care orders nine went initially or returned to observation and assessment centres, two were placed with relatives and three almost immediately were allowed 'home on trial'. Three months later the longer-term pattern had emerged with five of the residential subjects being allowed home on trial by case conference decisions and the other four going to community school. This sample is too small to reflect anything significant outside the City system. The relatively high number of adolescents allowed home after being through the care court is partly a reflection of the non-school attendance cases. However, for other clauses, a residential period, certainly for a couple of months before the substantive hearing, and again, for a reducing number, a period between two months and over a year is likely after the order is made.

The 'home on trial' tendency in our '1(2) (a), (c) and (d)' sample concerns the practical effects of the residential period of over two months, prior to the care order being made. In practice the interim orders acted as a 'cooling-down' period, in which either a particular crisis passed or a potential solution was worked out. We will illustrate such a process in the case studies in chapter 12. Those cases in which the adolescent went to community school will obviously involve a much longer in-care period, likely to be ended, according to the accounts of social workers, not by resolution of the 'difficulty' but by the adolescent coming to a particular birthday — often 16 for cases with moral danger, lack of parental control or truancy ingredients. Although 16 seems to be the key landmark in our sample, nationally the other anniversary of significance appears to be 18. It is significant that twice as many care orders in England and Wales simply lapse with the attainment of the 'maximum age' than are purposefully discharged by social services departments.

We will return to these issues in our final chapter but suffice it to say now that there are clear policy implications involved, whereby many 'status' adolescent cases can be 'resolved' within the three months *before* the substantive hearing and some of the remainder are merely managed in residential care, awaiting the day when the status condition rather than the defined 'problem' disappears.

DISCUSSION

In order to deal with the production of welfare justice as a sequential series of official decisions, that is as care and control is received by those processed, we have had to make certain assertions that we have not yet demonstrated empirically. First, we have claimed that the legal status of a care order or care proceedings is often only a partial representation of the actual reasons for state intervention being sought. The reality of this hidden agenda flows from our second assertion: that care proceedings involving adolescents are often concerned with knotty problems which are not easily resolved and which necessitate welfare officials making moral judgements about problem management in terms of choosing between the lesser of several evils.

City's care court, as we have demonstrated, copes with these moral dilemmas by simply sitting tight and steering cases through with minimal interference. City clerks, defence lawyers and magistrates baulk at delving into those cases pushed into court by case conference and social work decisions, preferring to adopt a passive role and merely rubber-stamping requests for care and supervision orders, in the belief that social workers normally act in the adolescent's best interests. Hence, once a case enters the legal arena, it tends to go all the way and receive a formal order.

If our analysis is correct, then clearly social workers can end up abusing the civil and legal rights of working-class families. We have no doubt at all that, from time to time, this does happen. Yet this is not our central point. On the contrary, given the expectations, yet permissive nature, of the present legislation and the passivity of the other key workers, the responsibilities placed upon social workers, using crude tools and limited resources which are available to them, seems a recipe for official misconduct and mismanagement.

In chapter 11 we shall consider the social worker's perspective on these matters. However, first we must look at the receiving of welfare justice and statutory care and control. In so doing, we will also be able to begin to lay out the evidence on which the assertions made in this chapter rest.

10

Receiving Welfare Justice

INTRODUCTION

Perhaps the most striking characteristic of the juvenile justice system is the extent to which the issue of non-school attendance pervades both criminal and care proceedings. Although it is much more explicit in care proceedings, it remains, as in criminal proceedings, an item which is always open to consideration by the magistrates and is often dealt with as being at least as important as the formal criteria for the proceedings.

Almost half of our sample of 14 girls and seven boys subject to care proceedings were formally proceeded against under Section 1(2) (e) of the 1969 Act and, while the rest of the youngsters were formally proceeded against under other criteria set out in Section 1(2), for many of them, education was also on the agenda. Hence in many of the cases in which the youngsters were proceeded against under another condition, their poor school attendance merely underscored their need for care and control and reinforced the local authority's case 'against' them.

The key variables which determine how their passage through care proceedings is perceived by adolescents and their parents are:

(1) The extent to which they acknowledge or accept that there is a 'problem' for which they require some kind of outside help or assistance.
(2) The extent to which they consent to any intervention or involvement.
(3) The form which such intervention takes.
(4) The manner in which it is carried out.
(5) The personality of the keyworkers. In particular, that of the social worker.

The dynamic inter-relationship of these variables determined the adolescents' and parents' comprehension of and satisfaction with care proceedings.

192

Education care proceedings were fundamentally differentiated from the other criteria for care proceedings by the fact that most parents and many of their children in our sample did not accept that non-school attendance was a serious problem which required the kind of statutory intervention which occurred. While most of the juveniles thought that their non-school attendance would eventually cause some response from the education authorities, neither they nor their parents voluntarily consented to such intervention and they were generally dissatisfied with the form that it took and the manner in which it was carried out. By contrast, many of the adolescents and parents subject to care proceedings, other than for genuine non-school attendance, did acknowledge that they had some kind of problem and they did consent, albeit reluctantly, to local authority involvement. In lacking this element of consent, education care proceedings were seen as essentially coercive and even perceived as unsolicited state intervention. For these youngsters formally subject to education care proceedings, their passage through the care process was usually different from those subject to other care criteria. Many of the adolescents in this latter group were placed on interim care orders for anything from one to three months and stayed in a residential unit, whilst those genuinely subject to the education condition tended to remain at home until summonsed to appear before the court for their case to be heard. If they were then placed in care, it was usually their first contact with the formal residential care system, rather than just another, if major, hurdle to be crossed, as was often the case with many of the other adolescents subject to care proceedings.

The sample

The average size of the families in our sample was seven, including parents. Half of the families were headed by a single parent, most often the mother. When the parents were still together, several fathers were unemployed and, in these cases, the mother often worked part-time and a few worked full-time. If the family was headed by a single parent, it was invariably dependent on supplementary benefit for financial support. Over half of the youngsters and their parents acknowledged that they had serious disagreements with each other and virtually all the girls said that their relationship with one or both parents was a constant source of acrimonious rows and much aggravation. Whilst rows are a normal characteristic of adolescent—parent relationships, the rowing which occurred in our sample cases was of a more serious nature and was causing both the adolescents and their parents a lot of worry and ill-feeling. The parents in the care sample, in contrast with those in the 'criminal' sample, did not feel that they had 'got to the bottom', of what was bothering their child and what was the central 'problem' that had contributed to care proceedings. Several admitted that they had difficulty in understanding and communicating with their daughters and felt that they could not 'fathom them out', or thought them 'very deep'. One mother even thought her daughter 'sick':

> She's sick, she knows she is . . . she doesn't like men [father, god-father or social worker] . . . she gets on all right with lads . . . she has no respect for authority . . . we've brought her home drunk at 12.30 at night. She needs help. She needs a psychiatrist.

The lack of rapport between mother and daughter meant that some mothers were dependent on their daughters' friends, and even the court itself, for knowledge about her difficulties:

> Found out from the other kids that she was bullied at school. I've been asking about special school for about a year but they [education welfare] were no help. The woman just said she's got to go to school. . . .

> She wouldn't tell me about school. . . . very silent . . . best to talk to strangers. It wasn't till we went to court that I got to know she was being called smelly and the girls were waiting for her at the bus stop.

Half of the youngsters' sample and a third of the parents had no previous dealings with a court before and, therefore, did not really know what to expect. Others had picked up impressions from other members of the family or from friends and a few had direct experience of juvenile court, mostly as a result of criminal proceedings. By contrast, though most of these families had previous dealings with a welfare agency, usually social services, only a few youngsters had ever been in a residential home or a similar institution before. Most of the sample adolescents had difficulty attending school regularly but only half were formally proceeded against for this reason.

THE PRE-HEARING STAGE

Slightly more than half our sample were on interim care orders and several of the youngsters were on two or even three interim orders before a full hearing was held to decide what should be done with them. The fact that many of the sample had been in care for two or three months prior to the final hearing and that several remained in care for another one or two months, before being allowed home after being placed on a care order, was perceived by many of the parents as a punishment in itself:

> I don't see why they should take so long.
>
> The interims are punishment enough.
>
> We had two interims of 28 days each.

Neither parents nor their children were present throughout any case conferences held during the interim period, or post hearing, although some of them were invited in at the end of a conference to be told what had been decided. The parents' and youngsters' view of the case conference will be discussed later, but suffice it to say at this point that the case conference during the interim care period is, as we have argued, only one stage of the 'incremental' or 'deferred' decision-making which characterizes the care process.

The majority of parents had some idea of what an actual juvenile court would be like, based either on their own family's experience or that of friends, but half of their sons and daughters had never been to court before and consequently had little or no idea of what to expect. A few of them had an image of *Crown Court* as portrayed on TV.

> I thought it would be like on the telly. It wasn't very nice. You feel out of place . . . everybody reading reports on you.

While some of them expected a Crown Court and got a care court, others expected a case conference and got a 'criminal' court:

> I didn't think I'd have to go up and read the words of the book. I thought I'd just go into the court and they'd give me the care order. I felt like a criminal . . . with everyone talking about me.

All the adolescents were accompanied by one or both parents or another significant adult. Although a few of them had to wait between one and two hours before they went into the courtroom, most went in within half an hour. Both parents and youngsters were anxious and tense about waiting:

Everybody was nervous. In the waiting room men were pacing up and down.

Most would concur that:

It's better short. Because there is an atmosphere of being in court.

However, despite the fact that many parents and their children felt that either they did not get any help or advice about what to do or say in court, or that the advice which they did receive was inadequate to prepare them for the experience, most were relieved that the court was not as formal as they expected.

Half of the youngsters expected that their behaviour would lead to a court appearance; most expected this because they were not going to school and they accepted that inevitably the 'crunch' would come. Although a few youngsters who were being proceeded against for something other than non-school attendance expected that 'something' might happen, they did not expect that 'something' would be a court appearance:

A conference would have been enough, 'cos I've never been to court for any trouble or anything.

Most of the juveniles proceeded against for not attending school did not have an acute sense of shock or surprise about ending up in court. They accepted, albeit reluctantly, that such behaviour would produce a court appearance *eventually,* if all other means had previously been tried to get them to attend. However, many of the parents did express resentment, feeling that their child had been picked out unfairly for 'prosecution' and insisting that from their experience all other means of resolving the problem had not been adequately tried prior to being summonsed to court. The non-school attendance issue upset and angered parents most of all, either because they saw the EWO was lacking in flexibility or because attempts to get help for a phobic or disturbed child had been ignored:

She should be able to go to any school, if she's willing, not just a choice of two bad schools.

The parents' negative assessment of the education department's behaviour and attitudes towards them built up into a resentment which tainted their perception of the whole proceedings. In many respects this resentment of the education department's role parallels the negative view parents had about the police's definition of the offence and the way they made the charge in criminal proceedings. In both situations the parents' assessment of that experience functioned to jaundice their perceptions of the rest of the process.

In many cases, in the care sample generally, it was the social worker who was seen, by the youngsters at least, as the person who had caused them to go to court. However, the social worker's role in this context was not necessarily seen in a negative light, as in several cases the adolescent or her parents were party to the process inasmuch as it was they, rather than the social worker who had 'started the ball rolling'. The police, members of the family and the EWO were also mentioned as being instrumental in their coming to court. Whether families had initiated the process or not, some felt that they certainly got more than they bargained for.

THE FULL HEARING

Impressions of court atmosphere and court officials

Most of the parents and about half of the adolescents in the sample had a good understanding of who the officials in the court were and could say what they did and where they were positioned in the courtroom. The rest of the youngsters had a fair grasp of who was who, in general terms, but tended to put people in the wrong role or in the wrong place. Half of the parents, but none of the youngsters, was aware of the lay status of the magistrates. While some thought magistrates were part-time, all thought they were paid and most thought they worked full-time. To the sample youngsters they were the 'judges' and were seen as being the most important people in the courtroom, competition coming, in a few cases, from the social worker, solicitor or EWO.

Despite the fact that for care proceedings the juvenile court becomes a 'care court', it was not generally seen by the young subjects as a caring court. It was somewhere where they felt out of place; it had an atmosphere which made them tense and nervous; it was essentially an unpredictable place where anything could happen and they were powerless to oppose it. As two girls put it:

> We were frightened — it wasn't fair 'cos we weren't expecting all this.

> I felt tense. They were all whispering, pulling faces. They looked like they were going to give a care order.

> It was all right — but them two can just say, 'Put away' and I can't do anything about it. No one is over them.

The parents shared their children's feelings of powerlessness and felt themselves to be 'on trial'. Many felt that someone was staring at them, being rude to them or appearing in one way or another to put them down:

> She smiled when the order was made.

They felt unable to intervene to correct a 'fact', deflect a slur, or dispute an innuendo. As one mother put it:

> You didn't have a say. They were just discussing you like a piece of paper.

Another mother, who had initiated social services intervention, remarked sourly:

> I was getting angry . . . all the high-faluting talk . . . getting nowhere. They don't know deep down what it's about . . . just sitting there in judgement like.

The children and their parents were on the 'receiving end' of the court process. They were hardly consulted while decisions were made about them; they were talked about rather than talked with; reports were read on them without their opinion being elicited; their presence rather than their involvement was what was required:

> I didn't get to say anything. Everybody else was doing all the talking and I was a bit nervous.

> It was fair but I had no say. It was all done on the social worker's report.

> I was mixed up.

> I was just sitting there. They told me to stand up and said, 'Care'.

> There was a lot of papers going round — the judges agreed and the clerk was reading the papers.

It was a bewildering experience for most of the young subjects, who were, in one way or another, happy to see the end of it all:

> I was relieved to get it over with.

> I went sick when I got my care order — especially when I had to come back here [assessment unit] — but I was relieved that I got my care order, that it wasn't being adjourned again.

Given their feelings of nervousness and anxiety about being in court, it is predictable that most of the youngsters did not want to have a say in such a forum or that the extent of their say was just to answer 'Yes' or 'No' to questions or at best to ask for 'another chance'. When minimum involvement was offered it was often gladly accepted:

> I was less scared because the social worker said, 'Just sit there, you don't have to say anything'.

> They were reading papers about me. I was only in there 15 minutes . . . but I knew I was coming home, the social worker told me.

Many of the adolescents and their parents felt that the atmosphere in court was not sympathetic and most of them identified at least one official as being antagonistic towards them and tended to identify him as a 'liar', an exaggerator, someone who 'twisted things' or was just plainly indifferent:

> They weren't bothered. It didn't really matter to them, they just read the reports. If they had wanted a care order they would 'ave got it. They gave me a supervision order to get rid of it.

> I didn't like the magistrate. He seemed to think I was a criminal. He said 'I hope you'll behave yourself' — as though it was all my fault.

> The woman judge was looking down her nose.

> They were trying to put me away. The social worker was trying to keep me out — my solicitor was — but the others. . . .

No official was identified as *consistently* helpful to them, although the social worker and defence solicitor were mentioned positively several times. Whether social workers were viewed as 'for' or 'against' them depended largely on the degree of consent which the family had given to the proceedings, the Section 1 clause under which the proceedings were being made, and, most significantly, as other receiving-end studies have found (see Thoburn, 1980), the personality and manner of the individual worker:

> The social worker, I don't know his name, he was helpful by what he said. He made a statement about everything; it was all true. And he helped me with my nerves.

Despite knowing who the officials were and what they were supposed to be doing, half the parents and adolescents admitted that they could not fully understand the proceedings. For the parents, this lack of understanding made them feel all the more vulnerable and unable to intervene for fear of 'incriminating themselves' and 'showing ignorance'. To many of them it was, 'like a trial', in many respects but a trial in which it appeared that it had been 'all decided before the day'. The 'punishment' might be decided in court, but the judgement had occurred elsewhere. Even those adolescents and parents who maintained that they understood what was being said were often confused as to exactly what was happening:

> The magistrates were whispering all the time.
>
> They never really said much. Just passed the reports around and gave a supervision order.
>
> They were talking to themselves.
>
> They weren't really talking to me.
>
> I wanted to know what they were reading ... what they were talking about what they were reading.

Access to, and understanding of, reports

Most parents had seen the SER and had a fairly high level of knowledge about its content, although their comprehension was somewhat diminished by the fact that they mainly saw the report on the day of the proceedings and had to read it in the tension of the moment. Parents, unlike their children, whose access to, and therefore understanding of the content and purpose of, the reports was limited, were under no illusions as to the significance of reports, despite many of them being denied sight of school and education reports. They correctly identified these documents as extremely influential.

Whether parents agreed with the reports or not was dependent on the unique dynamics of each case and these were largely determined by the degree of consent given initially to the proceedings. For some, the report was largely an articulate version of the truth, or even a character reference:

> I really thought it was for my benefit, so that there would be no recriminations against me.

For other it was a 'character assassination' and the authors were consequently seen as 'nosey', 'snoopy' and 'twisting':

> Whatever you told her she took it to mean something else.

Many parents felt that, although the reports were not negative, they lacked 'warmth' and could have been more positive and have included more about their side of the story:

> I saw the reports. I agreed with them but they were clinical and cold. I felt I was wicked when I'd read them.
>
> I never had a say in it. I would have wanted to say that 'City 9' is a notorious area and the schools are bad.

Only a few of the youngsters actually saw the SER via the social worker, although slightly more than half of them obtained some idea of its contents through other sources, namely their mothers, their solicitors and the court. Almost half of the sample youngsters had no access whatsoever to the reports. However, two-thirds said that they were told by the social workers what the outcome was likely to be, although only a third associated the predicted outcome with the recommendation in the social worker's report. Only two youngsters knew enough about the content of the report to say that they disagreed with it; the rest either could not answer or agreed as the result of ignorance.

Solicitor's role perceived

Virtually all the juveniles in the sample received legal representation funded by the legal aid scheme. Only a few knew their solicitor by sight, while in the majority of cases there was no continuity of solicitor involvement, a case being serviced by a firm rather than an individual solicitor. Despite the fact that the solicitor is funded to represent the child, not the parents, who are not eligible for separate representation, except if they can of course pay for it themselves, parents generally saw the solicitor as also representing their case. Most families declared themselves well satisfied with 'their' solicitor's performance. In relation to the adolescents, the solicitors did carry out an important role in giving their young clients some basis on which to develop an expectation of what would *ultimately* happen to them but few provided advice or help about how this would happen. They did not usually tell their young clients about what would occur in court and therefore did not provide them with a framework so that they could make sense of all that was happening. Their contact with their clients was generally brief and no great efforts were made to communicate with them, except perhaps to relieve their anxieties:

> He just said not to be scared. Said I wouldn't be in care until I was 18.

> He said that when you go in to stand up and the judge will tell you to sit down. That's all. I asked him if I'd go home. He said he didn't know, he would try his best.

> She tried to explain a little but I didn't really understand it.

Most of the youngsters were satisfied with their solicitor's performance and would chose to use the same solicitor if they had occasion to appear in court again, but many of these expressions of satisfaction were tinged with some bewilderment or scepticism about what exactly the solicitor had done in court. For some juveniles their solicitor's performance was clearly satisfactory, inasmuch as he was seen as on their 'side':

> He stood up for me 'n that. Instead of giving all bad points he gave good points as well.

But for others the basis on which to assess satisfaction or dissatisfaction was difficult to discern:

> He wasn't too bad. Could have spoken more. He was agreeing with the prosecutor — I think they're from the same firm.

> He never got the chance to say in any case. Just a few minutes then it was finished. A man on the left explained to the judge, then the solicitor got up and said 'All agreed', so they all agreed.

He didn't say anything. Think he did it all beforehand.

He tried his best to get me home 'n that — that was the first time
I'd been in court — they took no notice of him. The judge said it
was entirely up to me [i.e. future behaviour] if I went home or
not.

The first one was OK, but the second one didn't say anything.

For some adolescents it was clear that their solicitor had not performed
satisfactorily, either by saying nothing at all or failing to prevent them
being 'put away' or both:

He never said nothing. Two minutes after I went in they said care
proceedings [i.e. care order].

What solicitors were *seen* to do was often nothing, or very little but, for
both parents and youngsters alike, if the outcome was as they had expected then they *presumed* that the solicitor had done his job properly
or at least had not obviously messed things up. The solicitor who contradicted a few negative points presented by the 'opposition', or who
inserted a few positive points about the child or the parents, was assessed as being at least on 'their side' and was much appreciated for it.

Since in most cases the eventual outcome was seen by the children
and their parents as virtually predetermined, the good solicitor was not
expected to win the war but just to score a few minor victories, thereby
allowing their clients to retain their dignity:

He said the interim order was wrong, and he fought over that but
Joe still stayed in care. He said there was no chance of fighting
the full care order . . . that was inevitable.

RECEIVING COURT ORDERS

The disposition

Just over half the sample adolescents were aware that the magistrates
had given some kind of reason as to why they had made a particular
decision. This tallied with our own observations. The issue of school
attendance was mentioned as the magistrates' reason in most of the
cases, also in keeping with our own observations, but parental 'failure'
and the need for parents and youngsters to receive help was also men-

tioned in several instances. (Although a third of them thought, correctly, that no reason had been given for the decision.) All but two of
the sample knew what the court had decided:

> Said because I am in need of care because I was sagging — not
> because my mum ill-treats me or anything.

> So that if problems arise again they can just remand me — get a
> care order — help me. They don't have to go through all the thing
> again.

Whether or not they received some kind of formal magisterial comment
as to the reasoning behind the court's decision, most of the youngsters
in the sample were able to identify at least one significant factor which
they saw as strongly influencing the magistrates' decision in their case.

Several mentioned the social worker's role, her reports, the school
reports, the solicitor's performance or the prosecutor's contribution as
being highly influential in determining the outcome of their case:

> The social worker kept on bringing up about school about me and
> me mum. She wanted me back here [Assessment Centre]. I don't
> like my social worker. I tried to hit her with a 'phone a few weeks
> ago.

> They were given reports by the social worker and read that.

The social workers and both sets of solicitors were mentioned as having
most say in the cases, followed by the 'judges' and to a much lesser
extent, EWOs. Most of the adolescents mentioned that the court had
decided largely as they had expected and quite a few were thus reasonably 'satisfied' with the outcome. Those that were more deeply dissatisfied thought that the court could have been more lenient or considerate,
giving them a supervision order or a 'home trial' as an alternative to a
care order:

> They should have had a good discussion, not just accepted the
> care order.

For a few children the court's decision, although perhaps not unexpected, was received with resignation:

> As they did [but] ... I want to go home ... but my mum
> doesn't want me now ... I don't want to go into details.

Many of the children thought that their parents agreed with the court's decision:

> Yes I think they're happy . . . I've got a care order. It's doing me good. I went home for the weekend with my social worker.

> Mum was happy we was to come here and then go home.

> Yes, he thought care was OK. The best thing at the time.

It is perhaps not surprising that many of these juveniles accepted the court's decision and that most of them thought that their parents agreed with it, since half went home after the court hearing or after a short stay in an assessment centre. For several of those who returned home the court's decision marked the *end* of a period in residential care and so it was welcomed as such. For others who had been at home prior to appearing in court, the decision to allow them to remain at home was greeted with relief; they had avoided being 'put in care'.

Whether or not they ended up in care or were allowed 'home on trial' or on a supervision order, most thought that the very fact of having been to court could well have a negative effect on their future. Several were aware of employers' attitudes to young people who are deviant in any way:

> Like it might — say like a good job — they might not want anyone who's been to court.

> If it says I've been sagging school, they'll say he won't come to work — he won't come to work every day, will he? But I *will* — it's not like school. If you're in work you get customers . . . come in and talk . . . and you get paid. You don't get paid for reading and writing in school.

Some youngsters who had been 'prosecuted' for non-school attendance felt that they would now have to go to school as they were under surveillance all the time and under the threat of being whisked off into care:

> Being on a care order I can just get put away.

> I'm on trial. Say I stay off again, well there's nothing down for me — I'll just have to go into care.

> I now know I have to go to school. I'm getting watched now. Everybody knows now that I'm not going to school. The social worker can check up any time she likes.

For others the effect of the court's decision was immediate and personal:

> Things have changed at home already. My mum has changed towards me.

> Mum used to come and stay with us but they [grandmother and great-aunt] kept getting at her.

A few youngsters were concerned that the fact of having been to court made them a candidate for harassment, particularly by the police:

> I feel like a criminal. Police stop you for nothing and ask ... you say, 'I've got a care order', and they said, 'A little robber here'.

Nearly all of these adolescents felt that the stigma, surveillance and general insecurity which resulted from care proceedings would be with them for at least a couple of years. The effect of care proceedings was not just limited to the court hearing or being placed in a residential institution, foster care or allowed to return home; it lingered and would pervade their lives for several years and, for some, possibly for ever.

View of court's functions

Although most of the youngsters knew that the court dealt with criminal offences as well as care cases, only a few of them had a clear idea of the difference between care and criminal proceedings:

> Criminal proceedings are when you've done something really bad — you go to prison. Care proceedings you just go to a Home.

There was some disagreement and confusion as to whether the juvenile court was there to help or punish adolescents, or perhaps a bit of both. When asked, as many told us that being put in care was the worst thing the juvenile court could do to someone as said that Borstal was the worst; after all they both involved being 'put away' from home. The juvenile court's function then was to both help and punish you:

> It depends on what you go for. They helped me really.

> They're trying to help a bit — but they're not really.

> Help you — teach you a lesson.

The confusion between help and punish, care and control, abounds in these minors' view of the juvenile justice system:

> It's until you're 18 — taking years off your life — taken off your mum — taken to *their* school — then you've *got* to go to school then.
>
> It's to understand you, help you to stop doing wrong.
>
> It's if you get a problem at home, to help sort them out.

Many of these adolescents, although believing themselves that there is some basic difference between stealing from a shop or robbing a car and not attending school or having rows with your parents, seemed to grasp the concept that as far as the court and, by implication, society, is concerned, they are somehow fundamentally the same; both types of act can be subsumed under the category of 'doing wrong' and while the court's job in care and criminal proceedings may well be 'to understand you', its primary aim is to 'help you to stop doing wrong'. In the final analysis, perhaps it is, as one lad so acutely discerned, merely a question of method:

> Care is to help stop you doing things wrong; criminal is to scare you into stopping doing things wrong.

Receiving care and supervision orders

As a result of the full hearing decision half the sample youngsters were removed from their own homes to an assessment centre or placed with relatives other than their parents. All of them, with one exception, were able to be visited there by members of their family. For quite a few it meant a return to the assessment centre, rather than an initial placement, and many of these young subjects had already been there for anything from one to three months. Most did not particularly dislike their period in the centre and, got on reasonably well with the residential staff, sometimes they felt the residential workers had got to know them better than the field worker. While distinguishing between field work and residential workers in terms of function and power, many of the youngsters thought that residential workers had a lot of say about what would happen to them and found them informative about such things as the date of the case conference. Most youngsters were very aware that their behaviour in the centre would be taken into account at the case conference which, while being vague about its content, they perceived correctly as being the forum in which residential and social workers would decide what would happen to them:

> I played it cool. Trying to do myself a bit of good — to get home like.

> It all depends on how you're getting on.

> They said I had good reports.

None of the youngsters nor their parents were present during the case conference but most came in at the end to hear the 'verdict'. Their understanding of what occurred in the conference was based not on direct experience but was founded on the impressions they could pick up from the social worker, residential staff, other kids and the glance they obtained of who was there if they were invited in at the end:

> It's like a court. They were all talking about decisions and that — but it has more say for me [than court]. I went in at the end when they'd finished. They just said 'home trial'.

> They tell you afterwards. The people [in the assessment centre] say what you've been like, then the social worker says something — I don't know what. Then they decide.

> I went in at the end. They want to know what your behaviour's like. They know everything.

> I was told afterwards what they'd decided.

> I don't know — I didn't go — not allowed to.

Most of these captive clients were aware that the scrutiny of their behaviour did not end with their time in the centre and they understood that leaving care was ultimately conditional on their future performance. In this respect, although the conference was an important step in determining what would happen to them, it was not the final hurdle:

> I know it does get reviewed and it depends on your behaviour.

> I'm on a care order for four years but if I'm all right after a while they'll take the care order off. If I behave myself 'n that.

> They said that in six months' time, if I don't get into trouble, it [i.e. the care order] will be put aside — that if I get a job 'n that, it'll be all right.

We contacted 11 of the youngsters again three to six months after the court hearing and asked them what they thought about things. Most of them were *not* happy about being in care, or home on trial, or even on supervision but several accepted their situation, fatalistically or with resignation:

> They were doing their job. It's all turned out for the best now. It was OK there but you're not with your family. It's not the same.

> Just nothing – I'm not sad and I'm not happy.

Several of the youngsters had absconded from the assessment centre or residential placement but they were not generally critical of the residential staff nor of the level of schooling they had received, although some of them, with experience of more than one placement, constructed their own consumer guide:

> Went to a children's home – I just didn't give it a chance. Then I got sent back to the assessment centre. I kept running so I got sent here. Been here six weeks five days. I like it better than the assessment unit. Have a good laugh, sometimes . . . and some good fights . . . and you can wear what you like . . . jeans. At the assessment centre you had to wear a skirt.

The relative satisfaction or dissatisfaction which these youngsters felt about a placement was not related solely to the fact that it was residential but rather to the way it was run and the kind of rapport which developed between them and the staff. However, all of them wanted, above all else, to return home, with one sad exception:

> I've wrote a letter saying I don't want to see my mum any more. I'm not going near the place. It's all fading now . . . going from bad to worse.

While some of them thought that they would be in care, or home on trial, or on supervision for about six months, or until they left school in a few months time, most were reluctantly reconciled to the order lasting about two years and for a few it was an indefinite time, bounded only by their sixteenth or eighteenth birthday. These few children would never leave care, but merely outgrow it and escape rightly or wrongly into the legal freedom of young adulthood where they could chose to remain 'beyond care' and shed the adolescent status which had invited 'control' initially.

Perceptions of the social worker

All of the sample, with one exception, had a social worker allocated to
their case, and all but one knew the name of their social worker.
Except for 'genuine' education care cases, where social work involvement was, in our sample, limited to writing a report, most of the care
cases involved intensive social work involvement around the 'crisis'
which precipitated the initial referral. This continued during the following 'interim' period where the youngster was placed in care and had
often to make several court appearances and then in the aftermath of
the substantive hearing, when the youngster was committed for assessment or 'rehabilitation', home on trial or on supervision.

Most of the youngsters thought their social worker was 'OK' or
reasonable and several strongly liked them:

> She's OK. She's sometimes nice.
>
> She's a cracker.
>
> A nice person.
>
> I like her − she's great − she's nice to get on with.
>
> She understands − and she takes us swimming.
>
> I like her, she's very nice. She's trying to help me and she does a
> good job.

For some, their opinion of the social worker changed for the better
over time, while for others their present social worker was contrasted
sharply with his predecessor.

> After all the talks I've had with him now I think he's OK.
>
> He's all right. I like him. The one before was worse. He left.
>
> The other social worker wasn't as nosey as her.

Significantly, a high proportion of youngsters and their parents
thought that they needed a 'social worker'. They acknowledged that
they did have a problem which required someone from outside the
family to intervene and, inasmuch as that 'someone' turned out to be a
social worker, they accepted that they had a need for one. However,
the way in which the social worker met their need was not always to
their liking and in many cases the social work 'package' of involvement,
the stigma of being in court and the feeling, by parents in particular, of

being degraded, and the feeling of powerlessness and insignificance engendered by the care process, was experienced as a form of 'family punishment' rather than as care and consideration of the family's problems:

> It's a punishment if you're a *good* family.
>
> I miss her terribly and so does the baby.
>
> It must be a punishment; it takes away their freedom to be like other kids.
>
> It's affected the other girls having Karen taken away. And her grandparents they won't be OK . . . written her off as bad blood.

Where consent to social work involvement was lacking, and where there was no recognition by the family that they felt they had a 'problem', the social worker was usually disliked. In a minority of cases the youngsters and parents were sceptical about, or rejected, the idea that the social worker was trying to help them. They thought that what the social worker said or wrote misrepresented their situation and distorted what had happened. In their view the social worker was dishonest and disagreeable and was certainly not concerned with their idea of their 'best interests'. In some cases the adolescents' interests and their parents' interests were definitely in conflict and in such cases the social worker was hard-pressed to satisfy either party.

> I don't like him. He's just horrible. He's more with my mum and dad.
>
> I don't like him . . . his manner . . . he said 'It's up to your mother to take you to the Youth Club'. Kept asking me questions, called me a 'pathetic', twisted what I said.
>
> Don't like her 'cos when I was in court she was telling lies on me. She was trying to say that my mum told her that I was running up and down the lobby with a knife trying to stab my dad.
>
> They're supposed to help you but they don't all help you.

It is difficult to separate whether youngsters and parents liked or disliked what the social worker said, wrote and did from their liking or disliking the social worker's personality and manner. However, the general impression gained is that if the youngster or his parents liked the social worker as a person then, while perhaps disagreeing with some

of the things the social worker did, they would give him/her the benefit
of the doubt and assume that he/she had the 'best interests' of the child
at heart. If the social worker's personality was disliked then his motives
and actions were the objects of suspicion and mistrust. Since both
youngsters and parents were highly dependent on social workers to explain what was happening, to represent the family's situation accurately
in reports and generally to mediate between family and the formal care
process, a great deal of trust was required of them. If such trust was
lacking the possibility of families experiencing the care process as being
in their best interests was much reduced.

One family that had initiated social services intervention felt very
bitter:

> We asked for help and all we got was expense, court orders and
> our names on sheets.

They felt that the social worker had 'gone behind our backs' and set off
proceedings which produced an ordeal of several months' duration.
Consequently they concluded:

> I'd never recommend a social worker to anyone.

However, such biting criticism of social workers was not typical,
despite the fact that only a minority of parents felt that they had been
fully informed about remand decisions and none were present throughout the case conference at which major decisions were made. Most of
the youngsters thought that their social worker was 'for' them and liked
them for being an ally.

However, the picture changed slightly when we interviewed those
receiving statutory involvement three to six months on. By this time
the social worker, while still liked by many of the adolescents, was seen
in a different light. Most young subjects were no longer happy about
social work involvement. Although many of them acknowledged that
they *had* needed a social worker to help them sort out things during the
crisis period that led to care, only a few still saw the social worker as
necessary and some saw them as definitely irrelevant and an aggravation.

Some felt this because the situation which produced the local authority's intervention has been essentially resolved or had at least become
manageable, while for others who were still *not* attending school or
continuing to have difficult problems at home, the social workers'
statutory involvement with them was seen as adding to, rather than

ameliorating, their problems. For these young clients the social worker had become another person 'on their backs', who could put them away in care if they stepped too far out of line; the social worker symbolized their loss of freedom to deviate with relative impunity:

> Supervision makes you aware of how easy it would be to be put away. It's just something hanging over you.
>
> She hasn't done much. She just wants to know everything.
>
> I hide when she comes. I don't talk to the social worker.

Those youngsters happy to see their social worker reckoned that the social worker was there to help them sort out any problems with their family and that she was someone with whom they *could* discuss their problems:

> Any problems – particularly school.
>
> Anything. I can trust her to talk freely.

In the final analysis it was the person in the role of social worker who established or failed to establish a positive relationship with the young person or parent and who validated or negated their desire for continued social work involvement.

SUMMARY AND DISCUSSION

At the beginning of the chapter we identified five key variables which we have found to determine the youngsters' and parents' comprehension of, and satisfaction with or resignation to care proceedings. We have discussed the experience and views of our sample in relation to these variables.

Although, in general terms, parents agreed that the state or the 'authorities' should be able to intervene in those families which were unable, or unwilling, to provide adequate care for, and control of, their children, when they were the subject of such intervention themselves they deeply resented the stigma, and were bitter about the form that such intervention took and often the manner in which it was carried out. With the significant exception of those subject to 'genuine' education care proceedings, several parents and many youngsters acknowledged that there was a serious problem and consented to 'something' being done about it. However, for most of them that 'something' was far in excess of anything they had anticipated. The long duration of the care process and the degrading and alienating court hearing left many of them feeling powerless and bewildered. Once they had entered the care process, and for most of them this only occurred after a lot of pre-court negotiations, they had virtually no control over what would happen. They were very much dependent on local welfare and court officials to inform them about what was going on and to represent their views fairly and accurately. Being in such a powerless and uncertain position meant that their defence lawyer, even though he did not 'win' the case, was seen in a positive light as he was able to offer advice about the 'inevitable' outcome and present his clients in a more positive light to the court than would otherwise have occurred.

Whether or not youngsters and parents were satisfied with care proceedings is difficult to discern since the definition of satisfaction in this context is a complex issue. They were certainly dissatisfied with the form proceedings took and often the manner in which they were carried out. However, most parents, once the care process had reached the point of disposition, thought that the final decision regarding their son or daughter was essentially fair and accepted, usually with a strong sense of relief, that the right decision had been made. The youngsters were less sure as to whether the final decision was right for them. Although for two-thirds of them it was what they had expected, only a third of them fully agreed with it. Once the court hearing was over, the spotlight was no longer focused so strongly on the parents but, as we have indicated, many of the youngsters in receipt of statutory social work involvement were less than happy that for them the care process was not at an end. Indeed for some, in terms of surveillance and the monitoring of their behaviour, it had really just started.

Juvenile care proceedings are, then, characterized, in the eyes of our sample adolescents and parents, by their excesses. The formal court hearing was seen as greatly exceeding the 'something' which they had anticipated would be required to deal with the problem. The duration of the process, particularly the length of stay in residential care both before, and in several cases, after the full hearing was viewed as being unnecessarily long and was often seen as a form of punishment. For these youngsters allocated to a social worker, the extent of social work involvement, although often welcomed initially, was perceived as continuing beyond its relevance.

Despite these wide-ranging criticisms from those on the receiving end — clearly an indictment of the lack of sensitivity of a range of officials — we are still left with the fact that most of these families accepted that there were serious problems troubling them. The *raison d'etre* for outside care and even structure and control remains. The need for a positive support system for poor working-class families struggling to rear children, which was the clarion call of the 1960s, and even of Seebohm (1968), is still clearly required.

In documenting this acceptance by our sample that many are caught up in knotty problems often involving intractable dilemmas, we have offered some backing for the assertion made in the last chapter that resolving these presenting problems involves local statutory welfare workers making moral judgements, often in the face of chronic uncertainty. We showed in the last chapter how in City the responsibility for making these judgements and packaging them for the care court fell heavily on the shoulders of social workers. Clearly much of the indignity and unhappiness suffered by families subjected to welfare justice by the process itself can be laid at the door of social workers. Yet our understanding of the recent critiques of juvenile justice (e.g. Morris *et al.*, 1980; Taylor *et al.*, 1980) is that social workers are implicitly blamed for *actually making* difficult moral judgements not just for making them inappropriately or without due consideration. The former claim is unreasonable. Indeed, as we shall see in the next chapter, social workers are critical of lawyers and magistrates in the care court for not 'checking' their moral judgements more thoroughly. If one takes the views of those subject to care proceedings at all seriously and also analyses the nature of the problems these families face, it becomes patently clear that no statutory system, whether run by judges, lawyers or social workers, can avoid making moral judgements about often irreconcilable problems. In chapter 12 we will use specific case studies to illustrate further the nature of these problems. First we shall juxtapose our analysis of the care court and those on the receiving end of its jurisdiction with the perceptions of the key officials, the LA social workers, in order to see if social workers themselves are as ambivalent as their clients about the production of welfare justice and to try and tease out why they often misjudge some of the feelings and attitudes of their clients.

11

Orchestrating 'Care and Control': The Social Worker's Role

WEARING THE JANUS MASK

In care proceedings the social worker is a key figure representing, usually via a case conference, the local authority in its statutory child care and control responsibilities. The social worker is not only the key worker for 'the system' by orchestrating care proceedings but he or she is also the LA representative — the official that youngsters and parents perceive as 'the welfare'. He or she is the person who mediates between them and the formal system. He represents the welfare system to his clients but he also, often at the same time, represents his clients to the system. The social worker must, of necessity, wear a Janus mask in order to even attempt to fulfil this extremely ambivalent role as gate-keeper at the interface between the welfare system and the client.

The difficult role which the social worker is empowered to play is informed by a caring ideology mediated by organizational demands which stress both the value of individual dignity and freedom of choice and the need to over-rule these 'human rights' when a child or adolescent is, for one reason or another, not being provided with adequate care and control at home. Such an ideology contains inherent contradictions but in practice the social worker has to try to reconcile these contradictions — he has to be both the defender of child and parental rights and the usurper:

> The social control role is very central. You cannot avoid the role if you're a social worker.

However, the social workers' attitude towards their social control role differs, depending on whether it is played out in the context of care or criminal proceedings. Most of the social workers in our sample[7] felt that the atmosphere in court was distinctly different between care and criminal proceedings. While in criminal proceedings they tended to share the juveniles' sense of discomfort and anxiety about being 'outsiders' in a dangerous, unpredictable, even hostile, environment; in care proceedings, although appreciating that the youngsters were nervous about it, they generally thought the care court was there to help the subjects and was ultimately concerned to act in their 'best interests'. In the social workers' opinion, the atmosphere in the care court was caring rather than intimidating or hostile.

It is significant that, unlike in our criminal sample, where only half of the social workers attended and only one spoke to the court, in the care sample all of the social workers were present in court and the majority of them spoke to the bench, if only to give verbally a statement of evidence, details of the case, current developments or future plans. While in our criminal sample the social workers described their relationship to other court officials as, 'all very separate', or at least 'formal', in care proceedings the picture created was of the social worker working with other court officials, 'all as one', 'all working as a team'. This more intimate, almost collusive, relationship between social workers and court officials and the centrality of the social workers' role in care proceedings has, as we will see later in the chapter, a marked effect on the social workers' interpretation of what care proceedings mean to the youngsters and their parents.

ON BEING THE KEY WORKER FOR THE CARE PROCESS

Our sample social workers would largely accept the analysis of care proceedings we offered in the last chapter. They were well aware of the fact that most LA cases which went to court would be accepted by the magistrates as sound and their recommendations followed. The social workers were equally aware of their own strong influence on proceedings. Hence most of them thought that their presentation of a case should be thoroughly scrutinized and checked out by the magistrates and by solicitors. Such scrutiny at least afforded the social workers the possibility of a shared responsibility for the outcome in care proceedings, as well as giving the client some protection against the arbitrary use of social work opinion and discretion. While close magisterial consideration of a case did not absolve the social workers of their responsibility for taking care proceedings against a youngster, it could reassure them that the moral and professional judgements they were making were indeed in the youngster's best interest. It was thought that, rather than changing to a panel system, on the Scottish lines, a more representative and better trained magistracy could provide the necessary independent and sensitive arbitration required in care proceedings:

> I don't think many of them [magistrates] have much awareness of these people's lives or what brings them to court. They don't spend enough time on it. I can never work out how they have time to read and understand the reports they are given. Magistrates would be more useful if they were better informed and did their job better. . . . Improve them rather than find an alternative.

The social workers also fully accepted that youngsters should be legally represented to the extent that most of them claimed to have advised their clients to obtain legal representation, even when 'agreement' existed:

> Even though his mother agreed with the proceedings I advised her how to get legal representation to protect Christine's interests.

Most of the social workers saw the defence lawyer as a potential vehicle for the adolescent's own views, particularly since the youngster's lack of verbal skills and own insecurity stood in contrast with articulate, eloquent and well-schooled lawyers who could:

> Put over the feelings of the people better than the people themselves. They are used to court.

Indeed because of this social workers agreed:

> An adversary is necessary. We shouldn't be allowed to get away with things.

They were critical of the lack of legal representation for parents and what they saw as the rather shoddy service offered young clients. Lawyers were seen to abdicate their adversarial role, often in favour of a more 'caring' social work-type role which was much more concerned with judging what was in the youngster's best interests and avoiding 'hurting' the young client and his or her parents than it was concerned with a strict protection of their civil rights and liberties:

> Their job isn't to make the value judgements. They should represent their client. Solicitors often say one thing and mean another. They are instructed to oppose the care order but make it clear indirectly that they think the kids need care. It is the social worker's job to make the value judgements, not the solicitor's.

As another social worker put it:

> In care proceedings social workers have power — they are placed in the position of God. The court should *not* just rubber-stamp social workers' decisions and solicitors should take up the weaknesses in a social services department's case — that's fair enough. If it was my child I'd want a solicitor.

Despite these criticisms, most social workers thought that, given the present set-up, legal representation was necessary and useful. Many social workers appreciated that, like themselves, legal counsel had some very difficult decisions to make:

> I would hate to be a solicitor. He thought that a care order would be a good thing — to help her. But he did what the client wanted. That is he got her off. But his heart wasn't in it.

ON BEING THE KEY WORKER TO ADOLESCENTS AND PARENTS

Nearly all the social workers admitted that there were not always adequate reasons for youngsters being committed to care:

> Care — there's not always good reasons. We can't afford to take chances; we tend to play safe.

They acknowledged having reservations regarding certain types of cases, particularly non-school attendance. Yet it was a strong characteristic of our social worker sample that, with a few exceptions, they were generally confident that what *they* were doing for the subject youngsters was in their interests. These social workers believed that most of their adolescent clients 'agreed', if somewhat reluctantly, with what was being done on their behalf. Consequently, although most of the social workers thought that their young clients did not really understand what was going on in the care court, several were not particularly concerned about this lack of comprehension. Partly this was because the presence of a defence lawyer ameliorated the situation. However, drawing on their experience of care proceedings, most of the social workers knew that it was highly probable that their recommendations would be followed and so, as far as they were concerned, the outcome of the hearing was predictable. The hearing itself was thus seen as a 'formality' or 'straight-forward' and it was presumed that since their young clients knew the recommendation they would thus be reassured about the probable outcome of the hearing. In these circumstances, many of the social workers thought that there was no need to 'worry' their young clients unduly by informing them in detail about the proceedings or bothering to coach them about self-presentation:

> She was told before she went in what would happen so she wasn't bothered. The appearance was just a formality.

> He was there to be taken into care and it was almost a foregone conclusion.

The social workers were somewhat less confident of parental support for their actions but even here the level of assessed parental acceptance and 'satisfaction' was fairly high, most parents being thought to be satisfied that statutory intervention was necessary. Satisfaction was thought to be determined by a close relationship between expectation and outcome. Since most of the social workers claimed they had successfully conveyed an accurate expectation of the outcome to the family, they assumed relative satisfaction would follow. We have shown that most adolescents and parents not so much 'agree' as 'comply' with the care process which, regardless of whether they had originally initiated social work intervention, they had virtually no power to resist effectively. And, whilst there were elements of consent in the attitude of the youngsters and parents to care proceedings, clearly the social workers understandably latched on to and overemphasized these.

However, partly because of the social workers' own sense of 'belonging' in the care court, partly because to them it was a 'foregone conclusion', a 'formality' and, despite appreciating that the ordeal of a court hearing created anxiety and apprehension for the children and parents, it is our impression that the social workers tended to underestimate the feeling of being judged, degraded and derided, which the youngsters expressed, and, even more so, the parents. Many subject families were 'satisfied' with the outcome mainly because the fact of an 'outcome' meant that a negative and distressing experience had finally ceased. They may have wanted 'something' to be done to resolve their difficulties but they felt that the format in which it was done and the manner it was carried out was excessive and undesirable. (Yet most parents, when the whole business was substantially over and done with, did think that the social worker had their child's best interests at heart, although they did not always agree with the social worker's definition of 'best interests'.) This clash was particularly likely if 'the problem' involved some kind of interpersonal conflict between children and their parents and existed even when there was a degree of agreement from many of them that 'something' needed to be done to resolve or manage this conflict. Our sample social workers felt they intervened when a youngster's best interests were under threat. In this respect several of the parents were judged as deficient in some way and parental attitude to, and behaviour at, the hearing was often assessed in terms of whether or not it was supportive of, and sympathetic to, the son or daughter's situation. Again, like their assessment of client satisfaction with the proceedings, this issue was perceived as complex and the social workers, in the main, appreciated the parents' predicament. When they were asked whether or not the parents had acted in their child's best interests, their replies were sometimes critical but nearly always considered:

> When she gets emotional and mixed up in court it tends to go against her. They see her as an emotionally mixed-up person. She thought she was being protective, but she wasn't supportive — the kids supported her!

> Her mother obviously *thinks* she does. But I definitely don't.

> No . . . but . . . to the best of her ability. She came to the court wearing a low-cut dress — looking as if she was about to go soliciting.

> Yes, in the actual courtroom — because she just took a passive role. She was very different in the waiting-room. Mrs M came in bevied and got very maudlin towards J who was very upset. And when she was on a place of safety order, her mother told her she didn't want her any more and she wrote a letter — to *Miss* M from *Mrs* M.

Although we have argued that social workers and other court workers try to avoid the acting out of feelings and emotions in court — the 'dreaded performance' — there is a sense in which it is in the social workers' interests for some parents to show their 'true colours' in court, since such behaviour would visibly validate the local authority's case. Parents are placed in an invidious position. They run the risk of any strongly felt emotional outburst being viewed as a lack of concern for the feelings of their child but if they subordinate their own feelings to the needs of their youngster's security and reassurance in court, then they forfeit their right to express their point of view fully. In such a situation legal representation for parents, which was thought desirable by the social workers, at least would give parents a form of protection and provide some guarantee that the case will be considered on the 'facts' rather than the parents' social presentation.

The majority of our social work sample maintained that they showed or told the parents about the content and *recommendation* in the SER and told adolescents about the recommendation. This was not substantiated by the juveniles in our sample, although most of the parents acknowledged that the social worker was the main source of information about the content and recommendation in the report. As we stated in the previous chapter, most of the sample adolescents said that the social worker did tell them what the court's decision was likely to be but only a third associated this prediction with any recommendation in the report. As a result, they did not identify the social worker as the source of information about the report's recommendation and only a few knew anything about the report's content from the social worker. When youngsters got to know of the report's content, it seems that the triangular route of communication about the report — from the social worker to the parent to the youngster — which we noted in criminal proceedings, is repeated in care proceedings. Unfortunately such indirect communication with the youngsters appears to provide no guarantee that they will receive accurate information about the reports.

Indeed many of the social workers were ambivalent about just how much the youngster should know of the content of the report and appeared to convey to them, on any regular basis, only the recommendation. This does not seem to have been a thought-out policy in most cases, more the consequence of the lack of an agreed, systematic policy. The general pressure of work and inadequate typing facilities also prevented clients having access to reports before the hearing:

> I always discuss them. I used to show them but not now. Not for any particular reason — just pressure of work and limited typing facilities.

I was going to — but in this particular case I just didn't have the time. I don't have a set policy on it. It's a difficult area — it needs clarification.

Normally, I discuss it with the parents but not the child. I like to take it to the parents before it's typed and check it for inaccuracies with them. Then it's not a complete shock for them in the court.

Although SERs in care proceedings often contain quite sensitive and possibly embarrassing material, there appeared to be no distinction made, in terms of access to the reports, between care and criminal proceedings. The social workers in our sample gave basically the same reasons for providing or failing to provide juveniles and parents with full access to the reports in both types of proceedings. The minimal participation of the adolescents and parents in the courtroom and their limited access to court reports is mirrored in their status in the case conferences. As with adolescents placed in care via criminal proceedings, those routed through care proceedings shared a low level of involvement in case conference decision-making.

As we have pointed out, many of the adolescents in our care sample were on interim orders prior to the substantive hearing and half were placed for assessment in a residential institution after they had been made the subject of a care order by the court. A pre-hearing conference usually has the information of at least a partial assessment on which to decide whether 'care and control' is required and what form it should take, but the conference which occurs after the child has been made the subject of a care order is no longer concerned with whether 'care and control' is needed. Its function is to plan, on the basis of a relatively brief assessment and a consideration of the youngster's current circumstances, how best the care system can meet that need. However, in practice, the different stages of the assessment procedure and the care system's decision-making processes are not so clearly differentiated: from the social workers' point of view and from the perspective of the youngsters already on interim orders, care proceedings appear as almost a continuous process, punctuated only by the formality of the hearing.

The social workers in our sample tended to think that many of the youngsters did not strongly resent being in interim care nor in the assessment centre following the hearing. Some thought that a few of their young clients really liked it in one respect or another:

She didn't seem to mind that most of the girls were in there for criminal matters. She liked the schooling there because the classes were much smaller and she got a lot out of them [although] she absconded twice.

She liked it. She said it was like a holiday camp — being away from home. She got on with the staff.

He liked the assessment centre because it was more structured.

He enjoyed being there. He enjoyed the attention.

Although the social workers acknowledged the importance of the case conference and supported the idea that youngsters and their parents should be kept fully informed of when they were held, what they had decided and the basis for that decision, they were generally reluctant to accept the direct involvement of the family in the conference:

It's [participation] vital, but it's not welcomed in City. People fear that it would inhibit discussion since you couldn't say what you thought of the parents.

As it was, it was not always possible to keep youngsters and parents fully informed and some social workers admitted that some of their clients received information on the conference's decision from a variety of sources:

I think it's important that they should know. I didn't tell her but she knew about it from talking with the other girls and with the staff.

We did our best to keep them involved but it's sometimes difficult to really explain things.

The social worker's role in the post-hearing conference is usually influential but not necessarily so. While the social worker is 'responsible' for the adolescent, the residential staff are more initimately involved in the care and assessment and so the possibility of disagreement can arise. Several social workers indicated to us that, as time goes by:

They tend to treat you as the person who knows about the home, not the kid.

In these circumstances social workers have to make a considerable effort to retain contact with their young clients and:

> Try to build up a relationship.

The 'care plan' for a youngster tends to develop within the residential institution; the actual circumstances at home and in the community, and thus the social worker's contribution, can become very much a secondary consideration. This situation tends to apply particularly when an adolescent is in long-term residential care, but in many cases, as we have indicated, most stay in residential care for a relatively short time and for some it is merely for the purpose of assessment, after which they are allowed 'home on trial'. In the majority of our sample cases, the social worker retained the role of 'key worker' and continued to mediate between the youngster, the family and the welfare system.

In our follow-up sample, with 11 adolescents made the subjects of statutory social work involvement, it emerged that the problems which had trggered care proceedings largely continued in one form or another. The social workers acknowledged that the 'problem' had only been resolved effectively in a minority of cases and that the 'management', rather than the resolution of the problem, was usually their main concern. In several instances, other case conferences had been held to reassess and reconsider how the youngsters' needs could most appropriately be fitted to the available resources, which were thought by several social workers to be inadequate to the task. Some placements 'home on trial' or in a children's home had broken down and a vacancy in a community home was being sought, while for others the possibility of a return to the family home featured, particularly, if a local school would be willing to take them. Most of the social workers appeared to have a clear idea or plan of what they wanted to happen with particular cases, but the effective implementation of what 'should' happen was limited by the available resources, as well as by the complexities of the case.

In relation to those adolescents and their families in receipt of statutory involvement, particularly via care orders, the social workers were well aware that their responsibilities would stretch out beyond the substantive hearing and often after the first residential placement. Like their clients these social workers are themselves 'locked in' to a welfare-control relationship which, in many cases, will only subside when there is no longer the statutory demand for control: when the youngster can leave school legally, return home if her family are able to resume or reassert control and provide adequate care, or eventually just outgrow the period of adolescence which is so susceptible to state interference and control.

SUMMARY

LA social workers working on statutory cases are employed to represent a state welfare agency which has a legal duty and responsibility to provide care and control over those children and families whose social presentation is defined by themselves or, more usually, by LA agencies as problematic or deviant. The social worker's independence and discretion is therefore limited by the structure in which he or she operates. Although designated as the 'key worker' by the case conference to represent the departmental line in the care process, the social worker is also seen to be the key worker by the youngster and the parents, to whom he or she personifies the 'welfare' at a practical and local level. In reality, he/she mediates between the welfare system and the client, representing each to the other while being concerned primarily with his/her understanding of what is in the youngster's 'best interests'. This ambivalent and difficult role which the social worker is empowered to play is informed by a caring but contradictory ideology, which seeks to both defend and, when necessary, usurp the client's normal civil liberties and right to self-determination. Performing this task involves the social worker, and in theory the care court, in problematic professional and moral judgements. In care proceedings, social workers are an integral part of the court set-up and they feel fairly confident about their role in this context. They were aware that virtually all of their recommendations are supported by the magistrates and so were able to predict accurately the likely outcome of the hearing.

A consequence of their own relative security and their perception of the court hearing as already 'agreed', and thus essentially a formality, was that they saw no real need to involve families in the proceedings or coach adolescents about self-presentation. This was justified or explained in terms of there being no point in unduly 'worrying' or upsetting an adolescent or parent. Another feature of this approach concerned the low priority given to discussing the details of reports with families, particularly the young subjects. Social workers believed that, since families knew beforehand the likely outcome of the care process, this was enough to produce a reasonable degree of calm and satisfaction. This reluctance to discuss thorny issues fully with families was repeated in case conferences. Clearly this overall approach makes the immediate social work task in the care process less problematic yet the social workers displayed considerable ambivalence about their tendency to behave in this way, realizing it clashed with lauded principles in their own professional 'caring' ideology about face-to-face work with clients.

Their awareness of their own considerable powers in care proceedings and the fact that they believed the best guarantee of good practice was for their work to be subjected to thorough consideration led social workers to criticize legal counsel and magistrates for failing to scrutinize the LA case sufficiently. Such scrutiny would at least allow social workers to feel more sure that they were indeed acting, in the circumstances, in the best interests of the child — for they were also aware that they could not solve many of the problems inherent in their statutory child care cases. They often resigned themselves to problem management and 'containment', being aware that they would have to stay with the case, thereby being locked into a welfare-control relationship with the adolescent until the legal responsibility expired with the end of official adolescence. When we compare social work perceptions with those of the subject families it is clear that many social workers underestimated the extent to which families, especially parents, perceive the court as a degrading and humiliating ordeal. Whilst in some cases a high degree of consonance and empathy occurred between family and social worker, in others the social worker clearly assumed that because parents and/or child agreed there was a major problem requiring outside help that this gave the social worker and colleagues *carte blanche* simply to steer the case to its predictable court order. This false assumption, and hence insensitivity to the families' feelings about the degree of statutory intervention required and the manner in which it was executed, produced in certain cases, as we shall illustrate in the coming chapter, a massive gulf between social worker and those receiving welfare justice and statutory care and control.

12

Front-Line 'Care and Control'

In the two previous chapters we have aggregated and summarized adolescents' and parents' perceptions of the care passage and weighed these against the key workers' perspective. It has been extremely difficult to produce the resultant 'normative' picture without doing grievous bodily harm to the uniqueness and complexity of each case. In this chapter we will simply present some case studies and extracts from video'd roleplays made by the groupwork youngsters. These case studies are typical of our research 'triangles'.

'NOW YOUNG LADY YOU'VE GOT TO START GOING TO SCHOOL'

Our girls' group made a series of role-plays portraying their experience of being clients and of having been visited and dealt with by social workers and education welfare officers. As they ad-libbed and played out the task of these professional caretakers a key issue emerged: whether the welfare worker was going to 'send them away' into an institution or not? The EWO who threatened residential 'care' as a means of getting school attendance was seen as an ogre. One girl, taking on the role of her own EWO, 'acted' unscripted and unrehearsed for nearly half an hour, piling on the pressure as an extract illustrates:

> Don't tell me lies, you've been trying to come it with your mother. Your mother doesn't want this, does she? Does she? Your headmistress won't put up with this — do you think she will? Your teachers, are they bad to you . . . are they? Well, your headmistress isn't bad to you, is she? Your mother's good to you, isn't she?
> If you don't start going to school, Rose, you'll end up down the road in Rampton House [observation centre]. Your poor

mother must be worried sick with the school board calling round all the time. You'll end up in court you know. Did you know that? Did you know that? Well, you won't have to go to court 'cos you'll go straight to Rampton House. And, I'll have none of your lip. . . .

Yet a social worker (and a comparison is not intended) visiting for the same official reason but indicating that she would be trying to avoid the making of a care order is portrayed as kind, sensitive and reasonable by a girl who has had extensive experience of being on the receiving end. This social worker is 'made' in the role-play to offer baby clothes, bus passes and camping holidays. Even when the gritty issues of delinquency and truancy crop up the social worker can be seen as OK.

SW: I'm your new social worker. Glynis has gone on a 12-month course back to college. I've come to see about your eldest daughter Tracy. I believe she's been in quite a lot of trouble.

MOTHER: Yes, she's been truanting a lot from school.

SW: Have you been shoplifting lately Tracy?

TRACY: No.

SW: Pardon?

TRACY: No.

(*Later*)

SW: Your headmistress has asked for a case conference on you about a care order till you're 18.

TRACY: I wouldn't like to be stuck away.

(*Later*)

SW: How's Tony getting on in Borstal?

MOTHER: He's fine.

SW: Now Tracy. You'll have to start going to school you know because we're giving you one more chance. I'm going to ask for one chance or you'll get a care order. That means you'll be away two years, you know, and you'll only be coming home at Christmas and once every now and again — holidays. Mrs Lund said you didn't get on very well with the teachers — is that true? Why don't you like them?

TRACY: They get on me nerves.

SW: Particular ones or all of them?

TRACY: All of them.

SW: Beg your pardon?

TRACY: *All* of them.

SW: Well that's just something you'll have to put up with isn't it Missus?

MOTHER: Yes. She's been to several schools and found this in each school but nothing. . . .

SW: Well, everyone goes through this stage where they don't like the schools. I didn't like it myself . . . but you've just got to put up with it. It's either that or a care order, which I don't recommend either.

(*Later*)

SW: All I can suggest is that you go to school and just put up with the teachers. All the kids have the same.

(*Later*)

SW: At the case conference in three more days I'll stick up for you because me being the social worker I'll try and get you off this care order. The thing is you've been in trouble quite a few times with the law haven't you . . . you've got a court case coming up. What was that for? .

(*Later*)

SW: Oh Tracy I don't know what we're going to do about you. . . . I'll do my best anyway. (*Pause*) Are you going to school tomorrow?

TRACY: Yeh.

SW: Would you like me to come and pick you up, save you the messin' round?

(*Pause*)

SW: Where's your husband now Mrs Haydock, is he still with you?

MOTHER: No, we're separated. This is where all the trouble started you know. Tracy started playing truant like when her father went.

SW: Well we'll see what we can do for you. Just make sure you go to school for your mother's sake and your own sake 'coz it's the best way for you, you know. Whereas if you don't go to school you'll just get put away till you're 18. And when you go for a job or something people say ... they look at your background.

However, the same trio of girls played another scene, having in mind a social worker with a different outlook about the best course of action.

SW: When are you planning on going back to school?

TRACY: Monday.

SW: You sure? Would you like me to call up at the house on Monday and give you a lift up?

TRACY: No.

SW: It saves you getting the bus up.

TRACY: No. I want to get the bus.

SW: I can give you a lift up.

MOTHER: Your office is right by the school, aren't you in the Lybo Buildings?

SW: So I'll call up at nine o'clock Monday.

MOTHER: What will happen if she doesn't keep the promise of going to school?

SW: I reckon she should have a care order.

MOTHER: No. I don't agree with that, what do you think Tracy?

SW: It's got nothing to do with you love.

MOTHER: 'Course its got something to do with her. She's my daughter.

SW: Well I'm social services.

MOTHER: I couldn't give a shit what you are.

SW: I beg your pardon!

MOTHER: Well she's my daughter. You can't come here telling me you're going to take her into a home.

SW: Would you mind that language! I didn't come here to be sworn at.

MOTHER: You walk in here all high and mighty 'coz you're a social worker, think you've got the right to walk into somebody's home and take their child away.

SW: Well, you should send her to school.

MOTHER: Sometimes she stays off school, when I'm not very
          well to help with the young children. Otherwise,
          when I do send her, I send her at quarter to nine.

SOME SOCIAL WORKER! SOME CLIENT!

MRS E: I've been harassed with them all ... ever since I've
          been away from my husband ... social workers,
          school board — all of them. I feel I'm not even being
          a mother — they try to do that for you ... They
          won't let you get on with your life.

Mrs E understandably finds that bringing up seven children on
her own is a very difficult task ... In view of Mandy's very poor
school attendance and *obvious* problems at home, I feel she needs
to be in the care of the local authority. As past experience has
shown that voluntary care has not proved an appropriate method,
I respectfully recommend that a care order is made (from social
worker's report).

The E family score high on many indices of social deprivation — their
mother, who was cruelly knocked about by her ex-husband, suffers
from failing physical and mental health: She exists, now, on social
security, accommodated in an inadequate dwelling situated on a large
'sink' estate. She and her children have been known to local state agencies for as many years as she can remember — they are, without doubt,
the subjects of several voluminous files which could be condensed into
the shorthand of 'problem family'.

Mrs E's two eldest children, 'Mandy' who's 14 and 'Maria', 12, were
taken before the juvenile court, nominally on grounds of non-school
attendance. After three appearances, spanning about a month, Mandy
was made subject to a care order but shortly afterwards allowed 'home-
on-trial' and Maria was given a supervision order. Their school attendance had apparently been irregular for some time, whilst violent, punch-
drunk rows reverberated from their home and their mother, who like
most parents expressed a mixture of love and hatred for her daughters,
from time to time, low on barbituates and alcohol, made suicide gestures. Finally, Mandy's way of life, particularly the allegation by her
mother that she had taken to keeping company with 'known prosti-

tutes', galvanized the authorities into action: clearly, 'something had to be done'.

Accordingly, a case conference was called and local education and social services department officials decided to summons both girls before the juvenile bench on grounds of their non-school attendance. Again, it was felt this matter would be easier to prove and less hurtful to the family than any other Section 1 clause. Neither Mrs E nor her daughters attended this conference — which further fuelled their general resentment against the authorities. The social worker, with overall responsibility for this demanding and severely disadvantaged family, had apparently told Mrs E she would be invited but says that things moved swiftly and, when she called to inform Mrs E of the scheduled conference, she got no reply.

Given this background and her long and bitter experiences with officialdom, it is perhaps not surprising that Mrs E took issue with the social worker's courtroom evidence. Looking back on the tearful and emotion-charged hearing, the family as a whole felt that the social worker's evidence influenced the bench's decisions. Mandy, for example, regarded the social worker's tale as unfair and inaccurate:

> Social worker kept on bringing up about school, about me and my mum . . . she said I was staying out late . . . that I came in too late and couldn't get up in the morning. . . . I don't like my social worker.

Mrs E pointed out omissions in the social worker's evidence, particularly an instance when the social worker had, from Mrs E's perspective, allowed Mandy to stay with 'bad company' as part of an agreement:

> Social workers shouldn't make deals with children.

For her part, the social worker also referred to an omission. She says she deliberately censored the information that the E children were included on an 'NAI register', since:

> The magistrates would probably have taken them all into care.

The social worker's desire to avoid splitting up the family was not perceived by its members, however. Mrs E charged the social worker personally with causing her grief and chagrin throughout the proceedings. Here was a young, childless and professional middle-class woman who represented the very antithesis of her own way of life. Mrs E, who might have felt marginally less undermined by a male social worker,

concluded that this 'lady bountiful' who had come along with com-
pletely wrong-sized shoes for her daughters, and who thus could have
no idea about the practicalities of bringing up children, was, to her way
of thinking, quite unjustly empowered to remove Mandy from her care.
Mrs E told us she had threatened a further suicide attempt in the event
of Mandy being taken away from her. Even with Mandy back at home,
she continued to censure the social worker:

> She's only young . . . she's bit docile . . . doesn't have a bevvy
> . . . she'll be left on the shelf if she doesn't hurry up.

Mandy, perhaps taking her cue from her mother, held her social
worker responsible for the whole juvenile court business. She weighed
the social worker up personally and negatively. To Mandy, the social
worker bore little resemblance to her mother's probation officer — 'a
cracker'. Rather, Mandy felt the social worker:

> Just went along with the education . . . I know my social worker
> wanted me to get put away. I know she's punished me enough — I
> can't talk to my social worker without arguing . . . I know some
> social workers want to avoid putting you in care . . . my one
> wants me in care.

Consequently, Mandy did her utmost to avoid all contact with her
social worker, either by physically getting out of the house or by mentally distancing herself:

> I just sit there and day-dream when she comes.

The E family's story, however, cannot be written down as a totally
ineffectual and conflict-ridden encounter with welfare justice punctuated by mutual recriminations and communication barriers. For the
other daughter, Maria, apparently went back to school after the court
hearing and, some months on, had chalked up a regular attendance
record. As a girl made subject to a supervision order, not a care order,
she seemed less negative towards the social worker than her older sister,
although she too blamed her social worker for the court summons:

> 'coz she was supposed to make sure that I was going to school.

But was less ready to discuss the social worker personally:

> She's OK — she's sometimes nice.

Yet Maria too, tried to minimize her contact. The social worker responded with lax supervision. She told us she had been reluctant anyway to press Maria's case and, but for her sister's situation, might well have ignored Maria's erratic school attendance along with that of many other adolescents on her 'patch'. Thus Maria was 'in the shadows — almost an afterthought' and her renewed school attendance pattern enabled the social worker to conclude:

She seems to have worked something out for herself.

This social worker was not unaware or insensitive to any of the family's feelings. She too was a 'victim', directed to press for a care order by a case conference. She acknowledged that she had made little headway in terms of relationships and that her work with Mandy had proved superficial 'not very effective'. She simply got on with her statutory duties as best she could, working, in her terms, 'for' the family, despite them. She had had to face the invective, the changes of mind by the mother, the accusations and tears. She was aware that 'solutions' were certainly beyond her skills and resources and suspected they were probably beyond the resources and capabilities of her department. She tried both to keep the family together and to threaten to break it up, as instructed. She was not sorry when this messy case 'settled down' for a while.

'WE WENT FOR HELP BUT THEY LOCKED HER UP'

Joan Smith, a 14 year old with two younger brothers, was doing daily battle with her parents, when they both came home from work. These parents, in their early 30s, were having great difficulty with their daughter. There were regular rows for several months before 'the welfare' became involved, mainly over the 'bad company' Joan was keeping and her consequent tendency to 'stay out all hours'. Joan responded to the conflict with a series of suicide gestures and with 'behavioural problems' at school, which resulted in her being transferred to a special education guidance unit. Finally, in May, she ran away to London where she was picked up by the police and accommodated overnight in a local authority children's home before being returned to her parents. This episode prompted Mr and Mrs Smith to ask the local social services department for 'some help' and a breathing space. Joan was received into care on a voluntary basis for a couple of weeks. However, when her parents took her home, the inter-family frictions continued. Probably because Joan was now a 'case' to be watched by the various local welfare officials, some bruising on her leg was queried in July. Joan said her father had kicked her. The local social services were notified, and, using their established 'NAI' procedures they immediately convened a case conference. Neither Joan nor her parents were invited.

According to Joan's social worker, the conference expressed 'fears for her safety' and noted her father's 'excessive use of chastisement'. The case conference mandated the social worker to take out a place of safety order and begin care proceedings 'for' Joan.

Mr and Mrs Smith were both upset and angry. Their daughter had been removed from home and they found themselves subjected to a series of court hearings, culminating in the making of a full care order on Joan. Looking back on their court experience, the parents were particularly angry about the social worker's report. They found there 'twisted' information which failed to contextualize their long-standing problems with Joan. In particular, having the word 'assault' used in court by the social worker upset them. In their eyes the whole thing had escalated and avalanched out of their control: had they not gone for help no 'official' would have been any the wiser:

> We went for help but they locked her up and then we had to try and get her back. They made it twice as worse . . . like a hornet's nest. . . . I'd never recommend a social worker to anyone!

Nor was this a case of the social worker and young client siding together. Joan too felt the case had 'gone over the top':

> The social worker said my dad hit me and left a mark on my leg, that he attacked me . . . that wasn't true . . . he only hit me 'coz I stayed out late.

Joan thought the social worker 'just horrible'. Her parents felt similarly. In terms of 'personal social services' this case went badly wrong. The case began with a family seeking help but then, in their terms, finding the level and manner of intervention totally inappropriate. The social worker hardly enjoyed the case either. He was the front-line worker who had to carry out the case conference decision. And although he admitted he disliked statutory work with adolescent girls, once so instructed he set about 'winning the case'. He soldiered on, showing his court report to the family before the hearing. They in turn took exception to his choice of words and his claim that Mr S 'was unduly provoked by Joan's behaviour'.

Finally we should note that the Smith case rumbles on. Joan was actually allowed 'home on trial' to live with her grandparents soon after the care order was made — again 'objectively' a sign of the social worker's good intentions. However, this placement broke down with Joan again being picked up by the police. She was returned to residential care, with the intention of placing her in a community school.

'THEY KNOCKED ON THE DOOR . . . JUST BEFORE CHRISTMAS'

Joe Lynch had been in a lot of trouble. He'd been, 'through the mill' of both attendance centre and detention centre and he'd also been on a supervision order. His offences were not very serious, however, and tended to be the result of his 'mouth' (e.g. disorderly behaviour, insulting behaviour). As his father saw it:

> I'd say he's been harassed by the police. He tells them what he thinks of them for always getting on his back. That's what they do him for — for arguing.

Joe's social worker also resented his young client's 'arrogance':

> One day he came in and announced calmly that he was not going to be supervised. He looked me in the eye, a cool 15 year old, and said 'so don't waste your time'.

Having been to detention centre and come out on 'licence' to a probation officer Joe continued his 'defiant' ways by not attending school very often and by not keeping his supervision appointments with the probation officer. Joe's parents claimed to be largely unaware of this. Joe independently agreed that they were. The probation officer didn't like Joe's attitude. He liaised with the school. Although not unduly upset about Joe's absence, the school agreed he was truanting regularly. When eventually these 'failures' of their son became clear to Mr and Mrs Lynch, they too agreed that something had to be done. They accepted that the local authority had the right to take action. Mr

Lynch even thought Borstal might be appropriate. Joe himself 'knew something would happen' and accepted he'd 'been a bit wild'.

What upset both son and parents was the *manner* of intervention. We have already indicated the weakness of the probation 'office desk' approach to supervision. Mr and Mrs Lynch were not aware their son was failing to attend for his licence supervision. So when the probation officer, and social worker who'd been in charge of Joe's case previously, arrived with a place of safety order, these parents received an almighty shock:

> Just before Christmas they knocked on the door and took Joe away. They had some order signed by the magistrates. . . . Just before Christmas, and out of the blue.

Joe, wasn't too pleased either and responded by absconding, with some style, from the local secure assessment centre:

> Because I didn't think it was fair what was happening.

Joe's parents also took exception to the substantive care hearing which eventually took place. In particular they felt the probation officer 'told lies' and the 'evidence' by school officials about Joe's troublesome behaviour was merely hearsay. Joe, the subject of the 'inevitable' care order, was labelled during the proceedings as 'uncooperative and arrogant', 'aggressive and disruptive'. Indeed it was his 'attitude to authority' which was the focus of attention, although legally he was in court for non-school attendance.

In retrospect Joe's parents, at least, think's he's best off in community school until he's 16. They agreed something needed to be done. However several months after the hearing they still deeply resent the *manner* in which local welfare officials did that something.

'MY SOCIAL WORKER'S GREAT'

Colin

Colin is 16; his mother died a few years ago. Colin was living with his father, not the kindest of men, prior to being picked up by the police on account of a semi-public homosexual incident. He was made the subject of a place of safety order. Care proceedings followed by the local authority bringing evidence that Colin was in 'moral danger' and not receiving adequate care and control at home. City's magistrates found this case proved and as a result Colin was sent back to the observation and assessment centre he was first placed with. Several weeks lapsed before a case conference, rather short of placement options, and unhappy about 'letting him loose in a working boys' hostel' decided, by default, to allow Colin 'home on trial' but to reside with his elder sister, who agreed to this.

Colin's social worker, a local down-to-earth woman with several years' experience, saw this, in the circumstances, as the best course of action. In her eyes Colin's homosexuality was not a problem as such. She in fact was ambivalent about the need for statutory proceedings at all, but went along with her department's line. She worked conscientiously with Colin throughout the proceedings visiting him regularly and in his eyes:

> She's great . . . she tried her best all through. She told me not to be scared [in court] and what would happen . . . she doesn't tell me what to do, not pushy or bossy.

The social worker felt that Colin was ambivalent about her intervention, knowing he'd also felt that the court proceedings had been unnecessary and distasteful. In his eyes, as he'd admitted he was 'out of control' and 'out all hours', the court was unnecessary. Yet the social worker also realized:

> He enjoyed the attention in the assessment centre. Got on with the staff there.

Once Colin went 'home on trial' to his sister's, however, the social worker rather left supervision to chance. She expected Colin to drop in and see her every few weeks but nothing more. She saw her role as a friend rather than 'state parent'.

> I'm here if he wants to chat. I expect him to come in every couple of weeks. I think he should be in charge of his own life. . . . I think we've helped him through a bad patch. We gave him some attention when he needed it. He comes in here when he wants.

Colin accordingly *did* go in and see his social worker for a while.

The social worker was not blind to the fact that her young client

'tells me all sorts of lies'. So when Colin's sister rang up to say he had
left her home some two weeks before the social worker was not unduly
surprised. Her senior recommended she send out an escort officer and
return Colin into residential care on the grounds that the case conference decision was now in default. The social worker resisted this and
after some investigation found Colin was living with a boy friend and
working in a hairdresser's shop. She left things alone, arguing that
neither she nor her department had anything more to offer Colin.

In terms of a counselling relationship based on trust and self-determination, this social worker had achieved a high standard of practice
in a difficult situation. Both worker and client were 'satisfied' and the
high quality of the relationship had achieved a great deal. However, in
order to get it right with Colin, the social worker had wandered a long
way from her role as a local state official with statutory parental responsibility. She had left herself open to allegations of neglect of duty
and possibly even professional incompetence and hence placed her
department in a vulnerable position.

Carla

When both the family as a whole and the local authority come to agree
about what 'the problem' is and what should be done about it, only the
manner in which the necessary tasks are carried out remains problematic. We had several cases in our sample in which the need for intervention having been mutually agreed, it was the experience of the care
court and the quality of the relationship between social worker and
family that were the key variables in the 'satisfaction' formula; that is,
they represented the manner in which a family was dealt with. Mrs
Toon for instance, after a long and complicated series of dealing with
social services, eventually ended up accepting statutory care proceedings on her 13 year old daughter. Looking back on her family's passage,
and whilst resenting a few incidents during the care hearing, she had
nothing but respect for the social worker. The daughter felt similarly.
They both felt that the social worker had acted 'to help us sort it out'
and had kept them well informed throughout. Furthermore, he had
acted as an arbiter, a referee between mother, going through a difficult
divorce and settling into a new 'marriage', and Carla who had been out
and about the neighbourhood day and night and was not averse to
dipping into her mother's and a neighbour's purse. In particular the
social worker had only allowed Carla 'home on trial' when both parties
were ready for reconciliation.

From a 'practice' point of view the social worker did this by devising, with the residential home, a 'points system' whereby Carla could, through good behaviour, *easily* earn sufficient points to get a day or weekend or long weekend at home. This social work team noted that at first Carla did not earn sufficient points and indeed it was several weeks after the care order was made before she 'demonstrated' her readiness to go home for longer periods. The ground in the maternal home was carefully prepared and the reunion carefully monitored. Here was a case which perhaps should have been 'voluntary' anyway but the social worker felt that he would not have been able to get a place in the particular residential unit he wished to use for Carla without the status of a statutory order.

COMMENT

These case studies largely speak for themselves. They illustrate the complexity and uniqueness which characterized most of the care cases in our sample. The portrait of this 'side' of the juvenile justice system has a grey tone to it — not, we would contend, because we have failed to tease out the black and white texture but because the picture *is* grey, the issues are not simple and clear. Those of us who advocate radical changes in the present system must ponder long and hard. We must face the fact that, whilst problems can be solved, moral dilemmas can only be faced.

13

Making Nonsense of Juvenile Justice

CRIMINAL JUSTICE?

We have argued throughout that the 1969 Act, because of its partial implementation and consequent ambiguity, gave legitimacy to the extension of discretion in the criminal–juvenile justice system. Rampant discretion, in an area so politically important as the social control of working-class youth, has over the past decade led to a major *dissonance* between the intentions of the uncut Act and the actual sentencing patterns produced. We have shown how there is a clear 'push-in' tendency by the police as gatekeepers to the juvenile court. This push in of cases was strongly criticized by parents and juveniles, who also alleged that charges were routinely 'bumped up'. They perceived this tendency as a consequence of a 'battle' between urban policeman and streetwise youth – a view reinforced by our own present and previous (see Parker, 1974) research and studies of the police themselves (Jones, 1980). This tendency directly contradicts the intentions of the Act, which aimed at diverting and so decriminalizing large amounts of trivial delinquency. The citing of a formal caution on a juvenile's criminal record, recently introduced by law, and local developments such as the introduction of an 'informal' caution, to be recorded by police intelligence, all confirm this dissonance. The punitive sentencing patterns of the past decade, nowhere more dramatically illustrated than in our analysis of Countyside, merely sharpens this same portrait of juvenile justice as social control by punishment, involving the extensive use of custodial measures.

Discretion, in the hands of local police and magistrates, although they themselves do not always see eye to eye, will routinely produce punitive juvenile justice. However it will not do so across the board, since not all local officials will share exactly the same objectives. Hence, although the overall trend in England and Wales has been towards punitive juvenile justice, local 'productions' will vary sufficiently to give

242

the picture a quality of *diversity*. Our comparison of City and Countyside confirms the earlier findings of Anderson (1978) and illustrates how this phenomenon produces major inequities in sentencing, even within the same geographical region.

A third feature of the present juvenile justice system we have referred to is official *deviation*. Whilst we have illustrated rule 'bending' as an everyday occurrence throughout the system, undertaken by nearly all officials, if our respondents are to be believed it is with the police that official deviation occurs most frequently. Within the court process official deviance as it appeared in Countyside was a product of magistrates and clerks, in the absence of strict procedural rules, instituting a minimalist interpretation of the safeguards of due process by orchestrating and coordinating their extensive 'legitimate' discretion. What Countyside shows is that it is possible under the present legislation to produce a regime which can appear to operate against both the 'best interests of the child' and the principles of natural and criminal justice simultaneously. It leaves us in no doubt where the decision-making power lies.

We cannot be sure how City's contrasting approach to juvenile justice was initially created, although we are clear what operational rules and social interactions sustain it. City offers a clear model of how the spirit of the 1969 Act and the principles of due process and proportionality in punishment can be functionally combined to offer a version of justice for juveniles which has much to commend it − not least its general acceptability by its customers. City, compared with Countyside, offered young defendants and their parents more civility, more explanation, more legal representation and other legal safeguards embodied in due process, and a more consistent and proportionate sentencing policy. For liberal reformers keen to retain the juvenile court and who wish to extract policy implications from this comparative study some consideration must be given to the following areas. Stricter rules must be produced to govern the behaviour of clerks, with defendants being able to appeal against sentence if it can be shown, probably via the evidence of a defence lawyer, that such rules have been breached. The rules concerning the granting and refusal of legal aid should be much clearer, with the aim of making legal representation a right in most circumstances. Sentencing 'brackets' or restrictions should be introduced to reduce magisterial idiosyncracies (e.g. DC should not be available for a first time offender except for very serious offences) in sentencing − although we would anticipate the impact of such a framework would be badly undermined by the very same charge defining and 'bumping up' tactics our sample have described. Only the introduction of an independent 'sift', along the lines of the Scottish Reporter, would begin to solve this problem. The sentencing patterns of each juvenile court should be published, probably in Chief Constables' Reports and the Criminal Statistics (in Countyside even *magistrates* weren't informed of their annual sentencing pattern). These measures would go some way to preventing local responses to juvenile crime, which may well reflect inter-class antagonisms rather than 'the community response', from becoming grossly unjust.

We have analysed very carefully in this study the notion of 'welfare' or help as delivered by social workers and probation officers in the juvenile justice system. We did so because so much has been made of the supposed social work influence in the system. Although social workers do indeed have considerable power in care proceedings we found no evidence that this is the case in criminal proceedings. It seems more likely that the social welfare role has been scapegoated by what can increasingly be seen as the 'law and order' lobby of the New Right. This scapegoating has diverted attention from the fact that the power is really vested in the hands of local police and magistrates. It is they who are responsible for producing the expanding workload and punitive disposal patterns of the past decade, over and above the nature of reported crime. We have shown quite clearly that the social work—probation influence in court is marginal and *reflects* rather than creates the local production of juvenile justice. We have implied that the main reason for this rests again with the magistracy, since care orders and supervision orders are made at their discretion, although obviously usually with the encouragement of a welfare report. Yet even when community-based orders were made, we have shown that they have had little impact upon the lives of the juveniles and parents interviewed. This would seem to be largely the result of the confusion suffered by probation officers and social workers, concerning the objectives of their work and the failure of their agencies to resource more constructive programmes for young offenders.

Apart from community supervision only the '7 (7)' care order gives social workers any significant power in the decision-making processes. Their use of this discretion has not been impressive (see Thorpe *et al.*, 1980). Although they have been criticized for locking too many children up in community homes (see Taylor *et al.*, 1980), social workers have also been impuned by the magistracy for letting too many convicted juveniles 'home on trial'. Whilst the evidence suggests that the former criticism is more accurate (see Cawson, 1979), the fact that the 1980 White Paper *Young Offenders* backs the magistracy is a further proof of the dominance of the 'law and order' lobby of the New Right. Under the banner of 'returning' power to the magistracy, this latest intended renovation of the 1969 Act, along with the further watering-down of the police's need to consult with social services and probation over cautioning—prosecution decisions via criminal proceedings, will remove most of the social worker's discretion. These modifications, along with the removal of similar discretion from Borstal governors, the increase in the number of attendance centres, their introduction for girls, the probable introduction of community service orders and the extension of the use of detention centres and the 'shorter sharper shock' of a three-week order, can all be seen as a consistent trend, increasing and extending the local state's punitive control over working-class youth.

Juvenile criminal justice is patently about social control; it concerns the external imposition of influence or power to produce change in juveniles. Basically it requires them to change and to observe rules protecting private and public property. This is not at issue. Any society must make social rules and administer their observance. The real issue is *how* this control is exercised and how this mode relates to other social values and principles which underpin the particular social system. When the administration of social control clearly clashes with certain other social values, we enter the realm of conflict among different interest groups. The moral authority of the state is placed in question.

The hundred families who helped us carry out this research strongly backed the principles of 'law and order'; they accepted the idea of punishment being the prime concern of the juvenile courts. For this reason and the fact that their critique is so discerning we must take their condemnation of the local operation of 'law and order' very seriously. All the adolescents in our sample, and more surprisingly the vast majority of their parents, were deeply critical of routine policing practice. They delivered their critique with great anger and resentment. There was very little evidence that the police had any moral authority in the working-class neighbourhoods where our sample families lived. Although perplexed by being unable to consider how social order could be maintained without the police, these families clearly see the policeman as a powerful, unpredictable agent whose behaviour cannot be checked or made accountable. He is a source of alienation.

This alienation was carried over into the juvenile court in terms of, in the families' eyes, the 'push-in' and the 'bump-up'. In City, it had the tendency to partially undermine an otherwise valid and acceptable version of criminal–juvenile justice. For the Countryside 'customers' we spoke to this merely confirmed the class-based, biased, degrading and retributive nature of the practice of 'law and order'. Their passage through the process was perceived not as a prosecution but a persecution. The system undermined its own moral authority, which in principle its 'customers' were willing to give it.

The production of juvenile justice, in criminal proceedings, can thus clearly become the imposition of a form of social control which clashes with the very safeguards and principles of justice which are widely accepted as regulating society's criminal court apparatus. We have concluded this from our own analysis of local productions and it is borne out by the perceptions of those subjected to juvenile court appearances. The evidence makes nonsense of the notion of justice for juveniles.

We have contended that the history of post-war child care and delinquency control legislation is intimately related to the politics of government and consequently the ideologies underpinning the two main political parties. Just as the resistance to the 1969 Act and ongoing renovation has been politically motivated and administered by the New Right, so too the 1960s debate, linking delinquency prevention to the much larger ideal of *social justice,* was a socialist inspiration. This linking of social justice and, in particular, the notion of 'equality of opportunity' with child care and delinquency control rested on the premise that, in practice, the juvenile justice 'system' deals almost exclusively with working-class children – the most socially and economically disadvantaged. This is as true today as then and holds for the customers of care proceedings also (see Holman, 1976, Thoburn, 1980). Longford (Labour Party Study Group, 1964) saw delinquency as a symptom and manifestation of this deprivation and was encouraged to do so by a vociferous child care lobby. The notion of social justice is equally relevant to more sociological analyses of the conditions under which delinquency flourishes – for example, the relationship between legal and illegal opportunity pathways (Cloward and Ohlin, 1960) and the significance of neutralization techniques which the lack of legal pathways can cause. For instance, youth unemployment can 'encourage' delinquency, not just by blocking off legal pathways and so leading adolescents to resort to illegal routes, but the self-identity of being unemployed can 'neutralize' the social rules which normally restrain someone by providing an excuse for rule-breaking. A wide range of sociological theories about the conditions under which juvenile delinquency flourishes would support the view that socio-economic deprivation is relevant.

If we adopt this more radical position, which essentially argues that criminal justice cannot be applied fairly in a society lacking in social justice, then even City court, situated in one of the most deprived areas of Britain, becomes the product of 'unacceptable' social control. We noted how City court officials remained uncritical of the socio-economic position of their customers. They judged unskilled working-class juveniles on the basis that they and their families can live happily in poverty, that school is always a good thing and a gateway to upward social mobility. The jobs, they implied, are there for young people who look hard enough and have worked hard enough at school. In short you are where you are because of *your* own inadequacy not the social system's. City's liberalism was uncritical and nowhere more clearly so than in the court's unwavering belief, and consequent clash of beliefs with its customers, that the police are impartial, just do their job and objectively enforce the law. City officials can be nothing else. They must remain uncritical in order to perform their designated function: the upholding of social order in working-class areas, the protection of property and person, and the reaffirmation of the authority of the local state apparatus. City magistrates could not overtly accept that the juveniles paraded before them, as well as often being culpable for their crimes, were also, in terms of social justice, victims of disadvantage right across the board. To accept such ideas would involve accepting the relevance of social structural features and related social conflict and the final irony that delinquency may well be a rational response. Criminal—juvenile justice is at its best not concerned with social justice. Criminal—juvenile justice, at its worst, may not even be concerned with the minimal safeguards of natural justice.

WELFARE JUSTICE?

The children and adolescents who enter the juvenile justice system under the 'care' umbrella, whether through the '7 (7)' order in criminal proceedings or through care proceedings proper, to some extent pass into the system by chance. Whilst their situations may well merit referral, they are only a fraction of the number of youngsters who could be legitimately processed. We should not assume that the system picks up the greatest social need or the most problematic juveniles. Many youngsters are processed because of the nature of the school they attend (Reynolds, 1976; Rutter, 1979); or because one particular official rang a bureaucratic alarm bell — most often the social worker initially concerned with writing a court report on a young offender; or because their parents decide to contact the 'welfare' rather than soldier on alone. Generally, it would seem that adolescents (rather than young children) tend to enter the system when there are control issues on the agenda.

We have considered in some depth how these referrals are shaped up and further redefined by City's 'welfare justice' process. The hiding of real agendas, the use of certain primary conditions as vehicles to carry a case through the court successfully and the behind-the-scenes agreements among local officials have all been discussed. We have shown that, although such official deviance is usually perpetrated in the belief that it is in the child's best interests, in practice it can appear more functional for officials in and around the care court than for the families involved. For although some 'dreadful performances' are avoided, City's approach to welfare justice can appear to deprive families of the safeguards embodied in both due process and natural justice. The only justification for ignoring these safeguards in the production of welfare justice can be that it facilitates the best interests of the child by making 'care' more easy to offer. Yet if we define care, following Harris (1980), as 'concern for the well-being of another and a desire to sustain or enhance well-being in a manner and direction agreed between carer and cared for' we must remain sceptical, on the evidence of our case studies, that adolescents routinely receive care. The emphasis would seem to be on control, in which case traditional safeguards should not be waived.

We have seen how all officials in and around City's care court, including defence lawyers, do waive such safeguards, probably believing this to be in the interests of the child, by facilitating the 'smooth passage' approach to care proceedings. For the social worker once a case is pushed into the legal arena, it tends to go all the way, to the extent that she can be almost certain that her recommendation will be followed. Because of this, the social worker approaches the subject family in a particular way and misunderstanding often occurs.

In general terms, parents agreed that the 'authorities' should have the statutory right to intervene in families within which adequate care and control was not being exercised. With the exception of straight-forward non-school attendance cases which were not deemed by these families a sign of inadequate care and control, most accepted that they did have real problems and troubles which required something to be done. In principle, once again, the local state was recognized as a legitimate arbiter.

Yet, as we have seen, 'help' or care, as we have defined it, was not usually received because the form and manner of statutory intervention was out of tune with the wishes and expectations of all or some of the subject family members. The 'something' which was actually done was, in the eyes of these families, far in excess of anything they had anticipated. The resort to residential 'care' was seen by most parents and some youngsters as unnecessary, or unnecessarily long in duration, as was the overall court process itself. The court hearings were also seen as degrading and humiliating, particularly by the parents. This environment compounded the sense of powerlessness felt by families who consequently saw 'their' defence lawyer, even though he 'lost' the case, in a positive light because of his attempts to restore their dignity. For some of the adolescents, the post-hearing care and supervision orders also continued beyond their relevance (see also Thoburn, 1980).

It is clear that social workers, caught up in the key worker role of orchestrating care proceedings and desensitized by their own relative security in these proceedings and ability to predict the final outcome, badly misjudged the families' frustration. Hence families were not prepared by their social worker for the court hearings or 'coached' in any systematic way, but instead were treated for 'nerves' by being encouraged to simply 'sit tight', a tendency repeated in relation to seeing and discussing reports and participating in case conferences. In short, the social worker in particular and welfare officials in general were wrong to assume that, because parents and/or youngsters agree there is a major problem requiring outside intervention, this gives the local system *carte blanche* to mould and steer the case to some pre-determined outcome.

Having said this, social workers did appreciate their own considerable powers in care proceedings and realized that they would tend to produce their best practice if critically checked. This led them to criticize defence lawyers and magistrates for failing to scrutinize the local authority case. In City, not only does the responsibility for initiating statutory intervention rest with social workers, but, because of the ambivalance of the defence lawyers and magistrates and the clerk's low profile, the making of moral judgements, often in the face of chronic uncertainty, also weighs heavily and solely upon the shoulders of social workers and, at best, case conferences. Clearly much of the indignity and unhappiness suffered by families subjected to welfare justice can be laid at the social work door. Yet our understanding of other recent critiques of juvenile justice (e.g. Morris *et al.,* 1980; Taylor *et al.,* 1980) is that social workers are also blamed for *actually making* moral judgements. For City, at least, this claim is totally unreasonable and we cannot believe that the problems presented in other regions will be any more straightforward. Difficult moral judgements do have to be made and social workers have the *right* to have these judgements checked and scrutinized by lawyers and magistrates. City social workers at least partly understood this.

Although the present statutory apparatus clearly needs reforming, we should never lose sight of the fact that no system whether run by judges, lawyers or social welfare 'experts' can avoid making moral judgements about often irreconcilable problems. Improvements in legal representation and advocacy are vital. Clear guidelines about the writing of reports and the rights of families to see them are also much needed. There is also a strong case for an intermediate and finite intervention system. For cases involving adolescents, as we found, many of the 'crises' which led to outside intervention 'settle down' within the three months it took for the case to reach the substantive hearing. The court order was often made *after* the crisis had passed. Such an intermediate system would greatly reduce the 'excesses' of the present apparatus felt so keenly by parents and youngsters. A reform, which would be politically unacceptable but one which we would advocate on the basis of our research, would be the complete removal of non-school attendance as a discrete reason for initiating care proceedings.

Statutory care proceedings, whilst part of the juvenile justice system, are by implication also part of the child care services, themselves a part of perhaps the last epic dream of the post-war welfare state — the personal social services. The post-war creation of a 'preventative' child care service (see Packman, 1975), with the goal of positive family support, now seems far away. On the one hand, statutory child care services have been badly sidetracked by demands for social control and, on the other, badly undermined by the general pressure on and mismanagement of resources in social services departments. As a consequence, local authority intervention in the lives of working-class families has increasingly become synonymous with crisis intervention and resources are allocated accordingly. Hence social workers are often forced to initiate statutory proceedings to release the scarce resources they would otherwise not get. Furthermore, these resources are themselves often inflexible and inappropriate. The 'excesses' felt by families subjected to statutory care proceedings are partly due to this.

The *raison d'etre* for the welfare state and positive family support systems for working-class families remains therefore, as does the acceptance by these families that the state should provide such safety nets. In reality, however, such personal social services do not exist in sufficient quantity. Instead, we find an insensitive and under-resourced system, heavily involved in control rather than care, characterized by its inability to deliver meaningful help to working-class families encountering knotty problems. Once again, we are left with not just the personal misunderstandings and failures which we have documented, but a realization that they are largely a consequence of the politics of care and control and decision-making which takes place many miles away from the tense atmosphere in the waiting-room of City's care court. To receive juvenile justice is to receive a personalized political message.

Notes

1. Copies of the Schedules: 'Documentary Background'; 'Court Observation'; 'Juveniles on Criminal Proceedings I' and 'Follow-Up'; 'Juveniles on Care Proceedings I' and 'Follow-Up'; 'Selective Parental Interviews'; 'Social Work Interviews' and 'Follow-Up' can be obtained as a set within 12 months of publication subject to availability. Send £5.50 to H. J. Parker, Department of Sociology, Liverpool University, Liverpool L69 3BX.

2. Based on interviews with more than 80 adolescents and more than 30 sets of parents.

3. We will discuss the 'full tariff' in due course. Basically it involves magistrates voluntarily responding to recidivism by sentencing up a ladder of disposals one at a time. Table 5.1 (p. 79) shows the rungs of this ladder moving in practice from conditional discharge to fine, supervision order, attendance centre and detention centre. The reality is more complex than this but this general 'ladder' process underlies City's sentencing formula.

4. Interviews with some 60 adolescents and about a third of their respective parents and follow-up interviews with 17 adolescents form the basis of the analysis.

5. We interviewed 15 probation officers who were responsible for 17 subject youngsters and in the follow-up interviewed 6 probation officers who were responsible for 10 subjects. We interviewed 16 social workers, involved with 18 of our subject juveniles. We re-interviewed the 5 social workers who were in charge of supervision orders for 5 of our young sample. We have also included the social workers we interviewed vis-a-vis care cases in our more general comments in this chapter, since we administered the sections of our interview schedule concerned with criminal proceedings to them also, as they all had experience of such work.

6. Our sample of 21 adolescents (all between 13 and 15 years old) is the equivalent of about 6 months of City's new referrals with adolescents. Nine cases were officially '1(2) (e)' cases; the remainder a mixture of '1(2) (c)' and '1(2) (d)' and '7(7)'. We interviewed 11 sets of parents.

7. Again, whilst we asked all 34 social workers about their work in care proceedings, as a basis for our general findings, we specifically interviewed 18 social workers responsible for the social work intervention within our care sample.

Bibliography

Anderson, R. (1978) *Representation in Juvenile Court*, London, Routledge and Kegan Paul.

Balbus, I. (1978) 'An Essay on the Relative Autonomy of Law' in C. Reasons and R. Rich, *The Sociology of Law*, Toronto, Butterworth.

Baldwin, J. and McConville, M. (1977) *Negotiated Justice*, London, Martin Robertson.

Bean, P. (1975) 'Social Enquiry Reports — Recommendation for Disposal', *Justice of the Peace* 139.

Bottoms, A. and McClean, J. (1976) *Defendants in the Criminal Process*, London, Routledge and Kegan Paul.

Bottoms, A. and McWilliams, W. (1979) 'A Non Treatment Paradigm for Probation Practice', *Br. J. of Social Work* 9, 2.

Burney, E. (1979) *J.P., Magistrate, Court and Community*, London, Hutchinson.

Carlen, P. (1976) *Magistrates Justice*, London, Martin Robertson.

Cavanagh, W. (1959) *The Child and the Court*, London, Gollancz.

Cawson, P. (1976) *Young Offenders in Care* (preliminary report), London, Department of Health and Social Security.

Chesney-Lind, M. (1977) 'Judicial Paternalism and the Female Status Offender', *Crime and Delinquency*, April.

Cicourel, A. (1968). *The Social Organization of Juvenile Justice*, London, Heinemann.

Cloward, R. and Ohlin, L. (1960) *Delinquency and Opportunity*, Chicago, Free Press.

Coates, K. and Silburn, R. (1970) *Poverty: The Forgotten Englishmen*, Harmondsworth, Penguin.

Corrigan, P. (1979) *Schooling the Smash Street Kids*, London, Macmillan.

Covington, C. (1979). *'The British Juvenile Justice System — A historical perspective'*, London, 'Justice for Children'.

Crowe, I. (1979) *The Detention Centre Experiment*, London, National Association for the Care and Resettlement of Offenders.

Curnock, K. and Hardiker, P. (1979) *Towards Practice Theory*, London, Routledge and Kegan Paul.

Deem, R. (1978) *Women and Schooling*, London, Routledge and Kegan Paul.

Ditchfield, J. (1976) *Police Cautioning in England and Wales*, London, Home Office, HMSO.

Donzeldt, J. (1980) *The Policing of Families*, London, Hutchinson.

Emerson, R. (1968) *Judging Delinquents*, Chicago, Aldine.

Ericson, K. (1976). *Young Offenders and their Social Work*, Farnborough, Saxon House.

Evans, E. (1977) *City in Transition*, Liverpool, City Planning Department.

Fears, D. (1977) 'Communication in English Juvenile Courts', *Sociological Review* XXV, 1.

Geach, H. (1980) 'When Registers Lead to Abuse' *Community Care* June 12th.

Gill, O. (1974) *Whitegate*, Liverpool, University of Liverpool Press.

Gill, O. (1977) *Luke Street*, London, Macmillan.

Glampson, A., Glastenbury, B. and Fruin, D. (1977) 'Knowledge and Perceptions of the Social Services', *J. of Social Policy* 6, 1.

Goldberg, E. (1970) *Helping the Aged*, London, Allen and Unwin.

Hall, S. and Jefferson, T. (eds) (1976) *Resistance through Rituals*, London, Hutchinson.

Harris, R. (1980) 'A Changing Service: The Case for Separating "Care" and "Control" in Probation Practice', *Br. J. of Social Work* 10.

Holman, R. (1976) *Inequality in Child Care*, London, Child Poverty Action Group.

Home Office (1965) *The Child, the Family and the Young Offender*, London, HMSO, Cmnd 2742.

Home Office (1968) *Children in Trouble*, London, HMSO, Cmnd 3601.

Home Office (1979) and (1980a) *Criminal Statistics, England and Wales*, London, Cmnd 7670.

Home Office (1980b) *Young Offenders*, London, HMSO, Cmnd 8045.

Hugman, B. (1980) 'Radical Practice in Probation' in R. Brake and R. Bailey (1980) *Radical Social Work and Practice*, London, Edward Arnold.

Jones, J. M. (1980) *Organization Aspects of Police Behaviour*, Farnborough, Gower.

Jones, R. (1979) *Fun and Therapy*, Leicester, National Youth Bureau.

Kitwood, T. (1979) *Disclosures to a Stranger*, London, Routledge and Kegan Paul.

Labour Party Study Group (1964) *'Crime – A Challenge to Us All'*, London, Labour Party.

Langley, M. (1978) 'Youths' Perceptions of Juvenile Court', *Canadian J. of Criminology*, January.

Lerman, P. (1975) *Community Treatment and Social Control*, Chicago, University of Chicago Press.

McKay, A., Goldberg, E. and Fruin, D. (1973) 'Consumers and a Social Services Department' *Social Work Today* 4, 16.

McRobbie, A. (1978) 'Working-Class Girls and the Culture of Femininity' in Centre for Contemporary Cultural Studies, *Women take issue*, London, Hutchinson.

Marsden, D. (1973) *Mothers Alone*, Harmondsworth, Penguin.

Martin, F., Fox, S. and Murray, K. (1981) *Children Out of Court*, Edinburgh, Academic Press.

Mayer, H. and Timms, N. (1970) *The Client Speaks*, London, Routledge and Kegan Paul.

Matza, D. (1964) *Delinquency and Drift*, New York, Wiley.

Morris, A. and Giller, H. (1977) 'The Juvenile Court — the Client's Perspective' *Criminal Law Review* pp 198–205.

Morris, A. and Giller, H. (1979) 'Juvenile Justice and Social Work' in H. Parker (ed.) (1979).

Morris, A., Giller, H., Szwed, E. and Geach, H. (1980) *Justice for Children*, London, Macmillan.

Mungham, G. and Pearson, G. (1976) *Working-Class Youth Culture*, London, Routledge and Kegan Paul.

Mungham and Bankowski, Z. (1976) *Images of Law*, London, Routledge and Kegan Paul.

Who Cares?, (1977) London, National Children's Bureau.

New Approaches to Juvenile Crime (1979) London.

Packman, J. (1975) *The Child's Generation*, London, Blackwell and Robertson.

Parker, H. (1974) *View from the Boys*, Newton Abbott, David and Charles.

Parker, H. (ed.) (1979) *Social Work and the Courts*, London, Edward Arnold.

Parsloe, P. (1976) 'Social Work and the Justice Model', *Br. J. of Social Work* 6, 1.

Parsloe, P. (1978) *Juvenile Justice in Britain and the United States*, London, Routledge and Kegan Paul.

Pearson, G. (1978) *Welfare on the Move 1945–75*, Milton Keynes, Open University Unit 4, DE 206.

Polsky, N. (1971) *Hustlers, Beats and Others*, Harmondsworth, Penguin.

Priestly, P., Fuller, R. and Fears, D. (1977) *Justice for Juveniles*, London, Routledge and Kegan Paul.

Rees, S. (1978) *Social Work, Face to Face*, London, Edward Arnold.

Reynolds, D. (1976) 'When Pupils and Teachers Refuse a Truce' in G. Mungham and G. Pearson (1976).

Royal Commission on Justices of the Peace (1948), London, HMSO, Cmnd 7463.

Rutter, M. (1979) *Fifteen thousand Hours*, London, Open Books.

Sainsbury, E. (1975) *Social Work with Families*, London, Routledge and Kegan Paul.

Scott, P. (1959) 'Juvenile Delinquency — The Juveniles' View', *Br. J. of Delinquency* 9.

Seebohm Report (1968) *Report of the Committee on Local Authority and Allied Personal Social Services*, London, HMSO, Cmnd 3703.

Shaw, I. (1976) 'Consumer Opinion and Social Policy', *J. of Social Policy* V.

Tarling, P. (1979) *Sentencing Practices in Magistrates' Courts*, London, HMSO.

Taylor, L., Lacey, R. and Bracken, D. (1980) *In Whose Best Interests?*, London, Cobden Trust/Mind.

Thoburn, J. (1980). *Captive Clients*, London, Routledge and Kegan Paul.

Thorpe, D., Green, C. and Smith, D. (1979) *Punishment and Welfare*, Lancaster, University of Lancaster.

Thorpe, D., Smith, D., Green, C. and Paley, J. (1980) *Out of Care*, London, Allen and Unwin.

Thorpe, J. (1979) *Social Enquiry Reports: A Survey*, London, Home Office, Research Studies 48.

Voelcker, P. (1960) 'Juvenile Courts: The Parents' Points of View', *Br. J. of Criminology* 10.

Walter, J. (1979) *Sent Away*, Farnborough, Saxon House.

Williamson, H. (1977) 'Processing Juveniles—Defence and Mitigation in the Juvenile Court', unpublished.

Williamson, H. (1980) 'Juvenile Justice and Work Class Community', submission for PhD, Cardiff.

Willis, P. (1977) *Leaning to Labour*, Farnborough, Saxon House.

Index